Reading Audio Readers

Bloomsbury Studies in Digital Cultures

Series Editors
Anthony Mandal and Jenny Kidd

This series responds to a rapidly changing digital world, one which permeates both our everyday lives and the broader philosophical challenges that accrue in its wake. It is inter- and trans-disciplinary, situated at the meeting points of the digital humanities, digital media and cultural studies, and research into digital ethics.

While the series will tackle the 'digital humanities' in its broadest sense, its ambition is to broaden focus beyond areas typically associated with the digital humanities to encompass a range of approaches to the digital, whether these be digital humanities, digital media studies or digital arts practice.

Titles in the series
The Trouble With Big Data, Jennifer Edmond, Nicola Horsley, Jörg Lehmann and Mike Priddy
Queer Data, Kevin Guyan
Hacking in the Humanities, Aaron Mauro
Investigating Google's Search Engine, Rosie Graham

Forthcoming titles
Human Exploits, Cyberpunk and the Digital Humanities, Aaron Mauro
Ambient Stories in Practice and Research, Edited by Amy Spencer
Metamodernism and the Postdigital in the Contemporary Novel, Spencer Jordan
Herman Melville and the Digital Humanities, Christopher Ohge and Dennis Mischke
Listening In, Toby Heys, David Jackson and Marsha Courneya
People Like You, Sophie Day, Celia Lury and Helen Ward

Reading Audio Readers

Book Consumption in the Streaming Age

Karl Berglund

BLOOMSBURY ACADEMIC
LONDON • NEW YORK • OXFORD • NEW DELHI • SYDNEY

BLOOMSBURY ACADEMIC

Bloomsbury Publishing Plc, 50 Bedford Square, London, WC1B 3DP, UK
Bloomsbury Publishing Inc, 1385 Broadway, New York, NY 10018, USA
Bloomsbury Publishing Ireland, 29 Earlsfort Terrace, Dublin 2, D02 AY28, Ireland

BLOOMSBURY, BLOOMSBURY ACADEMIC and the Diana logo
are trademarks of Bloomsbury Publishing Plc

First published in Great Britain 2024
This paperback edition published 2025

Copyright © Karl Berglund, 2024

Karl Berglund has asserted his right under the Copyright,
Designs and Patents Act, 1988, to be identified as Author of this work.

For legal purposes the Acknowledgements on pp. x–xi constitute an
extension of this copyright page.

Cover design: Rebecca Heselton
Cover image © Number 86 / Shutterstock

All rights reserved. No part of this publication may be: i) reproduced or transmitted in any form, electronic or mechanical, including photocopying, recording or by means of any information storage or retrieval system without prior permission in writing from the publishers; or ii) used or reproduced in any way for the training, development or operation of artificial intelligence (AI) technologies, including generative AI technologies. The rights holders expressly reserve this publication from the text and data mining exception as per Article 4(3) of the Digital Single Market Directive (EU) 2019/790.

Bloomsbury Publishing Plc does not have any control over, or responsibility for, any third-party websites referred to or in this book. All internet addresses given in this book were correct at the time of going to press. The author and publisher regret any inconvenience caused if addresses have changed or sites have ceased to exist, but can accept no responsibility for any such changes.

A catalogue record for this book is available from the British Library.

Library of Congress Cataloging-in-Publication Data
Names: Berglund, Karl, 1983- author.
Title: Reading audio readers : book consumption in the streaming age / Karl Berglund.
Description: London ; New York : Bloomsbury Academic, 2024. | Series: Bloomsbury studies in digital cultures ; vol 4 | Includes bibliographical references and index.
Identifiers: LCCN 2023030492 (print) | LCCN 2023030493 (ebook) |
ISBN 9781350358362 (hardback) | ISBN 9781350358409 (paperback) |
ISBN 9781350358379 (pdf) | ISBN 9781350358386 (ebook)
Subjects: LCSH: Audiobooks–Sociological aspects. | Books and reading–Sociological aspects. | Streaming audio–Social aspects.
Classification: LCC ZA4750 .B47 2024 (print) | LCC ZA4750 (ebook) |
DDC 011/.384–dc23/eng/20230831
LC record available at https://lccn.loc.gov/2023030492
LC ebook record available at https://lccn.loc.gov/2023030493

ISBN: HB: 978-1-3503-5836-2
PB: 978-1-3503-5840-9
ePDF: 978-1-3503-5837-9
eBook: 978-1-3503-5838-6

Series: Bloomsbury Studies in Digital Cultures

Typeset by Integra Software Services Pvt. Ltd.

For product safety related questions contact productsafety@bloomsbury.com.

To find out more about our authors and books visit www.bloomsbury.com
and sign up for our newsletters.

Contents

List of figures	vii
List of tables	ix
Acknowledgements	x

Introduction: Audiobook reading on digital display — 1
    Digital book culture and digital methods — 5
    Books, audiobooks and book reading — 11
    A new way of studying digital private reading — 16
    Storytel and the Swedish context — 20
    Materials and methods — 21
    Data access and ethical concerns — 25
    Outlining the book — 26

1 Understanding book streaming services — 29
    Streamed audiobooks in context — 30
    Modelling subscription-based book streaming services — 33
    Reading and the reading data feedback loop — 36
    Book streaming services and content production — 39
    Bibliographic codes in book streaming services — 42
    Book subscription beyond the Nordic countries — 45
    Conclusion: Alterations on all ends — 48

2 Bestsellers and beststreamers: Genre reading — 51
    Popularity seen as finished streams — 54
    Print books versus streamed (audio)books — 56
    The segmentation of book streaming — 59
    Mapping nuances in book streaming through completion rates — 61
    Conclusion: Aligning publishing studies and reading studies — 65

3 The re-emergence of the old: Backlist and frontlist reading — 69
    Bestseller frontlist patterns in streaming services — 73
    The rule of topicality: Bestseller backlist in practice — 76

Alterations in the backlist–frontlist power balance	80
Digital steady sellers? Seriality, brand names and algorithms	84
Conclusion: The universal and the personalized	89

4 Voices leading the streams? Narrated reading — 93
Mapping performing narrators	97
The gender dimension in the choice of voices	101
Readers following voices?	105
The special case of *The Mirror Man*	108
Tracing readers who follow voices	112
Conclusion: The elusive significance of the voice	115

5 The reading hours of the day and night: Temporal reading — 119
Comparing ebook and audiobook reading	120
Reading what when?	123
Kinds of readers	126
Night readers – sleep trouble or graveyard shifts?	131
Day and evening readers – periodical reading	135
Coda: The aggregated literary year	140

6 Repeaters, swappers and constant readers: Expanded reading — 145
Three important groups of outliers	147
Typical audiobook reading?	150
Repeaters: Reading as entering the comfort zone	152
Swappers: Impatient customers in the digital economy	157
Constant readers: The always plugged-in	162
Conclusion: New reading practices and material effects	166

Conclusion: Listen up to the reading data — 171

References	178
Index	189

Figures

1.1	Model of subscription-based book streaming services	34
1.2	The reading data feedback loop highlighted within the model	37
1.3	Bibliographic codes highlighted within the model	44
2.1	Relative frequencies of finished streams	59
2.2	Average finishing degrees in the commercial top segment 2015–19 by genre and format	62
2.3	Average finishing degrees in the commercial top segment 2015–19 by country of origin and format	62
2.4	Average finishing degrees in the commercial top segment 2015–19 by subset and format	63
2.5	Average finishing degree and finished streams in the commercial top segment 2015–19 by genre	63
3.1	Finished streams per month for three crime novels by the Swedish writer David Lagercrantz	75
3.2	Finished streams per month for five historical novels by the Swedish writer Jan Guillou	75
3.3	Finished streams per month for five romance novels by the British writer Jenny Colgan	76
3.4	Backlist streaming pattern of previous bestsellers in the Malin Fors series by Swedish crime writer Mons Kallentoft	77
3.5	Backlist streaming pattern of previous bestsellers in the Fjällbacka series by Swedish crime writer Camilla Läckberg	78
3.6	Streaming patterns of the Me Before You series by British romance writer Jojo Moyes	79
3.7	Finished streams for three previous bestsellers by Afghan American writer Khaled Hosseini	80
3.8	Frontlist and backlist power balance for Camilla Läckberg's Fjällbacka series	81
3.9	Frontlist and backlist power balance for British romance writer Jojo Moyes	82
3.10	Frontlist and backlist power balance for Norwegian crime writer Jo Nesbø	82

3.11	'Find your next book' in the Storytel app	85
3.12	The Fjällbacka series by Camilla Läckberg, as presented in the Storytel app	86
4.1	Average finishing degree for readers with at least five books in the selection	107
4.2	Marketing campaign picture from the publication of *The Mirror Man* as an audiobook	109
5.1	Audiobook and ebook reading: percentage per hour of the day	121
5.2	Audiobook and ebook reading: percentage per day of the week	122
5.3	Audiobook reading divided by genre	123
5.4	Audiobook reading divided by subset	124
5.5	The book in the dataset with the lowest temporal diversity	125
5.6	The book in the dataset with the highest temporal diversity	126
5.7	Three subsets of day readers (6 am–6 pm)	128
5.8	Three subsets of night readers (12–6 am)	128
5.9	Three subsets of evening readers (6 pm–12 am)	129
5.10	Screen dump of the Storytel app in reading mode	132
5.11a–d	Four individual distinct day readers	137
5.12	Started streams of bestsellers and beststreamers in audiobook format (n=376) aggregated over four whole years, 2017–20	142
6.1	Individual audiobook users	147
6.2	One of three high-consuming segments of individual audiobook readers (>500 hours of reading)	149
6.3	One of three high-consuming segments of individual audiobook readers (>694 hours of reading)	149
6.4	One of three high-consuming segments of individual audiobook readers (>1,000 hours of reading)	150
6.5	Audiobook users with at least 100 hours of reading and with two strata of repeaters highlighted	153
6.6	Audiobook users with at least fifteen books started, and with two strata of swappers highlighted	158
6.7	Streaming pattern of reader 'Swapper A' for the thriller series Jordbunden (seasons 1–3) by Erik Thulin	160
6.8	Audiobook users with at least 100 hours of reading and fifteen books started, and with two strata of constant readers highlighted	163

Tables

0.1	Genre Distribution in the Selection of Titles	24
2.1	Books in the Commercial Top Segment 2015–19 by Subset	54
2.2	Genre Proportions in the Commercial Top Segment 2015–19 by Number of Titles and Percentage	55
2.3	Genre Proportions in the Commercial Top Segment 2015–19 by Finished Streams	55
2.4	Proportions of Translations in the Commercial Top Segment 2015–19 by Finished Streams	56
2.5	Finished Streams and AFDs for Elena Ferrante's Neapolitan Novels	65
3.1	Frontlist and Backlist Titles: Number of Finished Streams	83
4.1	Performing Narrators with More Than Fifteen Narrated Audiobooks in the Selection	98
4.2	Gender Correlations between Authors and Performing Narrators	102
4.3	Gender Correlations between Protagonists and Performing Narrators for Audiobooks with Gender Opposite Author–Narrator	102
4.4	AFDs for Lars Kepler's Crime Novels	110
4.5	Reading Patterns for the Two Audiobook Versions of Lars Kepler's *The Mirror Man*	111
6.1	Number of Hours and Number of Books	152

Acknowledgements

The research comprising this book was made possible by a four-year research grant from the Swedish Research Council (2019-02829, 'Patterns of Popularity: Towards a Holistic Understanding of Contemporary Bestselling Fiction'; PoP).

Parts of this book have appeared elsewhere and have been improved due to the criticism and collaborative thinking of others. An early version of Chapter 1 was published as 'Modelling Subscription-Based Streaming Services for Books' in *Mémoirs du livre/Studies in Book Culture*, vol. 13 (2022:1), co-authored with Sara Tanderup Linkis. Chapter 2 is based on a piece first published as 'Introducing the Beststreamer' in *Publishing Research Quarterly*, vol. 37 (2021). Some parts of that article also helped form the introductory chapter in this book. An early version of Chapter 3 first appeared in *LOGOS*, vol. 32 (2021:1) as 'Is Backlist the New Frontlist?', co-authored with Ann Steiner. Finally, two graphs and some arguments in Chapters 5 and 6 appeared in my *Public Books* essay 'Audiobooks: Every Minute Counts'. I want to express my deepest gratitude to Sara and Ann for letting me use parts of our joint research under my own name. I also want to thank all the editors, reviewers and proofreaders involved, who, with their constructive feedback, have helped me refine my arguments.

Mats Dahllöf, my fellow research partner in the PoP project, has helped me with computational expertise as well as in managing and curating the large datasets that provide the foundation for the analysis in Chapters 4 to 6. Also, our discussions over the years related to statistics, natural language processing (NLP) and other computational and linguistic questions have of great importance for both me and the project. A big thank you!

Furthermore, I want to thank Storytel, who enabled access to this unique dataset, with very few strings attached. A special thanks to Mikael Holmquist, who served as the contact person during the entire project, and to Salla Simola, who put together and delivered most of the data. I also would like to thank Måns Magnusson, who first established the connection with Storytel.

I have had the opportunity of having plenty of brilliant readers along the way, in particular, I would like to mention Sarah Allison, Angelina Eimannsberger, Ann Steiner, Johan Svedjedal and Melanie Walsh – thanks a ton! I have presented parts of this book at conferences (e.g. SHARP, IGEL, ByTheBook,

DHNB), seminars and other academic and public talks over the years. Thanks to everyone providing me with constructive feedback. I would also like to thank Ben Doyle and Laura Cope at Bloomsbury, the copyeditor Katherine Bosiacki and the anonymous reviewers of my book proposal and manuscript for their valuable feedback.

I have written this book whilst part of the Section for Sociology of Literature at the Department of Literature, Uppsala University, and as affiliated to the Centre for Digital Humanities Uppsala (CDHU). Both have been stimulating and friendly environments, which have benefitted the book tremendously in various ways.

A final thanks goes to Anna, Dagny and Bror. Without you it all would be pointless.

Karl Berglund
Uppsala, April 2023

Introduction: Audiobook reading on digital display

In the opening scene of Julia Whelan's romance novel *Thank You For Listening* (2022) the main character Sewanee Chester is headed to Las Vegas, where she is attending BiblioCon to host a panel on audiobook romances. This job is something that Sewanee – herself being a successful audiobook narrator – has been talked into by a colleague and unwillingly accepted. On the plane, she is listening to an erotic romance novel by one of the participants on the panel. Beside her is a curious five year old, Hannah, who is asking her all sorts of questions. She stops listening and responds for a while. When she gets fed up, she politely tells the child's mother that she needs to finish listening to something for work. Then, the following happens:

> She lifted the headphones off her neck and secured them over her ears. She pressed play on her phone. No sound. She turned up the volume. Still nothing. She turned it all the way up.
> In the peripheral vision, she saw the mother clasp her hands over Hannah's ears, pull her into her narrow chest, and bug her eyes at Sewanee.
> No.
> God, no.
> She ripped the headphones off in time to hear, at full volume:
> "He thrust her legs apart, splaying her open, exposing her secret place to his throbbing eyes. Already pulsing, glistening, her generous –"
> Sewanee stabbed so fiercely at the pause button the phone shot to the floor. She scrambled for it, the audiobook continuing:
> "'Say it,' he growled. 'I want to hear you say it.' He gave her one quick, teasing lick. She moaned. 'Say you want my –'"
> The phone had fallen under Hannah's dangling, light-up Disney-princess sneakers. Sewanee grabbed it, jerked upright, and – in three stabs – stopped the audiobook … just after the word 'cock.'

> She stared down at the phone, ignoring the glare drilling into her temple. She took, what she hoped, was a casual-seeming breath. Then, as if nothing had happened (denial was another skill she'd honed), she turned fully away from mother and child and looked out the window.[1]

The scene is hilarious, with its slapstick humour and awkward embarrassment in a physical space without escape. It also manages to capture a feeling that is likely familiar to many audiobook readers. Since reading is a private thing, the fact that audiobooks play the text aloud creates the uncertainty for the reader of whether this privateness is kept intact – especially if the passage currently being narrated contains explicit content of some kind, as in the Whelan example. I believe I am not alone in having taken off my headphones not once but twice to make sure that no one else can hear what I am listening to when reading an audiobook in a public place like a bus or a cafe.

This recognition-as-a-reader is what initially speaks to the readers of *Thank You For Listening*. It is a romance novel about audiobooks for audiobook readers, in manifold ways. Its protagonist is an actor turned audiobook narrator. It contains lots of scenes from within the world of audiobook publishing and audiobook narration. It is involved in meta-reflections regarding the romance genre. (In one scene, for instance, Sewanee expands on the difference between romance and women's fiction.) It contains a love story between two audiobook narrators who fall in love during a narration job for a romance novel, where they voice the female and male leads. And it has a happily ever after ending that would make the Smithton romance readers in Janice Radway's seminal study most content.[2] *Thank You For Listening*, thus, in the romance form thematizes the strong position of the audiobook medium in contemporary book culture. In doing this, the novel extends streamed audiobooks from being an increasingly popular format for consuming popular genre fiction into being part of the tropes and themes of popular culture itself.

The episode also touches upon classic questions in reading studies, such as who the readers are, what they read, where they read, why they read and when they read. It is often surprisingly hard to identify these basic facts, especially in a more systematic fashion. In the digital world of customer data, figures on book sales and consumer behaviour are usually closely guarded company secrets. However, I have been given access to datasets on audiobook reading

---

[1] Julie Whelan, *Thank You For Listening: A Novel* (New York: HarperCollins, 2022), 9–10.
[2] See Janice Radway, *Reading the Romance: Women, Patriarchy, and Popular Literature* (1984; London: Verso, 1987), 66–74.

behaviour from Storytel – the biggest book streaming service in the Nordic countries and a global platform that, second to Amazon's Audible, is among the largest in the market. The datasets, which were shared with me by Storytel, cover the consumption habits for all Storytel users in Sweden for all titles in the commercial top segment. These digital reading patterns are tracked both by title and by individual user and hour of the day when each reading session – measured in minutes – ended. This means that the patterns of each individual audiobook user can be followed: which titles users listen to; which titles they complete or abandon; when users listen and when they stop listening. The largest of these datasets covers nearly 75 million logged sessions of book streaming, distributed over approximately 430,000 individual readers. With these data as the foundation, this book explores the ongoing audiobook boom and its reading culture.

The audiobook has a long history. It has existed since the late nineteenth century, in a variety of technological formats and targeted towards different readers – not least in relation to people with reading disabilities and to children.[3] But what is new is its commercial impact. Today, the audiobook medium can no longer be seen as a niche market or a mere substitute for 'real' reading. It is competing with print books and ebooks for the attention of book readers in a large and diverse range of national book economies. In contrast to other book formats, audiobooks have shown a rapid and steady increase over the last ten years.[4] Most people in the trade expect that the audiobook share will continue

---

[3] For further insights into the history of audiobooks, see Matthew Rubery, *The Untold Story of the Talking Book* (Cambridge, MA: Harvard University Press, 2016). For a specific study on reading disabilities and neurodivergence, see Matthew Rubery, *Reader's Block: A History of Reading Differences* (Stanford, CA: Stanford University Press, 2022). Regarding children and audiobooks, see Ann Steiner and Karl Berglund, *Barnlitterära strömningar: Om ljudböcker för barn* (Stockholm: Swedish Publishers' Association, 2022).

[4] For comparison, the figures for 2021 from three national book trades: According to the Association of American Publishers (AAP), 8.1 per cent of the revenues of the total US book trade in 2021 came from digital audiobooks, which can be compared to ebooks (11.6 per cent) (Porter Anderson, 'AAP StatShot: The United States' Publishing Industry Gained 12.2 Percent in 2021', *Publishing Perspectives*, 26 January 2022). It should also be noted that the Audio Publishers Association (APA) reports higher figures for audiobook revenues than the AAP. In a less digitized Western book trade, namely France, for 2021, 15 per cent of book readers had listened to a physical audiobook and 12 per cent to a digital (downloaded or streamed) audiobook (Porter Anderson, 'France's "Digital Barometer": 27 Percent Trying Audiobooks', *Publishing Perspectives*, 4 May 2022). On the other end of the spectrum, the Nordic countries show high rates of audiobook consumption, due largely to the impact of subscription-based book streaming services. In the Swedish book trade, for instance, roughly 26 per cent of the total revenues in 2021 for all members of the Swedish Publishers' Association came from streamed audiobooks. Five years earlier, in 2016, the same figure was around 8 per cent (Erik Wikberg, *Bokförsäljningsstatistiken: Helåret 2021* (Stockholm: Swedish Publishers' Association and Swedish Booksellers' Association, 2022), 9). See further John B. Thompson, *Book Wars: The Digital Revolution in Publishing* (Cambridge, UK: Polity Press, 2021), 349–92, for a discussion of audiobooks on the US markets; Rüdiger Wischenbart and Michaela Anna Fleischhacker, *The Digital Consumer Book Barometer 2021: A Report on Ebook and Audiobook*

to grow in the coming years. 'We are observing a deep shift,' as the book trade analyst Rüdiger Wischenbart concluded his comment on the ongoing audiobook boom.[5]

At second glance, there are strong factors causing this change. A key circumstance is technical development. Although vinyl records, cassette tapes and CDs all worked fine for reading audiobooks, the conversion into first digital mp3-files for download, and then platforms for streaming audiobooks made the medium much more flexible and appealing. With the possibility to stream audiobooks, anyone with a personal device and an internet connection could potentially get instant access to large collections of titles. The technical shift also enhanced portability. Today it is possible to consume audiobooks while doing something else – working, exercising, commuting, doing the dishes, cleaning and so on – which enables new ways of reading and provides people with more reading time.

The audiobook boom has been driven by the simultaneous shift in reading medium (from text to audio) and distribution medium (from sales of individual physical or digital titles to sales of subscriptions to large catalogues of available titles), and it is the combination of the two that explains the success. These concurrent changes are altering the book business and reading culture in a multitude of ways that are hard to pin down, yet I will outline some of the key ways in this book.

'But audiobook listening is not reading', is an often-heard statement. Yes, one might argue that the rise of audiobooks is a sign of an ongoing crisis of our book culture, in which people no longer actively engage in books but lend them half an ear as a mere distraction. There may be some truth to this statement, but it is not entirely accurate. Though audiobook streams are skyrocketing, print book sales are not declining. What appears to be happening is that people are expanding how they make use of literature. Or, if you will, what reading is and can be. Perhaps streamed audiobooks are not primarily competing with print books and ebooks but with radio, podcasts and other audio media? If this is true, audiobooks could be regarded as a defender of our book culture rather

---

Sales in Canada, Germany, Italy, Spain, Brazil, Mexico (Vienna: RWCC, 2021), for data concerning Canada, Germany, Italy, Spain, Brazil and Mexico; and Johan Svedjedal, 'Läsning och lyssning i en mångmedial tid', in *Läsandets årsringar: Rapport och reflektioner om läsningens aktuella tillstånd i Sverige*, edited by Anna Nordlund and Johan Svedjedal (Stockholm: Svenska Förläggareföreningen, 2020), 20–3, 34, 36, 39–40, for a discussion on the relationship between publisher's revenues and reading practices regarding books and audiobooks in the Swedish context.

[5] Rüdiger Wischenbart, 'Deposing the King of Content: Understanding the Shift Triggered by Audiobooks and Subscription', *LOGOS* 32, no. 2 (2021).

than a threat. In any case, streamed audiobooks are changing our reading habits, which, in turn, are changing book production and distribution.

But *how*, more precisely, is book culture and reading affected by the age of streamed audio? And how does one investigate such changes? This is what this book sets out to explore. Drawing from the unique reader consumption data from Storytel, I map and critically discuss contemporary digital audiobook culture, both in detail and at scale. Through contextualized analyses of this data, *Reading Audio Readers* investigates how and when readers read in their everyday life. It shows how audiobooks and digital streaming platforms affect literary culture and offers an academic perspective on the kind of user data hoard typically associated with the tech industry. As Shoshana Zuboff, among others, has noted, tech companies with large customer bases notoriously keep track of their users with the aim of making money on predicting their behaviour.[6] Storytel and other book streaming services are no exception to this – to read books on these platforms is also to be read. In this book, I use this kind of user data to understand contemporary digital reading practices from a scholarly point of view. By reading audio readers, this book offers a computational window into the emerging private reading practices of contemporary digital culture. This data is an asset in understanding the underlying logic of book streaming; it makes it possible to study these platforms in an informed way, in their own habitat.

Digital book culture and digital methods

This book is empirically driven and deeply rooted in the traditions of sociology of literature and book history – the latter once humorously and accurately described by Simone Murray as 'an empiricist refuge from the high tide of post-structuralist-inspired abstraction'.[7] By combining computational methods from cultural analytics with theoretical perspectives from the sociology of literature, contemporary book history, publishing studies and media studies, this study aims to provide new insights into reader behaviour on digital platforms, the effects of the audiobook boom and the business models for book publishing and distribution based on streaming and subscription. The intervention proposed in this book thus derives from a deliberate and consequent merging of critical book

---

[6] Shoshana Zuboff, *The Age of Surveillance Capitalism: The Fight for a Human Future at the New Frontier of Power* (London: Profile Books, 2019).

[7] Simone Murray, *The Adaptation Industry: The Cultural Economy of Contemporary Literary Adaptation* (New York and London: Routledge, 2012), 31.

history, on the one hand, and empirical cultural analytics, on the other. Both perspectives, I argue, are necessary to understand the rapid alterations in reading practices that mark the book trade of today. In line with Lev Manovich, I believe that the amount of data produced in the digital world makes quantitative and mixed-method approaches increasingly significant – 'when we start studying the online content and activities of millions of people, this perspective becomes almost inevitable'.[8]

Equally crucial is that the analysis does not stop at showing off impressive results, a critique that can at times be justifiably directed towards cultural analytics work. In this book, I am careful to *use* the data to frame an informed critical discussion about contemporary reading practices; it is first and foremost a means to reach that end. Johan Svedjedal's definition of the sociology of literature as 'the systematic study of the relationship between literature and society' aligns well with this ambition.[9] The computational approach brings systematics and helps avoid bias and cherry-picking, but my main interest is in the interplay between reading and its book-trade context, not in the methods themselves.

The digitalization of the trade has naturally been a standard element in most scholarly work on twenty-first-century publishing and reading – starting with the discussions on books, ebooks and hypertexts in the 1990s, and following the steps of the digitalization of the book trade, including internet book retailing, ebook readers such as the Kindle, and streamed ebooks and audiobooks.[10] It is also not the first study that uses large-scale datasets to study contemporary

---

[8] Lev Manovich, *Cultural Analytics* (Cambridge, MA: MIT Press, 2020), 47.
[9] Johan Svedjedal, 'Det litteratursociologiska perspektivet: Om en forskningstradition och dess grundantaganden', in *Litteratursociologi: Texter om litteratur och samhälle*, edited by Johan Svedjedal, 2nd edn (1996; Lund: Studentlitteratur, 2012), 78. In the Swedish original: 'att systematiskt analysera relationerna mellan skönlitteratur och samhälle'.
[10] Some standard references in this tradition are Sven Birkerts, *The Gutenberg Elegies: The Fate of Reading in an Electronic Age* (Boston, MA and London: Faber and Faber, 1994); Michael Joyce, *Of Two Minds: Hypertext, Pedagogy, and Poetics* (Ann Arbor: University of Michigan Press, 1995); Johan Svedjedal, *The Literary Web: Literature and Publishing in the Age of Digital Production* (Stockholm: Kungl. biblioteket, 2000); N. Katherine Hayles, *Writing Machines* (Cambridge, MA: MIT Press, 2002); Ted Striphas, *The Late Age of Print: Everyday Book Culture from Consumerism to Control* (New York: Columbia University Press, 2009); Adriaan van der Weel, *Changing Our Textual Minds: Towards a Digital Order of Knowledge* (Manchester: Manchester University Press, 2011); Andrew Piper, *Book Was There: Reading in Electronic Times* (Chicago: Chicago University Press, 2012); Claire Squires and Padmini Ray Murray, 'The Digital Publishing Communications Circuit', *Book 2.0* 3, no. 1 (2013); Simone Murray, *The Digital Literary Sphere: Reading, Writing, and Selling Books in the Internet Era* (Baltimore, MD: Johns Hopkins University Press, 2018); and Thompson, *Book Wars*. See also the review articles Matthew Kirschenbaum and Sarah Werner, 'Digital Scholarship and Digital Studies: The State of the Discipline', *Book History* 17 (2014); and Rachel Noorda and Stevie Marsden, 'Twenty-First Century Book Studies: The State of the Discipline', *Book History* 22 (2019).

book culture, though such approaches are less common. In a recent survey of publishing studies, Rachel Noorda and Stevie Marsden claim that 'twenty-first century book scholars commonly use digital methodologies – such as data scraping or mining, online surveys and computational analysis'.[11] Although there are certainly examples of studies in this vein, especially when it comes to studies of digital social reading, a clear majority of the studies in the field are still qualitative.[12] In addition, prominent scholars have raised criticism towards quantitative perspectives. In *The Digital Literary Sphere* (2018), Simone Murray highlights several problems with computational methods. She warns of 'an inherent risk of naïve positivism', of weaknesses in the methods employed and of the fact that book history scholars might unconsciously internalize a culture of metrics, in a way similar to how actors such as Amazon understand book consumption.[13] Simon Rowberry relatedly claims that data collected from digital reading offers a poor substitute for reading, and that it is unclear how the metrics provided relate to the act of reading.[14]

Although Murray's and Rowberry's concerns should be taken seriously, they do not thoroughly discuss the inherent possibilities in such methods for studies of contemporary book culture.[15] It could be added that their objections are in many respects similar to previous criticisms in literary studies of large-

---

[11] Noorda and Marsden, 'Twenty-First Century Book Studies', 382.

[12] Computational studies on digital social reading include: Ed Finn, 'New Literary Cultures: Mapping the Digital Networks of Toni Morrison', in *From Codex to Hypertext: Reading at the Turn of the Twenty-First Century*, edited by Anouk Lang (Amherst: University of Massachusetts Press, 2012); Anatoliy Gruzd and DeNel Rehberg Sedo, '#1b1t: Investigating Reading Practices at the Turn of the Twenty-first Century', *Mémoires du livre / Studies in Book Culture* 3, no. 2 (2012); Federico Pianzola, Simone Rebora and Gerhard Lauer, 'Wattpad as a Resource for Literary Studies: Quantitative and Qualitative Examples of the Importance of Digital Social Reading and Readers' Comments in the Margins', *PLoS ONE* 15, no. 1 (2020); Federico Pianzola, *Digital Social Reading: Sharing Fiction in the 21st Century* (Cambridge, MA: MIT Press Works in Progress, 2021); Simone Rebora, Peter Boot, Federico Pianzola, Brigitte Gasser, J. Berenike Herrmann, Maria Kraxenberger, Moniek M. Kuijpers, Gerhard Lauer, Piroska Lendvai, Thomas C. Messerli and Pasqualina Sorrentino, 'Digital Humanities and Digital Social Reading', *Digital Scholarship in the Humanities* 36, no. 2 (2021); and Melanie Walsh and Maria Antoniak, 'The Goodreads "Classics": A Computational Study of Readers, Amazon, and Crowdsourced Amateur Criticism', *Journal of Cultural Analytics* 6, no. 2 (2021), 246. Other areas of computation within or bordering publishing studies include: Allen Riddell and Karina van Dalen-Oskam, 'Readers and Their Roles: Evidence From Readers of Contemporary Fiction in the Netherlands', *PLoS ONE* 13, no. 7 (2018); Karl Berglund, Mats Dahllöf and Jerry Määttä, 'Apples and Oranges? Large-Scale Thematic Comparisons of Contemporary Swedish Popular and Literary Fiction', *Samlaren* 140 (2019); and Corina Koolen, Karina van Dalen-Oskam, Andreas van Cranenburgh and Erica Nagelhout, 'Literary Quality in the Eye of the Dutch Reader: The National Reader Survey', *Poetics* 79 (April 2020). See also Kirschenbaum and Werner, 'Digital Scholarship'.

[13] Murray, *The Digital Literary Sphere*, 151–4.

[14] Simon Rowberry, 'The Limits of Big Data for Analyzing Reading', *Participations* 16, no. 1 (2019).

[15] To be fair, it should be noted that Murray has partly revised her judgement of the potential in digital methods for studying digital literary culture. See Simone Murray, 'Varieties of Digital Literary Studies: Micro, Macro, Meso', *Digital Humanities Quarterly* 16, no. 2 (2022).

scale computational methods, where scholars have warned about positivism,[16] troublesome methods,[17] and metrics and measuring culture.[18] Simon Rowberry's claim that 'metrics of consumption [...] fail to capture the complete reading process' is in many ways analogous to Stephen Marche's assertion that 'literature is not data', except transferred from literary studies to book history, from literary text to reader behaviour.[19]

In the most basic sense, I agree with both Marche and Rowberry: literature is not data; metrics of consumption do fail to capture the complete reading process. But this does not mean that it is not a useful way to study reading on digital platforms. From my perspective, large-scale book streaming data drawn from companies seem to be one of the more promising operationalizations of reading and book consumption that reading scholars have ever had access to. In the analyses throughout this book, I will show how this data can be used, and what it can tell us about reading and book culture in the age of streaming audio. The keyword here is operationalization, namely, the transformation of an elusive concept (such as reading) into something concrete that can be studied empirically. Operationalizations are needed in all studies of reading, and no single method manages to capture all aspects of what constitutes this complex activity. Historical reading studies have to juggle with a large variety of heterogeneous, scattered and time-consuming archival sources to draw conclusions on reading behaviour.[20] In fact, and as Matthew Rubery points out, 'there is no single activity known as reading'; it makes more sense to think about 'reading as a spectrum'.[21]

With that said, there are certainly limitations in operationalizing reading as streaming patterns in a digital platform. However, I seek to be upfront about these limitations and to discuss them critically. When approached in this transparent way, data points on book streaming can reveal a lot about contemporary reading

---

[16] See, for example, Daniel Allington, Sarah Brouillette and David Golumbia, 'Neoliberal Tools (and Archives): A Political History of Digital Humanities', *LA Review of Books*, 1 May 2016.
[17] See, for example, Nan Z. Da, 'The Computational Case Against Computational Literary Studies', *Critical Inquiry* 45, no. 3 (2019).
[18] See, for example, Stephen Marche, 'Literature Is Not Data: Against Digital Humanities', *LA Review of Books*, 28 October 2012.
[19] Rowberry, 'The Limits of Big Data', 237–8; Marche, 'Literature Is Not Data'.
[20] In his impressive *The English Common Reader* (1957), for instance, Richard D. Altick used a combination of sources – including bibliographies, sales figures, figures on periodical and newspaper circulation, statistics on social reform, economics, education and religion, and memoirs and autobiographical accounts – into a solid patchwork showing the social history of the mass reading public in nineteenth-century England. See Richard D. Altick, *The English Common Reader: A Social History of the Mass Reading Public 1800–1900* (Chicago: University of Chicago Press, 1957).
[21] Rubery, *Reader's Block*, 1, 3.

practices. In addition, this data helps enhance the understanding of how book streaming platforms perform and function. Sales figures enable publishing scholars to see which books have been popular only in the sense of what books sold the most copies. Streaming data has the potential of letting scholars see not only which books have been the most popular in digital streaming services but also how readers have interacted with these works. Although such measurements are in one respect always crude, they are more nuanced than figures on sales or library lending. Where sales figures are binary by nature (sold or not sold), the streaming data enables studying, for example, how far readers have read in books, when books are read and which books are frequently related to the reading of other books.

Furthermore, a firm demarcation between reading and book consumption is hard to draw when considering book streaming. In some respects, these things converge as publishers are getting paid per number of minutes streamed on these platforms. But only in some respects. What is tracked by Storytel is not reading in the sense of making meaning of the words in a particular audiobook. It is a measure of how the Storytel player has been used by a large number of platform users. This is not the same thing, and it has its shortcomings. As Simon Rowberry notes: 'In sum, unless data collected from the user agent can be correlated with some external evidence of reading, the resulting data map software usage rather than reading'.[22] Since I cannot correlate my data with any external evidence of reading, I cannot study reading, at least not in Rowberry's understanding of the concept.

But instead of being seen as a deficiency in tracking 'real reading', the discrepancy between data points ('software usage') and reading can be used to shed light on what people do with audiobooks in book streaming services. Even if they are not always 'reading' them, in the traditional sense of the word, and even if I cannot study how they cognitively perceive audiobooks, people are certainly doing something with books while they are playing them on the platform. And all book streaming patterns mean something, not least for the publishers who get paid based on these patterns. As I will show, some readers recurrently seem to use audiobooks for going to sleep or when sleeping. Likely, people do all kinds of things while they listen to audiobooks, and this affects, I argue, how 'reading' as a concept can be understood.

In the 1980s, Janice Radway proposed the following prompt to scholars of literary culture:

---

[22] Rowberry, 'The Limits of Big Data', 242.

By focusing on social process – that is, on what people do with texts and objects rather than on those texts and objects themselves – we should begin to see that *people do not ingest mass culture whole but often remake it into something they can use.*[23] (My emphasis.)

The necessity to focus on actual uses of literature is a perspective that I share with Radway, and with studies such as Leah Price's *How To Do Things with Books in Victorian Britain* (2012) and Rita Felski's *Uses of Literature* (2008) for that matter.[24] But where Radway uses interviews, Price historical records and Felski theory, I make use of large-scale data points on audiobook habits. Whether these data points can track reading or not can and should be debated, but they are in any case a tracking of literature use. Thus, turning to Radway again, the reader consumption data provides a way to 'listen more carefully to consumers of mass culture in order to detect the nature and source of their intense interaction with it'.[25] By blurring the practices of reading, literature use and consumption, then, the reader consumption data used in this study can highlight new aspects of literary culture in the age of streamed audio. Not all practices tied to these data are necessarily to be regarded as reading, but they are by definition to be regarded as both consumption and use of literature, and they *could* be regarded as reading practices, if the term is expanded.

Since reading and book consumption are overlapping categories in the book streaming economy, this book is consequently a simultaneous study of reading *and* publishing. More concretely, the first three chapters are mainly oriented towards publishing studies, while the final three chapters are mainly oriented towards reading studies. But it has been a deliberate goal to never separate those things; the ambition is to study reading and publishing in tandem.

Furthermore, the desire to separate digital reading contexts from digital methods, as suggested by Murray as well as Noorda and Marsden, is problematic.[26] Digital content and digital methods are intertwined. From my point of view, the best way to approach book streaming platforms is by investigating them on their own terms. This is exactly what reader data can provide. There is no conflict between computational methods and a critical perspective based on contextual knowledge.[27]

---

[23] Janice Radway, 'Reading Is Not Eating: Mass-Produced Literature and the Theoretical, Methodological, and Political Consequences of a Metaphor', *Book Research Quarterly* 2 (1986), 26.
[24] Leah Price, *How to Do Things with Books in Victorian Britain* (Princeton, NJ: Princeton University Press, 2012); Rita Felski, *Uses of Literature* (Malden, MA, and Oxford: Blackwell, 2008).
[25] Radway, 'Reading Is Not Eating', 27.
[26] Murray, *The Digital Literary Sphere*, 151–54; Noorda and Marsden, 'Twenty-First Century Book Studies', 382.
[27] See James F. English and Ted Underwood, 'Shifting Scales: Between Literature and Social Science', *Modern Language Quarterly* 77, no. 3 (2016); Ted Underwood, 'A Genealogy of Distant Reading', *Digital Humanities Quarterly* 11, no. 2 (2017).

When Noorda and Marsden argue 'that long twenty-first century research is in a unique position to use digital texts and contexts, such as websites, ebooks, apps, social media, and audiobooks [...] in its analysis of contemporary book and publishing culture', I completely agree, though I would add that most such datasets benefit greatly from computational methods.[28] In line with Melanie Walsh and Maria Antoniak, who are also responding to Murray in their data-driven analysis of tagging behaviour by Goodreads users, 'computational methods can supply a way of documenting, understand, and critiquing algorithmic culture and its effects'.[29]

Similarly, I support Simone Murray's claim that 'what is currently missing and is urgently needed is a digital literary studies that is both contemporary and contextual'.[30] However, complementary to Murray, I believe critically and contextually informed computational analyses of digital data points can be a feasible way to bridge this knowledge gap. Even though publishing scholars will likely never acquire the proprietary algorithms that respond to and steer consumption behaviour in digital platforms, as Murray rightly points out, analysing the outcome of these algorithms in terms of user interaction and streaming patterns can be a highly relevant alternative.[31]

Books, audiobooks and book reading

What is reading today? People are reading print books, journals and magazines as well as the digital counterparts of these things: ebooks, e-journals and digital magazines. They are also reading everyday texts such as signs, notes on medicine bottles, advertisements, mail and emails, social media, websites, blogs and micro-blogs – the list goes on. Reading is an impressively broad concept. As Naomi Baron notes, not even established ways of dividing different kinds

---

[28] Noorda and Marsden, 'Twenty-First Century Book Studies', 382.
[29] Walsh and Antoniak, 'The Goodreads "Classics"', 246.
[30] Murray, *The Digital Literary Sphere*, 9.
[31] Simone Murray, 'Secret Agents: Algorithmic Culture, Goodreads and Datafication of the Contemporary Book World', *European Journal of Cultural Studies* 24, no. 4 (2021), 976. All recommendation algorithms are however based on statistical models that cluster users together based on similarity patterns in consumption and interaction. Such algorithms can be biased in different ways – they can, for instance, favour the company's own titles (see Simon Rowberry's analysis of bias in Amazon recommendations in *Four Shades of Gray: The Amazon Kindle Platform* (Cambridge, MA: MIT Press, 2022), 55–60). But the technical details of each individual algorithm might not be the holy grail for contemporary book history. Instead, basic knowledge of how machine learning recommendation systems operate, paired with a critical mindset towards their output, is probably sufficient for most research questions.

of reading practices, such as skimming, scanning and linear reading, manage to map the complex diversity of reading methods.[32] I have not even mentioned 'reading' in the hermeneutical sense, as an interpretation of a literary work, or as methodology (reading 'close', 'distant', 'surface', etc.).

For fiction, more specifically, digital audiobooks have in the last decades been added to print books and ebooks as a popular reading media. The differences between books as text and books as audio are in many respects more fundamental than the differences among other book formats, since it is not only a change of medium or of material conditions, but also of the sense used when reading. While incunables (books printed before 1500), nineteenth-century three-volume novels, modern hardcovers and paperbacks and digital epub files diverge in many ways, they are all read with your eyes. Audiobooks, on the other hand, are perceived by listening with your ears. Although oral literature has a long history, the recent boom in audiobook reading and especially the turn towards book streaming services affects not only what kind of literature is being read but also the social contexts for reading. Following this development, the success of streamed audiobooks may be related to a broader turn towards aurality in contemporary culture, especially listening to podcasts.[33]

Whether listening to audiobooks should be understood as reading, though, is a matter of debate. Some scholars regard both book reading and audiobook listening as reading, but they claim that reading through different media enables different possibilities for perception, attention and immersion.[34] Others have proposed a more distinct line between 'reading by listening' and 'reading by seeing'.[35] Still others understand audiobook listening not to be reading at all, mainly since it involves no decoding of alphanumeric characters.[36] How one chooses to define reading also ties into questions concerning reading disabilities. A pure focus of reading as processing text visually excludes blind people, for

---

[32] Naomi Baron, *How We Read Now: Strategic Choices for Print, Screen, and Audio* (New York: Oxford University Press, 2021), 10.

[33] See, for instance, Dario Llinares, Neil Fox and Richard Berry, 'Introduction: Podcasting and Podcasts – Parameters of a New Aural Culture', in *Podcasting. New Aural Cultures and Digital Media*, edited by Dario Llinares, Neil Fox and Richard Berry (Cham: Palgrave Macmillan, 2018); Michael Bull, *Sound Moves: iPod Culture and Urban Experience* (New York: Routledge, 2007); Sara Tanderup Linkis, 'Reading Spaces: Original Audiobooks and Mobile Listening', *SoundEffects* 10, no. 1 (2021).

[34] Lutz Koepnick, 'Figures of Resonance: Reading at the Edges of Attention', *Sound-Effects* 8, no. 1 (2019); Birgitte Stougaard Pedersen, Maria Engberg, Iben Have, Ayoe Quist Henkel, Sarah Mygind and Helle Bundgaard Svendsen, 'To Move, to Touch, to Listen: Multisensory Aspects of the Digital Reading Condition', *Poetics Today* 42, no. 2 (2021).

[35] Elisa Tattersall Wallin, 'Reading by Listening: Conceptualising Audiobook Practices in the Age of Streaming Subscription Services', *Journal of Documentation* 77, no. 2 (2021).

[36] Birkerts, *The Gutenberg Elegies*, 146–49; Miha Kovač, Angus Phillips, Adriaan van der Weel and Rüdiger Wischenbart, 'What Is a Book?', *Publishing Research Quarterly* 35 (2019).

instance, both those who listen to audiobooks and those who use braille ('reading by touch'). As Matthew Rubery has noted, discussions of what reading is often use double standards, treating practices among people with reading disabilities as a separate discussion.[37] At the same time, of course, what is at stake in these debates is the possibility to identify as a reader *at all* for people with reading disabilities.[38]

These discussions are taking place beyond the scholarly community as well; there are long threads on, for example, Reddit, Goodreads and Bookstagram dedicated to discussing exactly this question: 'do you count listening to audiobooks as reading?'[39] Scholars of cognitive science and neuropsychology discuss audiobook listening as well, though more from learning perspectives. According to Naomi Baron, the cognitive difference between reading books and listening to audiobooks is a complex scientific question, not yet possible to answer in an easy way.[40]

Despite this extensive conversation, many recent book historical conceptualizations of reading and the reading process have not taken audiobooks into account or have treated them on the margin. In Leah Price's *What We Talk About When We Talk About Books: The History and Future of Reading* (2019), audiobooks are only mentioned a couple of times in passing and not really in connection to the main argument.[41] In their influential framework for reading in the age of digitalization, Anne Mangen and Adriaan van der Weel discuss all kinds of possible aspects of reading as human-technology interaction and embodied acts, but they never explicitly address audiobooks.[42] The same goes for Simone Murray in her otherwise excellent chapter on online reading in *The Digital Literary Sphere*.[43]

---

[37] Matthew Rubery, 'Introduction: Talking Books', in *Audiobooks, Literature, and Sound Studies*, edited by Matthew Rubery (New York: Routledge, 2011), 2.
[38] See further Rubery, *The Untold Story of the Talking Book*, 17–19; Anna Lundh, '"I Can Read, I Just Can't See": A Disability Rights-Based Perspective on Reading by Listening', *Journal of Documentation* 78, no. 7 (2022); Rubery, *Reader's Block*, 1–34.
[39] For one example, see 'Do you count listening to audio books as reading?', *Reddit.com*, https://www.reddit.com/r/books/comments/24pykt/do_you_count_listening_to_audio_books_as_reading/ (accessed 26 January 2022).
[40] Naomi Baron (*How We Read Now*, 164–79) provides an overview on cognitive research comparing print and audio reading, with focus on children and learning; see also Rubery, *The Untold History of the Talking Book*, 14–16.
[41] Leah Price, *What We Talk About When We Talk About Books: The History and Future of Reading* (New York: Basic Books, 2019). Audiobooks are also absent in her review article 'Reading: The State of the Discipline', which is less strange given that it was published in 2004. See Leah Price, 'Reading: The State of the Discipline', *Book History* 7 (2004).
[42] Anne Mangen and Adriaan van der Weel, 'The Evolution of Reading in the Age of Digitisation: An Integrative Framework for Reading Research', *Literacy* 50, no. 3 (2016).
[43] Murray, *The Digital Literary Sphere*, 141–67.

My point here is not to criticize these authors, but to highlight that within contemporary book history, audiobooks are not regularly a part of discussions of reading – not even when the focus is explicitly on digital reading practices and how new digital technologies affect reading.[44] Somewhat ironically, book historians focusing on reading before the audiobook was born are much better at highlighting the oral aspects of reading culture. As Robert Darnton succinctly expresses it: 'for most people throughout most of history, books had audiences rather than readers. They were better heard than seen.'[45] When audiobooks and reading *are* discussed, it is with an explicit audiobook focus and often within library and information science, media studies and sound studies.[46] Such studies are many times revealing, but they lack the connection to literary reading studies and book history. My ambition in this book is to try to bridge this gap by discussing streamed audiobook reading, both theoretically and empirically, within a book history framework.

This discussion also connects to how one defines a book. Are audiobooks books? It is obvious that the publishing industry understands audiobooks as books. They are, after all, generally published by book publishers, provided with an ISBN, called audio*books*, and distributed and sold through the same channels as print books and/or ebooks. But the treatment of audiobooks as books can and should be problematized. In 'What is a Book?', Miha Kovač *et al.* propose a hierarchical book definition, where print books are seen as the core – 'the purest form' – and audiobooks are found in the outer circles of the book definition, understood to be a border case.[47] Their definition is well developed

---

[44] I am not the first to point out that audiobooks are often overlooked when books and reading are discussed. See further Rubery, 'Introduction'.
[45] Robert Darnton, 'The First Steps Toward a History of Reading', *Australian Journal of French Studies* 51, no. 2–3 (1986), 164; see further Walter J. Ong, *Orality and Literacy: The Technologizing of the Word* (London: Methuen, 1982); and several of the chapters in Guglielmo Cavallo and Roger Chartier, editors, A *History of Reading in the West* (Oxford: Polity, 1999). For instance, Jesper Svenbro in his chapter 'Archaic and Classical Greece: The Invention of Silent Reading' (37–63) discusses what was meant by reading in the classical Greece, which ties in surprisingly well with today's discussions about whether audiobook listening should be regarded as reading or not. By examining Greek verbs Svenbro shows that they used three different verbs for the various practices connected to reading, and that people listening to oral readings – by far the most common reading practice in classical Greece – were actually not called readers but '"auditors" of the text': 'Apart from the reader, "who includes himself in the reading" and hears his own voice, Greeks read absolutely nothing. They simply listened to reading' ('Archaic and Classical Greece', 44).
[46] See, for example, Rubery, 'Introduction'; Lutz Koepnick, 'Reading on the Move', *PMLA* 128, no. 1 (2013); Rubery, *The Untold Story of the Talking Book*; Iben Have and Birgitte Stougaard Pedersen, *Digital Audiobooks: New Media, Users, and Experiences* (New York: Routledge, 2016); Koepnick, 'Figures of Resonance'; Elisa Tattersall Wallin and Jan Nolin, 'Time to Read: Exploring the Timespaces in Subscription-based Audiobooks', *New Media and Society* 22, no. 3 (2020); Tanderup Linkis, 'Reading Spaces'; and Tattersall Wallin, 'Reading by Listening'.
[47] Kovač *et al.*, 'What Is a Book?'.

and makes intuitive sense. Yet, all definitions come with problems. Should audiobooks produced by record companies and sold and marketed as records through music channels be counted as books? As both Matthew Rubery and Ann Steiner and Karl Berglund have shown, such releases have been common historically, especially for children's literature.[48] What about podcasts and born-audio audiobooks produced by book publishers? Or podcasts in general? Some podcasts have storylines that are very book-like, while some born-audio audiobooks are highly dramatized and influenced by the current wave of podcasts and the longer tradition of audio drama.[49]

I argue that the line between audiobooks and audio drama/podcasts is impossible to draw theoretically. 'Book' is an ontologically fuzzy concept in the contemporary digitized and mediatized reading culture, and the audiobook falls across several lines of possible demarcation.[50] Practically, however, the line between audiobooks and other audio media is drawn all the time. Audiobooks are titles emanating from the book publishing industry, which get ISBNs (or ASINs, for Amazon-only produced titles), and which are then included in book streaming services and other channels for book distribution, as well as in official book sales and reading statistics. Podcasts and radio dramas are not, they are therefore not considered books. Interestingly, this division seems to be quite accepted in society. Few laypersons would characterize podcasts as books, whereas most people would probably agree that audiobooks are in fact books. Not least the names of media are important. Of course, audiobooks must be books; of course, podcasts must emanate from the world of radio broadcasting.

In this book, I will take a pragmatic standpoint and follow book industry standards. I thus understand audiobooks coming from book publishers and with ISBNs/ASINs as books, and I consider listening to audiobooks as reading. But I want to emphasize that this standpoint is made with a sincere understanding that things are not at all that simple, and that choice of media deeply affects how books are perceived and consumed. Again, the simultaneous rise of audiobooks and book streaming and the effect of this joint development on reading patterns is the driving force behind this book. The tension between ontological discussions

---

[48] Rubery, *The Untold Story of the Talking Book*; Steiner and Berglund, *Barnlitterära strömningar*.
[49] Steiner and Berglund, *Barnlitterära strömningar*, 16–18.
[50] Of course, one can, as the media scholar Andrew Bottomley has, instead argue that all such audio media should be regarded as radio, audiobooks included. His inclusive definition of radio reads as 'any sound medium that is purposefully crafted to be *heard* by an audience' (Andrew Bottomley, *Sound Streams: A Cultural History of Radio-Internet Convergence* (Ann Arbor: University of Michigan Press, 2020), 14). From a book-history perspective, as well as from the point of view of the reader, this makes little sense, but to similarly label podcasts as books would be equally problematic.

on media forms and content (what is a book?) and industry pragmatism (this is a book!) will necessarily wave in and out of the analyses of this book.

A new way of studying digital private reading

Robert Darnton once famously claimed: 'Reading remains the most difficult stage to study in the circuit followed by books.'[51] For historical studies of reading, this is still true. For studies of contemporary reading, there are more methods and materials available, but up until recently, reading practices have been difficult to map, especially if one is interested in investigating larger patterns. With the emergence of large amounts of reader data, however, this is about to change.

Methodologically, previous studies of reading and readership can schematically be divided into three main areas. The first are historical studies that use archival materials to map and reconstruct the reading practices of earlier times. This can – and has – been done in a multitude of ways, including studies of marginalia, diary notes, letters, subscription lists and lending records. Some key studies in this vein include Richard D. Altick's *The English Common Reader* (1957), Rolf Engelsing's *Der Bürger als Leser* (1976), *A History of Reading in the West* (1999), edited by Guglielmo Cavallo and Roger Chartier, and Jonathan Rose's *The Intellectual Life of the British Working Classes* (2001).[52] Such studies have contributed immensely to the understanding of the developments of reading and readership, but they have their methodical limitations. In most cases, their sources can either provide detailed micro-historical accounts of certain readers (marginalia, autobiographical archival materials) or some ideas about what larger groups of people read at a certain point in history (subscription lists, lending records). As Darnton argues: 'to pass from the *what* to the *how* of reading is an extremely difficult step'.[53]

The second area of reading research has studied living readers with methods derived from the social sciences, using interviews, surveys and various kinds

---

[51] Robert Darnton, 'What Is the History of Books?', *Daedalus* 111, no. 3 (1982), 74.
[52] Cavallo and Chartier, *A History of Reading in the West*; Rolf Engelsing, *Der Bürger als Leser: Lesergeschichte in Deutschland 1500–1800* (Stuttgart: Metzlersche Verlagsbuchhandlung, 1976); Jonathan Rose, *The Intellectual Life of the British Working Classes* (New Haven, CT: Yale University Press, 2001). For overviews of this field, see Darnton, 'The First Steps Toward a History of Reading'; Price, 'Reading: The State of the Discipline'; Stephen Colclough, 'Readers: Books and Biography', in *A Companion to the History of the Book*, ed. Simon Eliot and Jonathan Rose (Malden, MA, and Oxford: Wiley-Blackwell, 2007).
[53] Robert Darnton, *The Great Cat Massacre* (London: Allen Lane, 1984), 222.

of field studies. This cultural studies-influenced research has several classics of its own: Janice Radway's *Reading the Romance* (1984), Elizabeth Long's *Book Clubs* (2003) and Danielle Fuller and DeNel Rehberg Sedo's *Reading Beyond the Book* (2013), just to mention three of the most canonical ones.[54] These and other studies have shown how people actually make use of books and why people say that they read certain books, emphasizing the social aspects of reading. Radway, for instance, uses a range of anthropological methods circulating around forty-two romance readers in a Midwestern American suburb to challenge the notion of the romance genre as merely sexist and reactionary. Instead of focusing only on the texts read, she argues, critical attention must be paid to what the complex social event of reading such texts brings to readers. Radway goes on to claim that romance novel reading actually can be empowering.[55] Fuller and Rehberg Sedo, somewhat similarly, use a combination of interviews and surveys to examine the phenomena of mass reading events and what readers get from them. The emergence and popularity of such events highlights the social aspects of reading, they argue, but there is a complex array of interests that is driving this development, including economical ones.[56]

The third and currently vibrant area of research investigates reading practices in digital- and social media-influenced platforms such as Goodreads, Wattpad and LibraryThing. Such work draws on qualitative approaches and computational ones – the latter involving scraping, mapping and analysing reader comments, reviews and networks at scale. One example in this vein is Melanie Walsh and Maria Antoniak's study of how one of the most popular tags on Goodreads – the 'classic' – is being used on the platform. By analysing 144 books tagged as 'classics' on Goodreads and their 120,000 accompanying reader reviews, they show that the classic label has multiple functions. For the readers, it is an inclusive label of well-known literary works that one 'should have read' – including popular genre fiction and books read in school. It also gives these readers a chance to reflect and partake in a literary discussion with others. For

---

[54] Radway, *Reading the Romance*; Elizabeth Long, *Book Clubs: Women and the Uses of Reading in Everyday Life* (Chicago and London: University of Chicago Press, 2003); Danielle Fuller and DeNel Rehberg Sedo, *Reading Beyond the Book: The Social Practices of Contemporary Literary Culture* (New York: Routledge, 2013). In a Swedish context, the works of Gunnar Hansson are important, see especially Gunnar Hansson, *Dikten och läsaren: Studier över diktupplevelsen* (Stockholm: Bonniers, 1959); and Gunnar Hansson, *Inte en dag utan en bok: Om läsning av populärfiktion* (Linköping: Linköping University, 1988).
[55] Radway, *Reading the Romance*.
[56] Fuller and Rehberg Sedo, *Reading Beyond the Book*.

Amazon, who owns the platform, the classic tag works as an advertising target value and marketing tool.[57]

Simone Rebora, Federico Pianzola and others have proposed the term *digital social reading* for such activities, as these digital platforms enable and foster reading practices that are social by nature and apply to the logics of social media: writing, posting, commenting, reviewing, linking and community-building. Furthermore, they argue that computational methods are especially well suited for conducting research in digital social reading, and that these platforms paired with digital methodologies enable new possibilities for understanding current reading practices.[58]

The methods and materials for studying reading proposed in this book most closely resembles the computational approach of the third branch, but there are significant differences. As Simone Murray notes, one needs to be aware of 'the degree of readerly performativity involved in online reading reports'.[59] What can be traced when mining digital social reading platforms is different versions of public reports written by readers with the deliberate aim of showing off certain reading behaviours and literary tastes to a larger crowd. While this is important to study, it only covers a specific aspect of reading – its public and social dimension. Although social reading platforms gather large amounts of readers, they are still biased towards people who are interested in communicating and discussing books and reading practices.

Reader consumption data drawn from reading platforms such as Storytel is a very different thing. This data provides a window into the digital private reading practices of large populations of readers at a granular level. Also, this data is biased (not all readers are audiobook readers), but not to the same extent as Goodreads reviews. If digital social reading is said to enable completely new possibilities for reading research, this is even more true when studying reading consumption data. As Mark McGurl puts it in *Everything and Less: The Novel in the Age of Amazon* (2021):

> Goodreads, with its more than 100 million users, may be the richest repository of the leavings of literary life ever assembled, exceeded only by the mass of granular data sent back to home base from virtually every Kindle device in the

---

[57] Walsh and Antoniak, 'The Goodreads "Classics"'.
[58] For an overview of this field, see especially the review article Rebora *et al.*, 'Digital Humanities and Digital Social Reading'; and Pianzola, *Digital Social Reading*. For a qualitative study in this vein, see Bronwen Thomas, *Literature and Social Media* (London and New York: Routledge, 2020).
[59] Murray, *The Digital Literary Sphere*, 152.

world. (We can only hope that literary scholars will someday be given access to all this data.)[60]

In this study, I actually have access to the kind of data that McGurl dreams of, though the data comes from Swedish users who are streaming books on the Storytel platform. This data can help answer questions about reading practices and literary culture that sociologists of literature previously only could speculate about, many of which are discussed in this book, including: which books do readers finish, and which do they abandon? (Chapter 2); when do readers read during the day? (Chapter 5); and which books do readers read over and over again? (Chapter 6). Though I have no personal or socio-economic data on these readers, the data does enable me to zoom in on individual readers and reading patterns.

Therefore, I argue that my approach in this book offers a new and fourth way of studying reading. I call this *digital private reading* to highlight the similarities and differences to digital social reading. It is indeed a question of *digital* reading practices (streamed audiobooks and ebooks), but it is the tracked patterns of *private* reading that are analysed, not public data or data accessible to anyone except the streaming platform. The method is computational at its core, but it combines quantitative and qualitative perspectives.

Just like digital social reading, the concept of digital private reading is used as a means to identify important aspects of what reading is and can be in the contemporary digital literary sphere. However, as Federico Pianzola has noted, private and social reading are not mutually exclusive practices but intertwined.[61] The Storytel platform steers reading by means that are social by nature. Algorithmic recommendations, for instance – a crucial part of any contemporary media platform – are statistical predictions based on what you have read and *what other people have read*. Correspondingly, textual reviews in online reading communities are affected by private as well as social aspects. The categorical distinction between social and private reading is thus a theoretical construct that can be analytically productive.

Furthermore, the streaming data offers new insights to the reading studies problem of differentiating between readers/reading and consumers/consuming. As Claire Squires puts it:

---

[60] Mark McGurl, *Everything and Less: The Novel in the Age of Amazon* (London and New York: Verso, 2021), 244–45.
[61] Pianzola, *Digital Social Reading*.

If a reader can read without having bought (by borrowing or stealing), and a consumer can buy without reading (buying on behalf of others or leaving the purchase languishing on a pile of unread books), how can patterns of consumption and reading be understood and meaningfully analyzed?[62]

With reading consumption data, the scholar empirically knows much more about this distinction than by means of book sales numbers or other data. And not only the scholar, naturally, but also publishers and authors. This fact will likely have large consequences on the book production of the future. As will be discussed further in Chapters 1 and 2, when books are no longer sold as entities, but per streamed minute, publishers will try to publish – and authors will try to write – books that are not sold, primarily, but streamed all the way through, ideally repeated several times.

Storytel and the Swedish context

As stated, the empirical foundation in this book is reader consumption data derived from the Swedish book streaming service Storytel. The company was founded in 2005 as 'Bokilur', literally 'book-in-phone'. After a change of name and some tough years initially, including financing through venture capital from the Swedish version of the TV show *Dragon's Den* in 2009, Storytel expanded rapidly. Most famously, they bought Norstedts in 2016, Sweden's oldest and second largest publishing house. This spurred an intense debate around the increasing market share of book streaming services and audiobooks in Swedish publishing that is still ongoing. Today, Storytel is the dominant book streaming platform in Sweden and Scandinavia, but also a global actor present in over twenty-five markets globally.[63] Their main competitor in the Nordic markets is BookBeat, a book streaming service owned by the Swedish publishing and book retailing company Bonnier Books.

In 2021, book streaming accounted for 26 per cent of the revenues for the members of the Swedish Publishers' Association.[64] Audiobook streaming constitutes the absolute majority of this market share – roughly 90 per cent

---

[62] Claire Squires, 'The Global Market 1970–2000: Consumers', in *A Companion to the History of the Book*, ed. Simon Eliot and Jonathan Rose (Malden, MA, and Oxford: Wiley-Blackwell, 2007), 406.
[63] Storytel, 'Om Storytel', https://www.storytel.com/se/sv/om-storytel (accessed 17 November 2022).
[64] Wikberg, *Bokförsäljningsstatistiken: Helåret 2021*, 9–10.

of the book streaming in Sweden emanates from audiobooks, the remaining 10 per cent from ebooks.⁶⁵ Streaming audiobooks is thus a big thing in Sweden.

Although similar in many respects, Storytel and BookBeat represent two different kinds of book streaming services. Storytel started out as a distributor of others' products. When they began to grow, they also acquired content producers, which in the world of books are generally called publishing houses. Apart from Norstedts, Storytel has so far acquired Swedish Storyside (2013), Lind & Co (2021), Danish People's Press (2017) and Finnish Gummerus (2019). BookBeat, on the other hand, is part of a large publishing company and thereby has firsthand access to all titles published by Bonnier-owned publishing houses, but it also distributes books from other publishers and thus holds a position as an independent actor in the market.

Moreover, both Storytel and BookBeat deploy a subscription-based business model for book streaming. They pay publishers (and accordingly also authors) per minute streamed on the platform, a fact that has raised a lot of criticism in Sweden, not least by the Swedish Authors' Association.⁶⁶ The subscription-based business model of book streaming and its implications for literary culture is examined in detail in Chapter 1.

Materials and methods

Given the nature and the uniqueness of the data studied in this book, I would like to clarify my methods and the data used, as well as address some of the ethical concerns involved in this study.

The reading consumption data received from Storytel covers reading behaviour for all Swedish users of the Storytel platform, for audiobooks and ebooks, and for all works of fiction for adults in the 'commercial top segment' (explained further below). Two main datasets have been used. The first covers reader consumption data *per ISBN and per day from January 2014 to April 2020*. It includes information about which books have been started and finished, as well as where in the narrative, on average, users stopped reading. This dataset enables studies of book popularity, book completion and the longer conjunctures of book streaming on the title level. In total, it contains data on

---

⁶⁵ Steiner and Berglund, *Barnlitterära strömningar*, 39.
⁶⁶ See Jerry Määttä, Ann Steiner and Karl Berglund, *Skilda världar: Kvalitetslitteraturens villkor i Sverige idag* (Stockholm: Swedish Publishers' Association, 2022), 63–5.

nearly ten million started and finished streams, and it is the main empirical source used in Chapters 2 and 3. The second dataset covers reader consumption data *per individual user and hour, for one year (May 2020–April 2021)*. The granularity of the data enables detailed studies of individual readers concerning how and when audiobooks and ebooks are read. The large number of readers covered (just over 432,000 users) enables studies of reading at a new scale. In total, the dataset covers roughly 74.5 million logged sessions of book streaming, and it serves as the main empirical source in Chapters 4 to 6.

Practically, these two datasets are giant matrix files that consist of a few columns and a very large number of rows. I have curated and analysed these datasets with the help of the programming language Python and standard Python libraries such as Pandas.[67] In the chapters that follow, I use basic data science approaches including descriptive statistics and linear regression. This is paired with highlighting revealing examples that are chosen by statistical means. In Chapter 2, for instance, I zoom in on the single outlier of prestige fiction that readers tend to read all the way through – Elena Ferrante's *The Story of the Lost Child* (2014) – to make an argument about literary series and reader devotion. In Chapter 5, I similarly zoom in on three clusters of readers with very distinctive reading hours by randomly selecting ten readers in each cluster and analysing their reading practices in detail. This approach of zooming in (on individual examples) and out (at general statistical trends) is indebted to cultural analytics methodology – especially Richard Jean So's *Redlining Culture* (2020) – but it likewise builds on and updates a long tradition of work in bibliometrics, sociology of literature and book history dating back at least to the 1960s.[68]

The reason for the limitation to titles in the commercial top segment of fiction is partly sociological: I am interested in the reading patterns of the many, and this segment of books – mostly popular genre fiction but also prize-winning books and books by well-known authors – engage the largest reader base. But it also makes sense from a data science perspective. Books with a large number of readers have a large quantity of reader consumption data tied to them, which in turn makes for a more statistically solid understanding of the observed patterns.

---

[67] Wes McKinney, 'Data Structures for Statistical Computing in Python', in *Proceedings of the 9th Python in Science Conference*, ed. Stefan van der Walt and Jarrod Millman (Austin, TX, 2010); the Pandas Development Team, *pandas-dev/pandas: Pandas* (Zenodo, 2020).

[68] For an early example in this tradition, see Alan Pritchard, 'Statistical Bibliography or Bibliometrics?', *Journal of Documentation* 25, no. 4 (1969).

In this book, 'the commercial top segment' is defined as:

1. All bestselling fiction, as defined by the Swedish Publishers' Association, for adults in print in Sweden per year 2004 to 2020 (319 titles).[69]
2. All additional 'beststreamers' (i.e. the twenty most popular fiction titles for adults) in the Storytel platform that were not already bestsellers, per year 2015 to 2020 (57 titles).
3. All born-audio works of fiction for adults in the Storytel platform (i.e. the 'Storytel Originals'), from their launch in 2016 up until 2020 (105 titles).[70]

In total, the titles in the selection comprise 481 novels, which covers the commercial top segment for fiction in its entirety and in all important formats in Sweden for the period 2015–2020, and for print bestsellers 2004–2014. The author gender balance is fairly even (51 per cent female, 45 per cent male, 4 per cent mixed-gender collaborations[71]), while Swedish originals are dominant (20 per cent translations). Since it is the commercial top segment that is being investigated, the selection naturally has a distinctive bias towards popular genre fiction, in particular crime fiction, which holds a very strong position in Sweden and thus account for most of the titles in the dataset. But the selection also contains prestige fiction by award-winning authors as well as middlebrow literary fiction (see Table 0.1).[72] These biases – especially apparent among the beststreamers and born-audio titles – are discussed in detail in Chapter 2. Here, it is perhaps enough to note that the increased dominance of genre fiction in digital formats is in line with discussions raised in both Mark McGurl's *Everything and Less* (2021) and Kim Wilkins, Beth Driscoll and Lisa Fletcher's *Genre Worlds* (2022).[73]

Since genre is an important parameter throughout this book, some notes on how these distinctions were made are also needed. Theoretically, I understand

---

[69] The bestselling titles are compiled from bestseller lists published yearly in the Swedish book trade magazine *Svensk Bokhandel*. All top 20 titles of fiction (hardbound and paperback) have been included, with duplicates removed.
[70] Storytel Originals were at the beginning modelled after TV series and published in 'seasons' of ten or more episodes, each with their own ISBN. Such seasons are lengthwise more or less equal to the normal length-span of novels. Therefore, one season is consequently treated as similar to one title, and all reader consumption data are correspondingly drawn together for all episodes in each season.
[71] There were no authors with non-binary or unknown gender in the dataset.
[72] For an elaborated discussion on crime fiction in the Swedish book trade and elsewhere, see Karl Berglund, 'Detectives in the Literary Market: Statistical Perspectives on the Boom in Swedish Crime Fiction', *Scandinavica: An International Journal of Scandinavian Studies* 51, no. 2 (2012); Karl Berglund, 'Crime Fiction and the International Publishing Industry', in *Cambridge Companion to World Crime Fiction*, edited by Jesper Gulddal, Stewart King and Alistair Rolls (Cambridge: Cambridge University Press, 2022).
[73] McGurl, *Everything and Less*; Kim Wilkins, Beth Driscoll and Lisa Fletcher, *Genre Worlds: Popular Fiction and Twenty-First-Century Book Culture* (Amherst and Boston: University of Massachusetts Press, 2022).

Table 0.1 Genre Distribution in the Selection of Titles

	Crime fiction	Romance	Prestige fiction	Other fiction	Total
Bestsellers	183 (57.4%)	35 (11.0%)	26 (8.2%)	75 (23.5%)	319 (100.0%)
Beststreamers	53 (93.0%)	3 (5.2%)	0 (0.0%)	1 (1.8%)	57 (100.0%)
Born-audio	44 (41.9%)	30 (28.6%)	0 (0.0%)	31 (29.5%)	105 (100.0%)
Total	280 (58.2%)	68 (14.1%)	26 (5.4%)	107 (22.2%)	481 (100.0%)

the concept of genre not as fixed categories of literary content but rather as labels that are constantly being reconstructed in the interplay between readers, authors and publishers, and as one of the more important communicative aspects on the book trade that 'includes formal aspects of literary texts, marketing strategies and other kinds of categorisations by the producers, and perspectives on how these labels are perceived by readers'.[74]

Practically, however, fixed categories are needed to enable quantitative approaches to genre. In this study, the categorization of 'crime fiction' follows the bibliography of Swedish crime fiction compiled by the Swedish Crime Fiction Academy, which applies an inclusive genre definition in line with book trade categorizations.[75] Defined as 'romance' is the broad array of stories within the realm of 'classic' historical and contemporary romance, erotic romance, romantic comedies and chick lit, that is, popular genre fiction where a love story is central and which is clearly marketed towards female readers. Since there is no bibliography or other reliable metadata markup that singles out romance in this wider sense in Sweden, the categorization has been made manually for all titles that have a Thema code markup of romance of any kind ('FR' and its sub-categories)[76] and/or peritextual attributes that are clearly connected to the tropes of romance.[77] 'Prestige fiction' is defined as all titles that have received or been

---

[74] Karl Berglund, 'Genres at Work: A Holistic Approach to Genres in Publishing', *European Journal of Cultural Studies* 24, no. 3 (2021), 758; see further Claire Squires, *Marketing Literature: The Making of Contemporary Writing in Britain* (Basingstoke: Palgrave Macmillan, 2007), 70–104.

[75] For further details, see Berglund, 'Detectives in the Literary Market', 40–1.

[76] Thema is a subject category scheme designed for global use in the book trade, in contrast to the BIC and BISAC classification schemes that have historically been more focused upon the United Kingdom and the United States specifically. Thema is used by all large actors in the Swedish book trade, including Storytel. For details concerning the Thema category scheme, see Editeur, 'Thema Current Version 1.5', https://www.editeur.org/151/thema/ (accessed 30 November 2022).

[77] 'Peritextual' here follows Gérard Genette's definition as everything apart from the literary text that is included in a book volume, including book covers, book cover texts and titles (Gérard Genette, *Paratexts: Thresholds of Interpretation* (1987; Cambridge: Cambridge University Press, 1997)). By clearly connected to 'the tropes of romance', I mean keywords in text such as *romance, love,*

nominated for a major literary award, namely, the Nobel Prize in literature, the Pulitzer Prize, the Booker Prize and the two most important literary prizes in a Swedish context: Augustpriset and Nordiska rådets litteraturpris. It should be noted that this is a definition of literary prestige that excludes some titles that probably would be regarded as prestige or literary fiction by most critics. The label 'other fiction' thus applies to all titles not belonging to any of the three specific categories. It covers popular genre fiction other than crime fiction and romance (e.g., fantasy, science fiction) as well as middlebrow literary fiction. Fantasy and science fiction were not separated out because they make up such a small share of the bestselling segment in Sweden.

Data access and ethical concerns

Access to the streaming data was enabled through a collaboration agreement between Uppsala University and Storytel Sweden AB that was set up for the research project 'Patterns of Popularity', which this book emanates from.[78] The agreement states that Storytel is to provide reader consumption data for the books of interest to the project group, in various levels of granularity. The project group is obliged to report back all published research and refined data emanating from the project, and to not share the raw source data to any third party beyond the research project group. Apart from these stipulations, the data comes with no restrictions. The project group is academically free to pose any kind of research questions and to conduct any kind of research on the data. It should perhaps also be explicitly stated that I do not have commercial interests or other relationships to Storytel of any kind, nor do any members of the project team. In many respects, the reader consumption data is similar to other book trade data coming from commercial actors and used for book trade research (e.g. Nielsen BookScan sales figures, internal reports from publishing houses, etc.).

Even so, access to this data raises some ethical concerns. The obligation not to share raw source data to third parties can be considered problematic for the ideals of open science. Since reviewers cannot access the raw source data

---

feelgood, cozy, heart-warming, dating, and so on, and/or images showing genre-typical combinations of couples or females, quirky handwriting and bright pastel colours (preferably on the pink-red-yellow-green spectrum).

[78] The project group consists of myself, who acts as principal investigator, and computational linguist Mats Dahllöf, who works mostly with text analysis in the project but who has also been involved in curation of the reader consumption data.

that the results are based on they cannot completely evaluate or reproduce the methods and results. Yet, this is far from the first project using commercially sensitive data, and many projects that use qualitative methods cannot share their raw source data either. For example, John B. Thompson's foundational studies *Merchants of Culture* (2010) and *Book Wars* (2021) are both mostly based on a large number of qualitative interviews. Thompson explains in method appendices that around 280 and 180 interviews were conducted respectively. But it is not possible to access transcripts of these interviews.[79] The same goes with Janice Radway's reading studies classic *Reading the Romance* (1984).[80] Thus, one has to trust the authors (which – I must emphasize – I completely do). In other words, research transparency is regularly achieved without providing complete access to raw source data.

Since the data includes information about the reading patterns of real individual readers, ethical considerations need to be thoughtfully applied. The dataset is completely anonymized, which means that the project group has no information regarding who the users are. Nevertheless, there is a risk of personal integrity intrusion if patterns of individual readers' book reading are showcased as examples. I therefore make use of user groups and proxy readers in all such sensitive cases, which guarantees that no individual reader can identify themselves.

Outlining the book

The book is organized into six chapters, one theoretical and five empirical. It covers the most important aspects of how the rise of streamed audiobooks has changed literary culture. Chapters 1 to 3 mainly highlight the publishing studies perspectives, while Chapters 4 to 6 focus more on reading studies, but my aim has been to blend these things throughout the book as much as possible.

In Chapter 1, book streaming is conceptualized by placing the ongoing structural changes and their effects within a book historical framework. More concretely, I propose a model that pinpoints how subscription-based streaming

---

[79] See the method appendices in John B. Thompson, *Merchants of Culture: The Publishing Business in the Twenty-First Century* (Cambridge, UK: Polity Press, 2010), 406–15; Thompson, *Book Wars*, 488–97.

[80] Radway, *Reading the Romance*, see especially the method discussion on pages 46–9, and the appendices on interview and questionnaire design on pages 223–40.

services function, and what effects they have on contemporary literary culture. In the context of streamed audio, the production, distribution and consumption of books are becoming increasingly interrelated. This also applies to the category of 'the book' itself: in streaming services it is hard to separate material books as objects from their distribution; books and book distribution have in some respects converged into floating, overlapping categories. The model highlights the consumption-data feedback loop, which allows streaming services to know much more about readers than publishers and authors do, or that has ever been known about them before.

In Chapter 2, I zoom in on the kind of fiction that currently dominates the audiobook format: popular genre fiction, predominantly crime fiction and romance. Building on streaming patterns of print bestsellers and 'beststreamers', I show how audiobook reading has become more or less synonymous with easy reads. This emerges clearly in which genres are consumed the most, but also which books that are completed by readers to the highest degree. The concept of completion levels is posited as a way for scholars to study readerly devotion, and to measure the ability of books to absorb their readers. In understanding the results, multiple explanations are highlighted, including media-specific aspects of audiobooks, customer base, platform design and the role of performing narrators. In the chapter, I also emphasize the need to talk about beststreamers: since book streaming services do not sell books, but access to books, the term bestseller no longer applies.

The book trade has long been driven by current and topical bestsellers, which in publishing are called *frontlist* bestsellers. In Chapter 3, I argue that understandings of the relationship between the frontlist and backlist have to be updated in relation to book streaming. By investigating data for reading patterns for old and new bestsellers, I observe a striking shift in the publishing balance between the frontlist and backlist. While the frontlist obviously retains an important position as the instigator of book consumption, the backlist has become important on streaming platforms. The development is related to the free-for-all-model introduced with subscription services as well as platform design and serialization. The chapter ends with a discussion of the more long-term effects on publishing and reading that these changes in reading behaviour might provoke.

Chapter 4 deals with the assumption that the performing narrators of audiobooks are crucial both for the audiobook experience and for which books readers choose. Some commentators go as far as to say that narrators might be more important than genres or even authors in the audiobook segment.[81] In the chapter, I empirically track the relations between individual audiobook reading habits and performing narrators. The rising stars of performing narration and their role as stakeholders in contemporary literary culture is taken up for discussion, as is the role of self-narrated audiobooks, and the correlation between author gender and performing narrator gender. The reading patterns for Lars Kepler's crime novel *Spegelmannen* (The Mirror Man) (2020) are discussed as a case study, since it was simultaneously released in two different audiobook versions, with the difference between them being the performing narrator (one male, one female).

The change of reading medium with the rise of streamed audiobooks alters where, when and how books can be read. In Chapter 5, I make use of the temporal information in the reading data to discuss questions concerning when people are reading books and what it means. I chart the peaks of reading activity during the day and night – as well as during the days of the week and the months of the year – and discuss the distinctly different temporal reading patterns observed between ebook and audiobook reading. Moreover, certain types of temporal reader clusters are identified and discussed in relation to theories on digital reading. 'Night readers' is a category of specific interest, since the dataset in general shows a correlation between reading quantity and night-time reading.

In Chapter 6, I dig deeper into types of readers. By clustering individual readers into groups, the ambition with the chapter is to capture some of the complexities involved in contemporary digital reading practices. Special attention is paid to three kinds of reader types: repeaters are readers that over and over again listen to the same books, preferably during the night; swappers are readers that try out lots of books, only to abandon them and move on to others; constant readers are binge-readers who listen to books all the time. These kinds of readers shed important light on digital reading practices, as they show habits fostered by the reading milieu studied, either due to the audiobook medium (repeaters), the subscription-based consumption model (swappers) or a combination of both (superusers). They also highlight that reading in the age of streamed audio can be something quite far from what is generally meant when talking about reading.

In the Conclusion, finally, the results and discussions are drawn together into a synthesized treatment of three particular aspects of how the data-driven age of streamed audio is affecting reading, publishing and literary culture.

---

[81] See, for instance, Rubery, 'Introduction'; Have and Stougaard Pedersen, *Digital Audiobooks*, 83; and Koepnick, 'Reading on the Move', 235.

1

Understanding book streaming services

The audiobook is booming globally, but currently the tendency is most prominent in the Nordic countries. One reason for this is the impact of subscription-based book streaming services in Scandinavia. They hold both ebooks and audiobooks, but it is audiobooks and not ebooks that are the driving force behind the market expansion of book streaming. Audiobooks constitute the overwhelming majority of the consumption on these platforms – roughly 90 per cent.[1] In 2021, book streaming accounted for 26 per cent of the book trade revenues in Sweden.[2] The figures for Denmark and Norway are similar.[3] And if book consumption rather than revenue is considered, the importance of book streaming is emphasized even further. In Sweden, roughly twenty-seven million print books were sold in 2021. This can be compared to the roughly forty-four million digital books that were streamed through the same year.[4] In short, platforms for streamed audiobooks have rapidly become power players in Scandinavian publishing and reading culture.

The popularity of streamed audiobooks is part of a bigger and ongoing shift in media consumption of music and video content, but it is also connected to previous technological shifts in the book trade. These simultaneous changes in book distribution, production and reading are effecting and disturbing all concerned parties: writers, publishers, readers, libraries and so on. In this chapter, I conceptualize streamed audiobooks by placing the ongoing structural

---

[1] See Steiner and Berglund, *Barnlitterära strömningar*, 39.
[2] Wikberg, *Bokförsäljningsstatistiken: Helåret 2021*, 9–10.
[3] Kari Spjeldnæs has reported that digital audiobooks made up 23 per cent of the revenues in the Norwegian book trade in 2021, and 34 per cent of the revenues in the Danish book trade in 2021 (Kari Spjeldnæs, 'Platformization and Publishing: Changes in Literary Publishing', *Publishing Research Quarterly*, September (2022)).
[4] Wikberg, *Bokförsäljningsstatistiken: Helåret 2021*, 31–6. When a book is counted as 'finished' differs on the detail level between the book streaming services reporting in to the statistics, but a best practice in the trade is when a user has completed at least 80–90 per cent of a book. See further, Steiner and Berglund, *Barnlitterära strömningar*, 40.

changes and their effects within a book historical framework. More concretely, I propose a model that pinpoints how subscription-based book streaming services function, and what effects they have on the production, distribution and reading of books. As the proposed model will demonstrate, these analytical categories are becoming increasingly interrelated, and harder to distinguish from each other. The ambition is to contribute to a broader discussion of the impact of new digital distribution models on the contemporary book market. Claire Parnell, who has studied the social reading and writing site Wattpad, emphasizes that publishing and platform studies '*must be conceived of together* to understand how technology models are influencing praxis in contemporary book culture and consider reading and writing applications that do not limit themselves to forms of digital literature that closely resemble codices'.[5] I agree and believe it also holds true for Storytel, BookBeat and the other book streaming services currently thriving in the Nordic countries. My empirical focus rests on these services, but since similar platforms are growing in importance elsewhere as well, the scope is broadened towards the end of the chapter into a comparison with US-based counterparts.

Streamed audiobooks in context

The emergence and popularity of digital book streaming services has affected the function and cultural status of the audiobook. The previous role of audiobooks as a mere support to the print book – well described in Matthew Rubery's *The Untold History of the Talking Book* (2016) – is currently being questioned. Audiobooks are increasingly considered to be a medium worthy of recognition, and such research is developing into a field of its own.[6] Also models of digital

---

[5] Claire Parnell, 'Mapping the Entertainment Ecosystem of Wattpad: Platforms, Publishing and Adaptation', *Convergence* 27, no. 2 (2021), 527.
[6] In *Digital Audiobooks* (2016), Iben Have and Birgitte Stougaard Pedersen examine how the digitalization of audiobooks leads to new users and new modes of literary experience, and they have, following this trail, published several articles on related topics. In the last few years, a range of studies have expanded the knowledge of streamed audiobooks, in various directions: regarding production and born-audio works (see Iben Have and Mille Raaby Jensen, 'Audio-bingeing', *Passage* 83 (Summer 2020); Sara Tanderup Linkis and Julia Pennlert, 'Episodic Listening: Analyzing the Content and Usage of Born-Audio Serial Narratives', *Journal of Electronic Publishing* 23, no. 1 (2020); Steiner and Berglund, *Barnlitterära strömningar*; Tanderup Linkis, 'Reading Spaces'); textual patterns in streamed audiobooks (see Karl Berglund and Mats Dahllöf, 'Audiobook Stylistics: Comparing Print and Audio in the Bestselling Segment', *Journal of Cultural Analytics* 11 (2021)); and reading practices for streamed audiobooks (see Tattersall Wallin and Nolin, 'Time to Read'; Steiner and Berglund, *Barnlitterära strömningar*; Sara Tanderup Linkis and Julia Pennlert, 'En helt annan upplevelse: Ljudbokens band till sina läsare', *Tidskrift för Litteraturvetenskap* 52, no. 1 (2022)).

audiobooks and streaming services have been proposed, but there has not yet been any studies conceptualizing specifically the effects that subscription-based book streaming services are causing in the book trade.[7] This is the ambition here.

In studying this impact, I build on theories developed in textual scholarship and book history about how the medial and material framing of literature affects how it is perceived. In *The Textual Condition* (1991), Jerome McGann proposes that literary works consist of linguistic codes (i.e. the text) as well as bibliographic codes (i.e. the material framing of the text, the book), and that both of these things together constitute the work.[8] McGann's terminology can be related to Gérard Genette's concept of *paratext*, which he defines as everything sanctioned by the author and/or publisher that circulates around a literary text, embeds it and helps the reader to interpret it.[9] Moreover, McGann, and to some extent Genette as well, addresses the fact that publishers and authors in tandem affect the outcome of the work. In book streaming services, however, the distributor plays a crucial role in the framing of literary works. Thus, the line between production and distribution of books is blurred. This calls for an updated understanding of books as material objects in a digital streaming environment.

In this context, two perspectives are key. First, subscription-based book streaming services are based on digital platforms, and it is essential to consider the structure of these platforms, the algorithms at work behind their web interfaces and how these things affect reading practices. Personalized recommendation systems are turning the art of selling books upside down. Everyone gets their own custom-made book shop, based on what they have already read, instead of being exposed to the same titles as all the other customers. As several scholars have pointed out, this risks fostering reading practices where you stick to what you already know, and what complements your tastes, even though 'everything'

---

[7] Terje Colbjørnsen, 'The Streaming Network: Conceptualizing Distribution Economy, Technology, and Power in Streaming Media Services', *Convergence* 27, no. 5 (2021); Iben Have and Birgitte Stougaard Pedersen, 'The Audiobook Circuit in Digital Publishing: Voicing the Silent Revolution', *New Media & Society* 22, no. 3 (2020); Tattersall Wallin, 'Reading By Listening'.
[8] Jerome McGann, *The Textual Condition* (Princeton, NJ: Princeton University Press, 1991).
[9] Genette, *Paratexts*. Genette furthermore separates two levels of the paratext according to how close they are positioned towards the literary text: peritexts are paratexts found within the same volume as the literary text (e.g. book covers, typography, forewords, etc.), whereas epitexts are all paratexts found elsewhere (e.g. advertisements for books, author presentations, etc.) (Genette, *Paratexts*, 1–12). These two layers of the paratexts are impossible to fully separate, as parts of the peritext (for instance the cover) are often used in advertising. In a digital world, this demarcation line is increasingly difficult to draw, if not an artificial construct (see Nadine Desrochers and Daniel Apollon, 'Introduction', in *Examining Paratextual Theory and Its Applications in Digital Cultures*, ed. Nadine Desrochers and Daniel Apollon (Hershey, PA: IGI Global, 2014).

is potentially available.[10] Second, readers primarily read books in digital formats when there is no intrinsic value in owning or keeping the book after reading it. The paradigmatic example of this trend is the subscription-based model, where subscribers pay for temporary access to a whole catalogue of books. Subscription-based access thus facilitates reading of literature, but has potentially negative effects on other significant parts of bookish culture, such as books as signifiers of taste, books as gifts or books as furnishing in bookshelves.[11] Since Storytel uses such a model, all data analysed in this book is emanating from readers having a monthly subscription to the platform, with access to all titles in Storytel's vast collection.

Over the years, numerous models and schemas to describe the chain of book production and distribution have been published. The most well known is doubtless Robert Darnton's 'communications circuit' (1982), and others of note are Lars Furuland's 'literary process' (1970), Hans Hertel's 'media elevator' (1996), Johan Svedjedal's 'professional functions in the book trade' (2000) and Claire Squires and Padmini Ray Murray's 'digital publishing communications circuit' (2013),[12] as well as more recent models for audiobooks specifically.[13] The ones thematically closest to my model, which I will go through in some detail below, are Iben Have and Birgitte Stougaard Pedersen's (2019) audiobook focused reworking of Squires and Ray Murray, and Terje Colbjørnsen's (2021) generic model of media streaming services.

In 'The Streaming Network', Colbjørnsen presents a model of media streaming services that maps out the power relations involved. Basically, a streaming service controls a database with content that can be accessed by users through a device and/or interface, by paying a fee. It is not primarily the streaming service itself that produces the content, however, but content publishers, who enable access to their work in the streaming service database in return for payment.[14] An important part of the model is that it highlights both flows of payments (from users to streaming service, and from streaming service to content publisher) and

---

[10] See Chapter 3, but further also, for example, Ann Steiner, 'The Global Book: Micropublishing, Conglomerate Production, and Digital Market Structures', *Publishing Research Quarterly* 34 (2018); Murray, 'Secret Agents'; Thompson, *Book Wars*: 176–94.

[11] See further the discussion in Chapter 2; cf. Thompson, *Book Wars*: 43–8.

[12] Darnton, 'What Is the History of Books?'; Lars Furuland, 'Litteratur och samhälle: Om litteratursociologin och dess forskningsfält', in *Litteratursociologi: Texter om litteratur och samhälle*, edited by Lars Furuland and Johan Svedjedal (Lund: Studentlitteratur, 1997); Hans Hertel, *500.000 £ er prisen: Bogen i mediesymbiosens tid* (Stockholm: Svenska Bokförläggareföreningen, 1996); Svedjedal, *The Literary Web*, 114–32; Squires and Ray Murray, 'The Digital Publishing Communications Circuit'.

[13] Have and Stougaard Pedersen, 'The Audiobook Circuit'; Tattersall Wallin, 'Reading by Listening'.

[14] Colbjørnsen, 'The Streaming Network'.

parallel flows of data. While Colbjørnsen's model is accurate and flexible, it is too generic for analyses of the book trade.

Have and Stougaard Pedersen's 'digital audiobook circuit' is a close reworking of Squires and Ray Murray's 'digital publishing communication circuit', which in turn is based on Darnton's model from 1982.[15] It moves from author to publisher, distributor, retailer, device, reader, then back again to author. Have and Stougaard Pedersen have modified the scheme by inserting audiobook publishers (between publishers and distributors), as well as increasing the emphasis on the significance of social media platforms in the feedback loop from readers back to authors.[16] They make a point of the model being media sensitive, that is, working only for audiobooks. However, all steps in their model apart from the 'audiobook publishers' would also apply to ebooks, and the media-specific aspects of the audiobook, such as the performing narrator, are not visible in the model. Furthermore, they put little emphasis on the power of the streaming services platforms, and the subscription-based model of selling (audio)books.

Modelling subscription-based book streaming services

I propose a conceptual circuit where the book streaming service is placed in the centre (see Figure 1.1). Obviously, this model does not cover the entire book trade. The production, distribution and reading of print books fall outside of its scope, as do audiobooks and ebooks sold as entities, as well as libraries, literary agents and other important actors in the trade. Rather, by placing the book streaming service in the middle, the intention is to highlight how this specific part of the book trade operates, and how it can be understood within a publishing and book historical framework.

In relation to previous models, three aspects stand out. First, the 'product' – audiobooks and ebooks – is highlighted in the model, which enables more in-depth material analyses of literary works (and their linguistic and bibliographic codes).[17] Second, the 'streaming service platform' highlights the importance

---

[15] See Squires and Ray Murray, 'The Digital Publishing Communications Circuit'; Darnton, 'What Is the History of Books?'.
[16] Have and Stougaard Pedersen, 'The Audiobook Circuit'.
[17] The product itself is only implicitly present in earlier communication circuit models, and it is only made visible as part of the flow between actors in Colbjørnsen's actor-based model. See further Have and Stougaard Pedersen, 'The Audiobook Circuit'; Colbjørnsen, 'The Streaming Network'. 'Product' is a term in the model that can be debated. It is related to *content*, which is a term

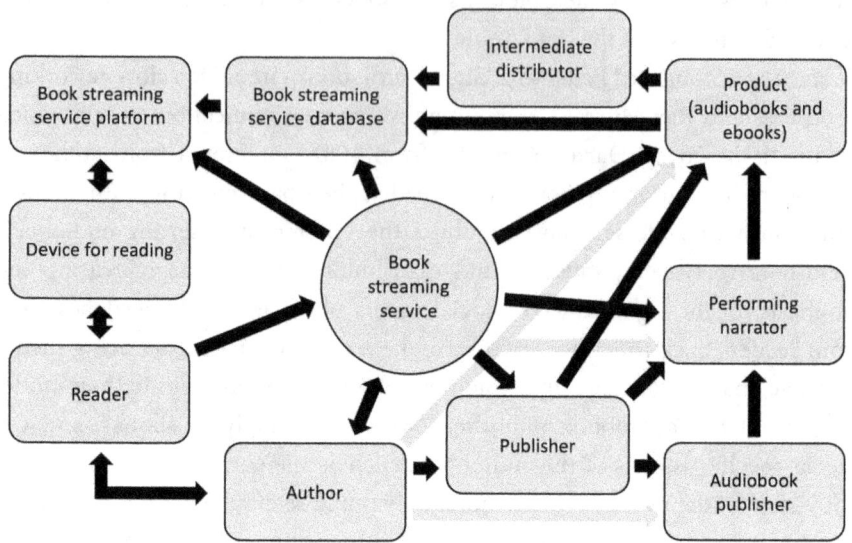

Figure 1.1 Model of subscription-based book streaming services. Boxes represent key actors and entities, black arrows represent flows of data and/or communication. Grey arrows represent flows of data and/or communication that are uncommon.

of interfaces, underlying algorithms and recommendation systems. Third, the model also calls attention to the 'performing narrator', as this is a significant part of audiobooks. The model is not reading media specific, as it works for both audiobooks and ebooks, but book streaming specific.

The model works as follows. A *book streaming service* provides a *database* of *digital products* (i.e. audiobooks and ebooks). The database consists of titles from *publishers, audiobook publishers*,[18] publications from the book streaming service themselves and possibly also from self-publishing *authors*. The arrows concerning self-publishing are grey in the model as this is not common in book

---

frequently used in the publishing industry. However, content is a rather vague concept that is in constant flux, whereas the product is more fixed; it is the content in its ready-to-publish form, if you will. In fact, the arrows in the model visualize how content is circulated between actors and changed along the way – manuscripts are edited, technical formats are decided and so on. With a textual criticism nomenclature, products might instead be understood as a category similar to the *work* in its *text* representation, and in two different *versions* (i.e. ebooks and audiobooks). For a thorough explanation of the nomenclature of textual criticism in a digital context, see Anna Gunder, *Hyperworks: On Digital Literature and Computer Games* (Uppsala: diss. Uppsala University, 2004), 155–94. Although these terms offer theoretical advantages, I have chosen to stick with the less abstract term 'product', as it manages, Ie argue, to capture what is at stake in the streaming-service business model.

[18] In principle, independent *ebook publishers* could also have been highlighted in the model. Because most publishers produce their own ebooks, and because audiobooks are so dominant in the Nordic streaming services for books, I have chosen to not do this, but instead keep a simplified model.

streaming services in Nordic countries yet. This is a major difference from Kindle Unlimited, for instance, which relies heavily on self-published ebooks.[19] When audiobooks are produced, a *performing narrator* (most often an actor) is hired for the recording. A publisher or self-publisher who wants to make their titles available on the platform can either negotiate directly with the book streaming service or go through an *intermediate distributor*.[20] In practice, all large publishing houses negotiate their own deals, while smaller actors often need to use intermediate distributors, and this works in favour for the large actors.[21]

The database is accessed through a *platform*, which is an app that *readers* download to their smartphone (or tablet, laptop or other *device*) to seek, browse, choose and finally read books – either as streamed sound files (audiobooks), text files (ebooks) or both. The platform also provides the option to switch between these formats as you go along. To gain access to the platform you pay a monthly fee to the book streaming service. This is the subscription part of the business model; instead of choosing and paying for specific books, you subscribe to the entire catalogue.

The subscription costs are constantly changing, and currently three alternatives are offered depending on how much you want to listen. In January 2023, a 'basic' Storytel account, with a limitation of 20 hours of listening per month, costs 129 SEK (around $12), a 'premium' account, with a limitation of 100 hours of listening per month, costs 169 SEK ($16) and an 'unlimited' account with no upper limit in listening hours costs 229 SEK ($22). The prices for the main competitor BookBeat are similar: a basic account with a maximum of 20 hours of listening per month costs 99 SEK ($10), a premium account with a max of 100 hours of listening costs 149 SEK ($15) and an unlimited account costs 249 SEK ($25).[22] The pricing levels are low, roughly comparable to buying one hardcover title a month, or to subscribe to a streaming service for other media, such as Netflix or Spotify.[23]

---

[19] See Thompson, *Book Wars*, 319–48.
[20] In the Nordic countries, such intermediate distributors include Bokinfo, Bookwire, Publit and Publizon. It can be noted that publishers may also use an intermediate distributor for the distribution of titles, while still having a direct agreement with the streaming service.
[21] In fact, books from many small presses are relatively absent in the Nordic book streaming services, especially concerning literary fiction. See further Määttä, Steiner and Berglund, *Skilda världar*, 64–5.
[22] Storytel, 'Storytel', https://www.storytel.com/se/sv/ (accessed 4 January 2023); BookBeat, 'BookBeat', https://www.bookbeat.se/ (accessed 17 November 2022).
[23] The low pricing levels has led to heated debates in Sweden, where among others the Swedish Authors' Association has accused the book streaming services of not paying authors enough per finished stream (see further Määttä, Steiner and Berglund, *Skilda världar*, 63–5). As Johan Svedjedal has noted, the pricing levels might be a reason to regard digital streaming services as a new low-cost format for books (see Svedjedal, 'Läsning och lyssning i en mångmedial tid', 20–3). It should also be noted that the three levels of subscriptions, with limitations in listening hours, were applied by

Apart from the price, the attractiveness of the subscription model for readers is related to the number of titles in the database. The larger the better, and the theoretical ideal is to hold 'all books', or at least all popular and recently published books. In Sweden, book streaming services have succeeded quite well in this respect. While 'all titles' are certainly not available,[24] all major publishers collaborate with these services, and most new releases that are also produced as audiobooks are included, as well as many titles as ebooks only.[25]

These book streaming services can sustain large numbers of available books paired with low subscription fees mainly because the revenues that go back to publishers and authors are lower than for books sold as individual items. Although there are certainly debates around these revenue models, publishers agree to the lower rates because subscription services seem to boost book reading in general by expanding the total market,[26] and because visibility on the lists of subscription services is becoming increasingly important. People now expect new books to be available on these platforms – at least popular fiction – which means that not having your titles included on these platforms is a problem, at least for large and mid-sized publishers.[27] Additionally, book streaming services such as Storytel are supported by venture capital, with the aim of growing rapidly. It is therefore not necessarily a problem if they do not generate profit immediately, since their investors believe that they will be profitable in the future, when they will control large shares of the market and have access to giant customer databases (such as Amazon, Google, etc.).[28]

Reading and the reading data feedback loop

The interest in collecting data on readers connects to an important aspect of book streaming that is a precondition for this book: the reader consumption

---

Storytel in January 2023. Before this – and thus for all users and reader consumption data which this book is based upon – the unlimited account was the only alternative offered, with a pricing level just above what is now called the 'premium' account.

[24] Especially literary fiction from smaller presses is less well represented in the Swedish book streaming services, both as ebooks and audiobooks (Määttä, Steiner and Berglund, *Skilda världar*, 60–72). For a mapping of the availability of classics and prestige fiction in Swedish book streaming services, see Jerry Määttä, 'Kvalitetslitteraturen i luren: Utbudet av Nobelpristagare och Augustnominerad skönlitteratur som strömmande svenska ljudböcker', in *Från Strindberg till Storytel – korskopplingar mellan ljud och litteratur*, ed. Julia Pennlert and Lars Ilshammar (Gothenburg: Daidalos, 2021).

[25] Both Storytel and BookBeat claim that they provide access to around 700,000 books in total, see Storytel, 'Om Storytel'; BookBeat, 'BookBeat'.

[26] Wikberg, *Bokförsäljningsstatistiken: Helåret 2021*, 26–7.

[27] Cf. John Thompson's description of American publishers' dependence on being available from Amazon as a 'faustian pact' (Thompson, *Book Wars*, 437–40).

[28] Cf. Thompson, *Book Wars*, 445–48.

data created by user interaction with these platforms and aggregated by the book streaming service. Datafication is of course a major trend in digital culture and the phenomenon of 'tracked reading' can also be observed more broadly, for instance in relation to Amazon's Kindle.[29] However, I argue that subscription-based book streaming relies to a larger extent than other forms of book distribution on user data, in ways that influence the whole chain of book production.

In the model, the reading data feedback loop is illustrated by the arrow from the reader back to the book streaming service. (The whole loop is highlighted within the model in Figure 1.2.) This arrow should be read as representing a flow not only of money but also of data. This data is used by the book streaming service to refine its platform by producing increasingly accurate recommendation algorithms and in other ways customizing the platform design for each individual user. Since the book streaming service owns this data, it can also serve other purposes. It can be used to adjust textual content according to user demand (as discussed below) and as part of the payment to publishers for making their titles available on the platform. It can also be sold to third parties who seek to reach specific customer segments through advertising. Companies are not yet selling data in this way, but it represents a possible way of generating more profit.

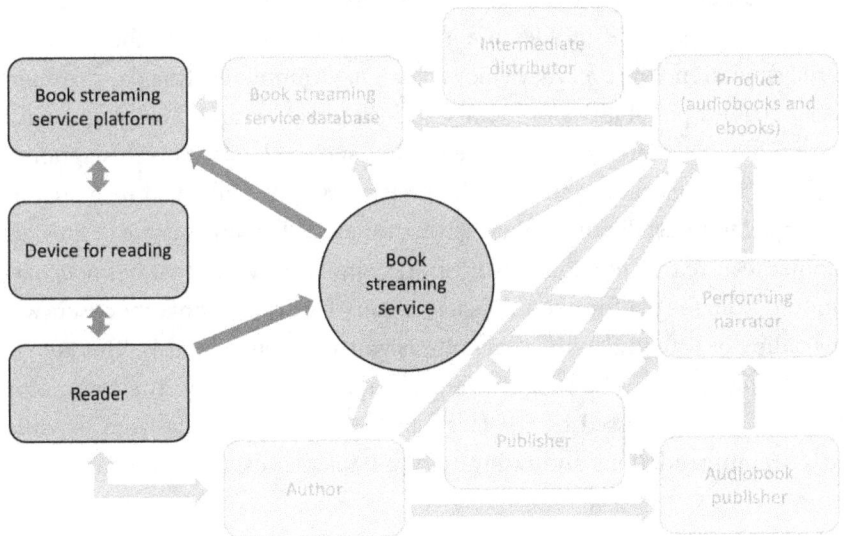

Figure 1.2 The reading data feedback loop highlighted within the model.

[29] See Whitney Trettien, 'Tracked', in *Further Reading*, edited by Matthew Rubery and Leah Price (Oxford: Oxford University Press, 2020).

What should be emphasized is that book streaming services, through this data, know much more about readers than publishers and authors do, and more than the literary industry have ever known before. In earlier book circuit models, the loop bites its own tail by connecting the readers back to the authors (through various kinds of feedback, physical as well as digital).[30] While the connection between the readers and authors remains important (and is also accounted for in the model), I argue that the feedback loop from readers back to the book streaming services is *decisive*, and something that is likely to have substantial consequences on publishing in years to come. As John B. Thompson notes, in the digital economy it is the distributors that know readers the best, not the publishers or the authors.[31] This discrepancy in terms of knowledge makes the distributor much more powerful and puts the distributional aspects at the forefront of contemporary publishing.

In the Storytel app, carefully curated selections from the reading data are also fed back and presented to the readers themselves as 'statistics'. For instance, the app will tell you which hours of the day and which days of the week you have used it, or which reader tags ('cosy', 'heartwarming', 'funny', 'page turner', etc.) have appeared most frequently on the books you have finished on the platform. In this way, Storytel allows the reader to become aware of parts of the machine learning 'profile' made by the company of their reading behaviour. The idea is, arguably, to create an appealing atmosphere of participation as well as self-recognition for the user, as these profiles are framed under suggestive labels such as 'Vardagsnjutaren' (the everyday enjoyer) or 'Dagdrömmaren' (the day dreamer). It also enables possibilities of literary self-presentation and 'bookfluencing', if such profiles are shared on social media sites such as Goodreads, Instagram or TikTok. Showing reading statistics in a harmless way could also be a strategy by Storytel to forestall potential criticism of their collection and use of the data. Another feature that previously worked in a similar way, but that has now been removed from the platform, is the visualization of the number of other users who are reading or listening to the same title as you are simultaneously. This appeals to readers who like to be part of a larger reading community. The community aspect is further stressed by the fact that the app features statistics on other users' recommendations and ratings of the books. Thus, users are encouraged

---

[30] Darnton, 'What Is the History of the Book?'; Squires and Ray Murray, 'The Digital Publishing Communication Circuit'; Have and Stougaard Pedersen, 'The Audiobook Circuit'.
[31] Thompson, *Book Wars*, 172–4.

to navigate the app by following the recommendations of other readers and listeners.[32]

The parts of the model that represent user interaction are key to grasping how book streaming affects reading. The platform design and its recommendation systems are one important aspect here, as highlighted in previous studies. Another is the subscription model itself. On the platform it is possible not only to browse books, as in a traditional bookstore or through an internet retailer, but also to start reading any book to try it out. This is something very different from carefully choosing a specific title and paying for it. In subscription-based book streaming the book shop and the private reading couch converge and can be anywhere, from a work commute to a remote mountain cabin.

The third and final point relates to what Thompson labels the *possession value* of books. In book streaming, it is only the actual reading of literature that matters: there is no show-off value or cultural prestige in streaming books, apart from what the reading itself gives.[33] Bookish social media such as BookTok and Bookstagram, however, complicates this reasoning. Such practices can be understood as a way for readers to create digital substitutes for the loss of the physical book's possession value. A challenge for book streaming services in the future will be to try to boost similar digital substitutes connected on their own platforms. The visibility of the user's own statistics is one way of adding value that stays after book completion. Other approaches might include book community building, in relation to social media, obviously, but perhaps also directly on the streaming platform. The cultural value of books and reading is likely to remain, while the ways of communicating this value change.

Book streaming services and content production

Book streaming services influence not only the relationship between readers and distributors but also literary content. A central aspect of the subscription-based business model is that it allows the book streaming service to bypass external publishers by producing their own content, which is exclusively available on their own platform. This option puts the streaming service in a strong position,

---

[32] See further Chapter 3, and also, for example, Steiner, 'The Global Book'; Murray, 'Secret Agents'; Thompson, *Book Wars*, 176–94.
[33] Thompson, *Book Wars*, 43–8; see further discussion in Chapter 2.

as it makes them independent of, and therefore less vulnerable to, external actors: it allows each platform to create a self-sufficient system for the literary process, covering production, distribution and consumption – to control the entire supply chain through what economic theorists call *vertical integration*.[34]

In the model, an arrow leads directly from the author to the book streaming service, indicating that the content producer collaborates directly with the author. This construction arguably influences the relation between the actors in a rather significant way and departs from the logic of traditional publishing (no external publishers, agents or editors). Storytel's own literary content is called 'Storytel Originals'. These are narratives written directly for the audiobook format and produced through close collaboration between editors and authors. In their presentation of the Originals brand, the company describes how they use a 'writer's room' approach, stressing collaborative writing, a concept associated with television production.[35] Furthermore, Storytel, rather than the author, holds the copyright for their original productions. The reduced status of the author is also highlighted by the centrality of another actor: the performing narrator. In the model, the performing narrator is placed between the book streaming service and the content, reflecting how the narrator works as a crucial mediator of content produced by the streaming service. This, of course, is true of any audiobook production, but the position of the narrator is particularly important in the services' original productions. On their webpage, directed at potential authors, Storytel emphasizes how the production of the Originals stories actively focuses on matching stories and narrators:

> At Storytel, we know from experience that it's key to connect the right voice to the right story for the right customer … We are experts at matching these three together: we have a lot of data on popular narrators in relation to different types of stories …. With our Storytel Original publishing process, we […] optimise stories for narration from the ground up.[36]

In order to 'optimise' products for the audio format, the streaming service makes use of data on audience behaviour. Storytel producer Anna Öqvist Ragnar emphasizes that they seek to produce original content that is adjusted to what the reader wants. Data analysis is used to secure this connection:

---

[34] For a discussion on vertical integration in relation to publishing, see Anna-Maria Rimm, 'Conditions and Survival: Views on the Concentration of Ownership and Vertical Integration in German and Swedish Publishing', *Publishing Research Quarterly* 30 (2014).
[35] Have and Raaby Jensen, 'Audio-bingeing'.
[36] Storytel, 'Storytel Original', https://publishing.storytel.com/storytel-original/ (accessed 21 June 2022).

We haven't made a lot of Originals that are supposed to attract new customers at Storytel. Our data analysis has rather involved saying, 'Hm, what are they listening to? Okay, then we will make something similar, only a little bit different.'[37]

The outcome is a certain kind of literature. Öqvist Ragnar notes that authors are instructed to write according to specific guidelines: the Originals series is characterized by straightforward, dialogue-driven and plot-centred storytelling.[38] On Storytel's webpage, the brand is presented as stories written directly for audio narration. The webpage further highlights that Originals stories should not contain too many metaphors and unnecessary digressions.[39]

The straightforward style of the Originals series is, however, not specific to born-audio works but reflects a broader relationship between the audiobook format and popular genre fiction. As will be discussed in Chapter 2, genre fiction, and especially crime fiction, is extremely popular on these platforms. Moreover, moving beyond the question of genre, a recent study has detected notable differences in style between works that are bestsellers in print format and the most popular audiobooks on Storytel. These results give reason to talk about a specific *audiobook stylistics*, where books that are popular in audiobook format on streaming service platforms are shorter, more straightforwardly written and appear to highlight plot and dialogue more than books that are popular in print format.[40] The streaming audiobook format arguably influences which styles and modes of storytelling become popular.

Notably, Storytel is competing not only with distributors of books but also with distributors of other media, including streaming services such as Netflix, for TV and film, or Spotify, for music and podcasts. The podcast format especially is a competitor. Elisa Tattersall Wallin has described how young audiobook readers more or less seamlessly switch between audiobooks, podcasts and music in their daily lives.[41] Storytel Originals may be understood as an attempt to attract a podcast audience, offering stories that include sound effects and music to a larger extent than other audiobooks.[42] The presentation of many Originals

---

[37] Anna Öqvist Ragnar, Storytel, Zoom interview with author, 28 January 2021. Translated from Swedish.
[38] Öqvist Ragnar interview with author.
[39] Storytel, 'Storytel Original'.
[40] Berglund and Dahllöf, 'Audiobook Stylistics'.
[41] Tattersall Wallin, 'Audiobook Routines'.
[42] This blurring of media boundaries is also reflected at the level of distribution, as Storytel offers podcasts as well as audiobooks. Furthermore, major streaming services for music and podcasts, such as Spotify and Soundcloud, are beginning to distribute audiobooks. In May 2021, Storytel announced that they had entered a partnership with Spotify which would enable Storytel subscribers

stories in 'episodes' and 'seasons' also reflects an orientation towards an audience used to TV series and podcasts.[43] Öqvist Ragnar acknowledges that Storytel is imitating the format of the streamed television series, but she also noted that this strategy has its limitations. When they launched the Originals brand in 2016, Storytel presented an Originals season in ten separate episodes. By 2021, they had shifted in most of their markets to publishing each season as one audio file of 9–10 hours, thus returning to a traditional average audiobook length:

> The episodic format has proved harder to implement than we thought it would be. [M]y hypothesis from the beginning was that the episodic format functions very well in television series [...] People are used to it. You don't have to promise to be listening for ten hours straight but can just try it out for an hour. And it is very possible that people do that, but the problem is that then, they quit, they kind of get nine chances to quit the series [...]. The competition is too fierce for us to allow that anymore. So now, we just want to get them going and not give them a single chance to quit.[44]

Rather than keeping listeners on the platform, Öqvist Ragnar believes that the ten-episode format involves a risk that people will abandon the series between episodes. This is because audiobooks are consumed in different ways and with different expectations than television series. Thus, while Storytel and other book streaming services may imitate trends in television production and other media industries, they still adjust production for a reading audience that is accustomed to long formats. Original productions might challenge the understanding of the audiobook as a remediation of the printed book. Yet, streamed audiobooks are still primarily defined by and closely connected to traditional book culture.[45]

Bibliographic codes in book streaming services

A final aspect of the model is that it enables analyses of the bibliographic codes and material aspects of literary works by capturing the intersections between

---

to listen to audiobooks via Spotify's platform, but at the time of writing nothing in this direction has yet happened. On streaming as a cross-industry tendency, see also Vilde Sundet and Terje Colbjørnsen, 'Streaming Across Industries: Streaming Logics and Streaming Lore Across the Music, Film, Television, and Book Industries', *MedieKultur: Journal of Media and Communication Research* 37, no. 70 (2021).

[43] See further Tanderup Linkis and Pennlert, 'Episodic Listening'.
[44] Öqvist Ragnar interview with author.
[45] This conclusion supports Sundet and Colbjörnson's observation that 'while informants across industries [...] emphasise the need to learn from other industries, solutions to challenges are typically sought within industry-specific frames' and 'that even if streaming is a cross-industrial trend, strategies are based on industry-specific logics and notions' (Sundet and Colbjörnson, 'Streaming Across Industries', 12.)

'books' (as objects) and book distribution in streaming services. The 'product (audiobooks and ebooks)' box in the model is an obvious starting point, but in line with McGann and others who emphasize the material aspects of literary works,[46] a complete analysis of 'books' as material objects in streaming services should also cover the streaming service platform and the hardware device used for reading.[47] The app design and its functionality is arguably the more important of the two, but hardware devices also matter. Literary works look slightly different depending on whether they are read on a smartphone, tablet or laptop. Even more significantly, audiobooks are read as sound through headphones or speakers, via the mediation of a performing narrator, while the reader interacts with ebooks through a touchscreen or a screen. When books are distributed through streaming services, accordingly, the book as it is produced by the publisher is not the same object as the one that the end consumers receive on the platform. Rather, its bibliographic codes, in McGann's sense, are a mutual creation of the publishers and the platform.

Indeed, both the platform and the reader's hardware device are part of the distribution of streamed books. It covers all the steps from the publish-ready product to when the mediated text reaches the readers' eyes and ears. This includes: integration in the book streaming service database, potentially via an intermediate distributor; visibility on the (software) platform; and concrete access through a (hardware) device. The model makes it clear that it is hard to separate material books as objects from their distribution when it comes to streaming services. Books and book distribution have in some respects converged into indistinct, overlapping categories.

When analysing literary works in streaming services, McGann's 'linguistic codes' are found in the 'Product (audiobooks and ebooks)' category, while the 'bibliographic codes' are found in several places: 'Product (audiobooks and ebooks)', 'Book streaming service platform' and 'Device for reading' (see Figure 1.3).[48] McGann's concept of bibliographic codes thus works quite well within the model as a tool for analysing the materiality of texts distributed through streaming services – though one could raise objections about whether aspects such as app design and recommendation system output should really

---

[46] See McGann, *The Textual Condition*; cf. Genette, *Paratexts*.
[47] I argue here in line with Anna Gunder, who emphasizes the materiality of electronic/digital texts and, accordingly, the relevance of a bibliographic approach to them. See Gunder, *Hyperworks*, 81–118. With a strict bibliographic approach, however, the term *book* is understood as the *physical text bearer*, which in the context of streaming services equals the hardware device, that is, most often a smartphone (cf. Gunder, *Hyperworks*, 98–111).
[48] Cf. McGann, *The Textual Condition*, 60–7.

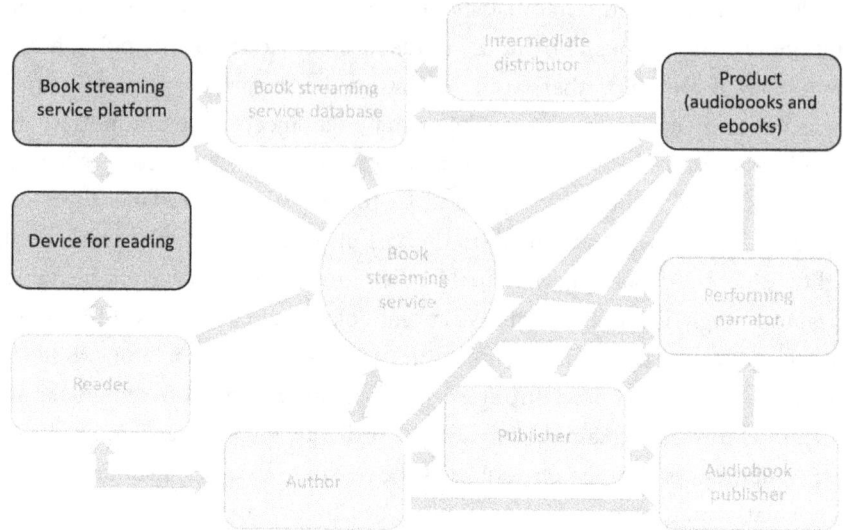

Figure 1.3 Bibliographic codes highlighted within the model.

be understood as parts of literary works per se. In any case, what the model visualizes is a power shift surrounding the bibliographic codes where streaming services are concerned. For print books, the bibliographic code is determined entirely by the publisher. For digital books sold as entities, it is determined mostly by the publisher, although the software and hardware have the potential to make changes in some respects. In book streaming, however, the material reading frame is arguably decided more by the book streaming service itself (i.e. the distributor) than by the publisher. Additionally, the reader is able to affect the bibliographic code of a given text as they interact with it, for example by choosing to speed up the pace of the narration.

Genette's distinction between peritext and epitext is more difficult to apply to book streaming services.[49] In one respect, all the information that is contained in a digital work when it is published (i.e. title, cover, author presentation, book presentation, performed narration) could be considered peritexts, but when this information is transferred into the book streaming service platform a lot of typically epitextual information gets blended with it and presented in the 'peritextual space' for each book. For instance, when you click a title in the Storytel app to read more about it, you get all the publisher's peritexts above,

---

[49] Cf. Genette, *Paratexts*, 1–12.

but also things such as average ratings by Storytel users, user reviews, users' top tag categories and recommendations of similar titles based on machine learning algorithms that use reading data, in other words, something that in accordance with Genette's terminology could be labelled 'the distributor's peritext', or even 'reader peritext', created by the many through reviews and ratings.[50]

Books sold through online retailers also appear at first alongside ratings and tags and other similar features. The big difference with book streaming services is that the reader only interacts with the literary work through the platform – books are never visible without this added information (as print books and downloaded ebooks and audiobooks are). If one talks about peritexts in book streaming services, it is crucial to understand that this category is a compilation of information from the publisher, the distributor and other readers (with the reader data provided indirectly, filtered through the book streaming service algorithms), which leads far away from Genette's original understanding of the peritext. If one, like McGann, believes that bibliographic codes should be seen as an important part of the literary work, then it must also be acknowledged that platform design and other aspects of the distributional frame shape the outcome of the literary work itself.

It is thus possible to analyse bibliographic codes and material aspects of literary works in book streaming services, as long as one is aware of the fact that the platform plays a pivotal role in determining how the end user will interact with the book, and thus how its material dimensions will contribute to its meaning.

Book subscription beyond the Nordic countries

Many national book trades have seen the establishment and growth of different types of book streaming platforms in recent years, but in most markets they are still more niche segments. In the United States, John B. Thompson calculates book streaming to account for only 2–3 per cent of the total book trade, and he believes that this will not change:

> [I]t seems likely that subscription will continue to play a relatively minor role in the evolution of the ecosystem of books in the Anglo-American world. Despite the many announcements of the arrival of the Netflix for books,

---

[50] Cf. Genette, *Paratexts*, 16, 347.

subscription services in the book industry have not acquired anything like the significance they have in music, film and television industries.[51]

I would not be so sure about that. First, Storytel, BookBeat and other similar actors are establishing themselves in new markets all the time, so far primarily in Europe, Asia and South America.[52] Storytel also recently acquired Audiobooks.com and thereby entered the US market.[53] Although this development is starting from small market shares, book consumers are gradually getting used to the idea of also consuming books by subscription (as the majority do with film, TV series and music).

Second, with the concurrent rise of digital audiobooks – a book format few people nowadays would like to own and keep after completion – the attraction of a digital subscription and easy access are increasingly transferred to books. It furthermore blurs the line between books and sound-based media such as podcasts. Interconnections between the music industry and the book industry have been present throughout the twentieth century, but such tendencies are amplified in the contemporary mishmash of digital media. A signal in this direction is that the music streaming service Spotify is starting to focus on audiobooks. 'A new chapter for listening. Audiobooks on Spotify', as they phrase it in their slogan.[54] But prior to this Spotify was also an important actor for streamed audiobooks. Children's literature in particular has a long tradition of audiobooks (or music sagas) released by record companies, and such books have been available to Spotify users for a long time.[55]

Third, in the Amazon-dominated Anglophone markets, the most important book streaming services at the moment are Amazon's Kindle Unlimited (KU) (for ebooks), Amazon's Audible (for audiobooks) and Scribd (an independent platform for both ebooks and audiobooks). KU provides unlimited access to their titles for their users, but the platform does not contain most titles from the major publishers. Instead, the 'over 2 million digital titles' available to users are mostly self-published titles or titles published by Amazon-owned companies

---

[51] Thompson, *Book Wars*, 348; for the whole account on subscription-based business models for books see the chapter 'Bookflix', 319–49.
[52] In November 2022, for instance, Storytel was launched in twenty-five markets, including important ones such as Germany, the Netherlands, Russia, India and Brazil.
[53] 'Storytel Enters the U.S. with Acquisition of Audiobooks.com', *Reuters*, 12 November 2021, https://www.reuters.com/business/media-telecom/storytel-enters-us-with-acquisition-audiobookscom-2021-11-12/ (accessed 28 November 2022).
[54] Spotify, 'A new chapter for listening: Audiobooks on Spotify', https://www.spotify.com/us/audiobooks/ (accessed 28 November 2022). Audiobooks are not included in the Spotify subscription though; each title needs to be paid for separately.
[55] Steiner and Berglund, *Barnlitterära strömningar*, 25–6.

as well as a limited selection of attractive megasellers such as the Harry Potter series and the Hunger Games series.[56] On the other hand, Audible (and Spotify's new audiobook launch works in a somewhat similar fashion) provides access to most audiobook titles by most major publishers, but instead has a restriction of only one free audiobook per month, with the possibility to buy additional titles separately. Access to the growing catalogue of Audible Originals, however, is unlimited and emphasized in the platform's own marketing: 'Unlimited listening to thousands of select Audible Originals, podcasts and audiobooks'.[57] Scribd, finally, provides unlimited access to lots of titles from several major publishers, but with some restrictions: 'there's no limit on the number of books or audiobooks that you can read or listen to each month', they state, followed by the more cryptical:

> That being said, you may sometimes notice that a title you have saved indicates it will be 'Available Soon'. Once your subscription renews for the next month, your library will refresh and you'll be able to select from our full library once more.[58]

It means that Scribd applies an unidentified consumption maximum per month – a threshold – to most of the titles from major publishers. When users hit that ceiling, they need to wait until the next month to read titles from that part of their catalogue. The threshold model is not very transparent, but its function is easy to understand: it hinders the top consumers from reading too much, as this would cause Scribd to lose a lot of money to rights owners. As Thompson describes it, the threshold model has been developed by Scribd over the years, 'more by trial and error and continuous iteration than by virtue of some fully formed plan'.[59]

None of these platforms offer unlimited access to most titles by all major publishers, the same as Storytel and other book streaming services in the Nordic countries. Nevertheless, they are in their heterogeneity pointing towards a probable future of the book trade: different book streaming services, with different offers targeted for different kinds of users. While it might be unlikely that one book streaming service in the UK or the United States could 'provide it all' to their customers, the market may evolve in similar ways to film and TV

---

[56] See further, McGurl, *Everything and Less*; Wilkins, Driscoll and Fletcher, *Genre Worlds*, 42–56; Steiner and Berglund, *Barnlitterära strömningar*, 25–6.
[57] Audible, https://www.audible.com (accessed 25 January 2022).
[58] Scribd, 'How many books does Scribd have? Are you adding more', https://support.scribd.com/hc/en-us/articles/210135406-How-many-books-does-Scribd-have-Are-you-adding-more (accessed 28 November 2022).
[59] Thompson, *Book Wars*, 330.

series streaming, where several major and competing platforms offer partly unique content (often self-produced) and partly overlapping content (acquired by deals with the rights owners). Disney and HBO can compete with Netflix mainly due to their strong back catalogues. The major book publishers could do the same. Perhaps the 'Big Five' publishers will start their own book streaming services, competing with KU and Audible; perhaps smaller and more niche platforms will appear.

In any case it seems likely that the subscription-based logic of cultural consumption will increasingly affect the book business. As Vilde Sundet and Terje Colbjørnsen claim, book streaming services can already be understood as a part of the wider digital media distribution of streaming.[60] Of course, books are not the same as music or TV series, and reading is not the same as listening to music or watching TV series. Yet, there are similarities, especially when it comes to the consumption of audiobooks, which shares many features with the consumption of music or podcasts.

Conclusion: Alterations on all ends

By proposing a model to conceptualize subscription-based book streaming services, I have in this chapter tried to account for ongoing developments in the production, distribution and reading of literature, especially in relation to the audiobook boom. These alterations, I argue, are affecting contemporary book culture and reading practices at its core, and some of these alterations will be studied in the following chapters. Using the model as a tool makes it possible to study how the increasing centrality of book streaming transforms established concepts and power relations in contemporary publishing and reading culture at all levels.

With regard to *reading*, the model enables investigations of the feedback loops and new forms of interaction between distributor and reader (via the device). The following chapters are all based on data emanating from this feedback loop for Storytel. Regarding *production*, the model visualizes how the relationships between authors, publishers and distributors are altered when streaming services are involved, as the book streaming service itself may act as producer of original content as well as distributor. This transforms the conditions for literary

---

[60] Sundet and Colbjørnsen, 'Streaming Across Industries'; cf. Colbjørnsen, 'The Streaming Network'.

production, shifting the power concerning who produces, controls and owns the text. Finally, concerning *distribution*, the model highlights that distributional aspects are both more complex and more important when it comes to book streaming services than they are in traditional book retailing. Where books previously could be understood as finished products (print or digital) that were distributed to an audience, book streaming services not only distribute books but also shape their bibliographic codes as they do so. In a book streaming service, the distributional frame and the final product are the same thing; all aspects of book consumption and reading start and end on these platforms.

By capturing the intersections between the reading and distribution of books, the model furthermore enables examinations of the bibliographic codes and material aspects of literary works in book streaming services. I argue that it is possible to understand books in streaming services as ontologically unstable per se, since their distribution and consumption are increasingly converging on these platforms. There is no longer any real material difference between seeing a book, 'buying' a book (or, rather, choosing a book for reading), reading a book, commenting on a book and switching the format for reading. What separates those activities is only a click or two within the same digital platform. By creating a model of the book circuit that applies McGann's concept of bibliographic codes to streaming services, it is possible to see how streaming services influence not only modes of reading, book production and distribution, but also the very constitution of books in our contemporary digital culture. How this, more concretely, is affecting reading practices is what will be discussed in the rest of this book.

2

Bestsellers and beststreamers: Genre reading

To study the commercial top segment of the book trade is to a great extent to study popular genre fiction. This holds true – at the very least – for most Western book trades.[1] In the Nordic context, this in particular means to delve into crime fiction. The global success story of Stieg Larsson and Nordic Noir is well recognized, but also back home the domestic writers in this genre are highly successful and have been so for at least two decades. Paired with the large import of crime fiction mainly from the UK and the United States, it is logical that crime fiction is by far the most commercially important genre in the Nordic countries.[2]

In this chapter, I zoom in on which kinds of literature are read the most in book streaming platforms, and if any differences on the genre level can be noted between streamed audiobooks and print books. I approach these reading practices with two main questions. The first is straightforward: which kinds of books are the most popular in book streaming platforms, and to which genres do they belong? The second is closely related but different in nature: which kinds of streamed audiobooks are readers most, and least, likely to finish?

Where the first question resembles the way quantitatively oriented strands of book history and sociology of literature for long have mapped popular books by means of sales figures, bestseller charts and library lending records, the second asks for a new kind of knowledge about book reading. Instead of the binaries of sold or not sold, lent or not lent, it provides a continuum. In so doing, the question brings to the fore the small revolution that reader consumption data can bring to reading studies. Upon a closer inspection, though, also answering

---

[1] See, for instance, Clive Bloom, *Bestsellers: Popular Fiction Since 1900* (Basingstoke: Palgrave, 2002); John Sutherland, *Bestsellers: A Very Short Introduction* (Oxford: Oxford University Press, 2007); Jon Helgason, Sara Kärrholm and Ann Steiner, editors, *Hype: Bestsellers and Literary Culture* (Lund: Nordic Academic Press, 2014); Wilkins, Driscoll and Fletcher, *Genre Worlds*.

[2] See further Berglund, 'Detectives in the Literary Market'; Berglund, 'Crime Fiction and the International Publishing Industry'.

the first question means something quite different from traditional quantitative bibliometrics. Instead of measuring books sold or lent, it tracks audiobooks completed in the sense of streamed all the way through.[3]

To answer these questions, I need to introduce two concepts for publishing and reading studies. The first is the concept of *the beststreamer*. In the most obvious respect, it works analogously to the bestseller, namely the books that have been streamed the most in a particular region and period of time; in the era of subscription-based book streaming that equates, more or less, to the digital bestsellers. Beststreamers should, however, not be understood as separate from bestsellers. On the contrary, titles popular in book streaming services are often also popular in print. As the analysis in this book will show, bestsellers and beststreamers both converge and diverge. In this respect, the beststreamer concept takes Simone Murray's claim that '[a]nalysts of the contemporary book world thus need to cease conceptualising the analogue and digital as ontological opposites and instead examine the two domains' complex patterns of coexistence' seriously, and it offers a way to concretely achieve this.[4]

Furthermore, and as I have already touched upon, the beststreamer has a second dimension, namely, it tracks actual literature use. That is, streaming rates in terms of started streams and finished streams as well as, potentially, any level of completion between these two outer delimiters. The concept of the beststreamer unites publishing and reading studies in providing a measurement of book impact based on literature use and not, as earlier book history metrics, based on book sales or library lending. As is commonly known, not all books that are bought are read. Finished streams are therefore a more accurate metric to track consumption in the sense of reading books instead of merely in the sense of buying (or lending) books.

To make use of the more nuanced information available in the reading data, I introduce the concept of *completion rate*, which is a measure of how well a book has been able to keep its readers. Such rates can be calculated in different ways, for instance, the number of finished streams of a title in a streaming-service platform divided by the number of started streams of the same title, or as the point in a narrative between the first word (0) and the last (1) where all readers in

---

[3] Or at least mostly all the way through. In the Swedish book trade, book streaming services report books that have been streamed to at least 80–90 per cent of their length as 'finished' (Steiner and Berglund, *Barnlitterära strömningar*, 40).
[4] Murray, 'Secret Agents', 971.

a platform who have started a specific title on average have ended their reading, the so-called average finishing degree (AFD).⁵

Since Storytel in their internal statistics make use of the latter, this is also the measure of completion rate that I will use in this chapter. The reason for this choice is partly to reduce the amount of data work involved, but, more importantly, it makes intellectual sense to not depart from the metric used by Storytel. If a scholar who studies a book streaming platform does so from the same points of view as its own engineers do, it increases the possibility of understanding how the platform and its categorizations and recommendations work. The completion rate is powerful in its simplicity, and it enables a fresh approach to the study of book popularity. As an addition to counting popularity (books sold, finished streams), the completion rate measures readerly devotion and books' ability to engage and keep their readers. Thereby, it avoids binaries and moves closer to real reading patterns. It should also be regarded as a starting point for further, more fine-grained approaches to analysing digital reading.

In the chapter, I try to showcase the utility of these two concepts – the principal beststreamer and the more operative completion rate – for publishing and reading studies by putting them to empirical use on Storytel's reading data, with a special focus on genre.

The reading data investigated is the first dataset as it was described in the introduction. The dataset covers all Storytel users in Sweden for all literary works that during the period 2015–19 have been either a bestseller in print (according to the Swedish Publishers' Association's annual lists), a beststreamer on the Storytel platform (according to Storytel data) or both (see Table 2.1). Apparently, the dataset is constructed mainly with regard to the comparative angle between print bestsellers and audiobook beststreamers.⁶ It covers consumption of audiobooks and ebooks, but audiobooks constitute 90 per cent of the traffic.⁷

---

[5] Thus, if a particular book has the AFD of 1, it means that all users who started the book also completed it. This is the absolute and theoretical maximum AFD, which no book in practice can achieve. To exemplify how the metric works even further, think of a book that has four readers in total, where one streamed a quarter of the book, one streamed half of the book, one streamed two-thirds of the book and one streamed the entire book. This would give an AFD of (0.25 + 0.5 + 0.67 + 1) / 4 = 0.605. What the AFD does not manage to capture is readers jumping around in narratives and people rereading the same books. The AFD is simply the average point in the narrative where each reader was located at the time when the dataset was compiled from the Storytel reader consumption data.

[6] For a 'twin' study to this chapter, departing from the same comparison of subsets but instead measuring differences between the two on a textual level, see Berglund and Dahllöf, 'Audiobook Stylistics'.

[7] Steiner and Berglund, *Barnlitterära strömningar*, 39. An official figure from some years ago on the audiobook share regarding consumption on the Storytel platform, covering all consumption in Sweden in 2020, is 92 per cent audiobooks (Mikael Holmquist, Storytel, email interview with author, 10 February 2021).

Table 2.1 Books in the Commercial Top Segment 2015–19 by Subset: Number of Titles, and Finished Streams and Finished Streams by Title on Average

Subset	Titles	Finished streams (000s, rounded)	Finished streams per title on average (000s, rounded)
Bestsellers 2015–19	81	1,545	19.2
Beststreamers 2015–19	49	2,318	47.4
Books popular in both formats	40	2,445	61.0
Total	170	6,309	37.1

Storytel has collected finished streams for the whole period studied, but the more fine-grained user data only since October 2018. This means that finished streaming rates are measured from January 2015 to April 2020, and AFDs for the shorter period from October 2018 to April 2020. Although it is unfortunate that the AFD scores do not cover the whole period studied, the limitation does not affect the discussion concerning the usefulness of the measure.

The empirical analysis is divided into two parts. In the first, bestsellers and beststreamers are compared and analysed according to the number of finished streams, that is, popularity in terms of digital reading. In the second, a similar comparison is carried out, but now departing from the AFD metric, focusing on reader devotion and the ability of narratives to sustain reader interest. In the final section, these two quantitative approaches are brought together and discussed in relation to publishing and reading studies.

Popularity seen as finished streams

What is then discovered when finished streams are compared for bestsellers and beststreamers? To start with, comparing the titles' attributed genres reveals important differences. Although bestsellers are a category of books dominated by popular genre fiction, especially crime fiction, it is nevertheless a mixed category that also contains a significant amount of prestigious and prize-winning fiction as well as middlebrow titles. Beststreamers, however, can almost be equated with crime fiction (see Table 2.2).

If the title-based numbers are transformed into streaming rates, the pattern emerges even more clearly. For the whole dataset, crime fiction constitutes

Table 2.2 Genre Proportions in the Commercial Top Segment 2015–19 by Number of Titles and Percentage

Genre	Bestsellers	Beststreamers	Crossovers	Total
Crime fiction	31 (38%)	45 (92%)	34 (85%)	110 (65%)
Romance	15 (19%)	1 (2%)	3 (8%)	19 (11%)
Prestige fiction	12 (15%)	0 (0%)	0 (0%)	12 (7%)
Other fiction	23 (28%)	3 (6%)	3 (8%)	29 (17%)
Total	81 (100%)	49 (100%)	40 (100%)	170 (100%)

Table 2.3 Genre Proportions in the Commercial Top Segment 2015–19 by Finished Streams (in 000s, Rounded) and Percentage

Genre	Bestsellers	Beststreamers	Crossovers	Total
Crime fiction	664 (43%)	2,167 (93%)	2,150 (88%)	4,981 (79%)
Romance	374 (24%)	37 (2%)	145 (6%)	556 (9%)
Prestige fiction	101 (7%)	0 (0%)	0 (0%)	101 (2%)
Other fiction	406 (26%)	114 (5%)	150 (6%)	670 (11%)
Total	1,545 (100%)	2,318 (100%)	2,445 (100%)	6,309 (100%)

65 per cent of the titles and 79 per cent of the finished streams, while prestige fiction constitutes 7 per cent of the titles and 2 per cent of the finished streams (see Tables 2.2 and 2.3). If looking only at bestsellers, prestige fiction constitutes 15 per cent of the titles but only 7 per cent of the finished streams.

The outcome shows that crime fiction in the commercial top segment is streamed to a notably higher extent on the Storytel platform when compared to print sales, and that prestige fiction conversely is streamed to a notably lower extent. The pattern is visible when looking at genres at the top of the lists for the respective subsets and is amplified when finished streams are counted. Thus, there is not only more crime fiction and less literary fiction in the digital charts compared to the print ones – the titles of literary fiction that were bestsellers are consumed less when compared to other bestsellers in print that did not make it to the top charts of the streaming platform.

If the finished streams are broken down into individual titles, all top titles are domestic crime fiction, with those written by David Lagercrantz, Lars Kepler and Camilla Läckberg at the absolute top. At the bottom there are several books by authors awarded major literary prizes, for instance, Olga Tokarczuk, awarded

Table 2.4 Proportions of Translations in the Commercial Top Segment 2015–19 by Finished Streams (in 000s, Rounded) and Percentage

Translations	Bestsellers	Beststreamers	Crossovers	Total
Swedish originals	900 (58%)	2,089 (90%)	2,177 (89%)	5,166 (82%)
Translations	646 (42%)	229 (10%)	268 (11%)	1,143 (18%)
Total	1,545 (100%)	2,318 (100%)	2,445 (100%)	6,309 (100%)

the Nobel Prize in Literature, Hanya Yanagihara, shortlisted for the Booker Prize and awarded the Kirkus Prize, and Johannes Anyuru, awarded the Swedish August Prize. Even more apparent is the dominance of translated works, including translated popular fiction written by authors such as Anthony Doerr, Armando Lucas Correa and Louise Doughty. If looking at the whole dataset, the bias concerning translations and Swedish originals is apparent. While the distribution is at least fairly balanced among the bestsellers in print (roughly six to four), the Swedish originals constitute around nine out of ten of the finished streams both among the beststreamers and the titles popular in both formats (see Table 2.4).

Importantly, the distribution of finished streams in the beststreamer category resembles the distribution in the category of cross-format popularity concerning both genres and translations. While pure bestsellers in print are a very different category of books compared to beststreamers, the bestsellers that also work well in book streaming platforms seem to be more like the pure digital beststreamers. This indicates that bestsellers in print are a mix of high- and lowbrow, whereas digital beststreamers are much more homogeneous, heavily dominated by Swedish popular genre fiction, especially crime fiction.

Print books versus streamed (audio)books

There are several, interconnected explanations for these apparent differences between book formats. One is that digital audiobooks are the driving force behind the vast impact of book streaming services and that this is a format best suited for straightforwardly narrated and streamlined popular fiction, while more complex and stylistically advanced prose perform less well. This aspect is frequently highlighted in debates around the rise of streaming services in Sweden, mainly because it worries advocates of literary fiction. The former CEO of Sweden's largest publishing house, Bonniers, for instance, stressed such points in an interview that gained considerable attention in Sweden.[8] Together with Mats Dahllöf I have empirically tested this assumption by means of a stylistic computational text analysis, with a corresponding result: bestsellers and beststreamers do differ regarding prose style, regardless of genre. Print bestsellers are long and syntactically complex and varied, by contrast beststreaming audiobooks are short, more straightforwardly written and focused on plot and dialogue.[9] Iben Have and Birgitte Stougaard Pedersen, however, claim that audiobooks work equally well for focused reading as for easy reads and distraction.[10] Even if this might theoretically be true, the data tell a different story: literary fiction, prestige fiction and more complex narrative constructs do not attract readers on book streaming services to the same extent as they do with print books.

A second explanation, which relates to a more thorough discussion in Chapter 3, is that the differences between print bestsellers and streaming rates make visible the distinction between literary consumption in the sense of buying books and of actually reading them. Many people probably recognize themselves in the description of having bought an award-winning book or having received it as a gift, and then letting the book sit on the shelf, completely or partially unread. Such behaviour is explained by the intrinsic value in owning or giving away books by prize-awarded, prestigious authors, regardless of whether they are read or not. Books by Nobel Prize laureates such as Herta Müller or Olga Tokarczuk – who are both parts of the dataset investigated here – on a bookshelf signal education and good taste. Popular genre fiction works differently – if you buy a detective story or a romance novel, you usually do so because you want to read it. When similar behaviours are transferred to a digital book streaming service, the difference between genres emerges with brutal clarity: with the status consumption of print books taken away, the figures for literary fiction simply plunge. There is little prestige connected to streaming a book that goes beyond what the actual reading provides. From this perspective, book streaming might be regarded as a new low-cost format for books, a digital version of the mass-market paperback.[11]

A third explanation of the homogeneity of the beststreamers might be found in the customer base of the book streaming services. In Sweden in the year 2021, around 13 per cent of all book readers used book streaming services for audiobooks on a daily basis, which can be compared to the corresponding

[8] Sverker Lenas and Georg Cederskog, 'Konflikt om ljudböcker på Bonniers: "Nobelpristagare underpresterar digitalt"', *Dagens Nyheter*, 22 March 2018.
[9] See Berglund and Dahllöf, 'Audiobook Stylistics'.
[10] Have and Stougaard Pedersen, *Digital Audiobooks*, 25–60.
[11] See further the discussion in Chapter 3; Thompson, *Book Wars*, 176–94.

number of 34 per cent for printed books.[12] Although audiobook reading has been growing constantly over the last five years, it is still a minority of readers that read audiobooks regularly. It is therefore likely that the Storytel users are not representative of the book-reading community in Sweden in general. Frequent readers of literary fiction might prefer reading in print, and readers of both popular and literary fiction might choose Storytel as a substitute for buying mass-market paperbacks of popular fiction, while sticking with print editions for their literary reads. Added to this is the fact that the selection of popular fiction in the audiobook format is much larger than literary fiction; the marketing of book streaming services has largely been about audiobooks as a time-saving and efficient way to read while doing something else; and much of the debate around audiobooks has focused on either textual adaptations and simplifications to attract broad audiences or the authors' low remuneration levels.[13] In short, there is much about both the digital audiobook and the debate that surrounds it that discourages many of those who read, write and/or work with literary fiction. This has likely affected the customer base, but currently there is unfortunately no data available about such biases.

A final explanation relates to the Storytel platform design. Several commentators have discussed how interface design and functionality in book streaming platforms affect and shape consumption behaviour, and how the availability of seemingly endless numbers of choices makes readers increasingly dependent on suggestions from recommendation systems.[14] Similar patterns are likely at work here. If the customer base of readers is skewed towards popular fiction in line with the above, it produces effects in the platform's recommendation systems and general design. Since most Swedish Storytel users at the moment read crime fiction and other genres of popular fiction, such titles are recommended to a large extent and placed strategically in the app design in terms of suggested reads and categories. Beststreaming lists in themselves, moreover, tend to work in a similar fashion, since such rankings are not only a listing of popular books but a marketing tool in themselves, they attract more readers to the already-popular titles.[15] In fact, literary fiction is not that easy to locate in the app, since it is not organized into a category of its own.[16]

---

[12] Jonas Ohlsson (editor), *Mediebarometern 2021* (Gothenburg: Nordicom, 2022), 78–9.
[13] See further Määttä, Steiner and Berglund, *Skilda världar*, 60–5, 72–5.
[14] See, for instance, Ted Striphas, 'Algorithmic Culture', *European Journal of Cultural Studies* 18, no. 4–5 (2018); Steiner, 'The Global Book'; Murray, 'Secret Agents'; see also further the discussion in Chapter 3.
[15] Cf. Laura J. Miller, 'The Best-Seller List as Marketing Tool and Historical Fiction', *Book History* 3 (2000).
[16] See further Määttä, Steiner and Berglund, *Skilda världar*, 66–7.

The segmentation of book streaming

Another viable approach to the finished book streaming rates concerns the diachronic perspective. That is, how the reading proportions of print bestsellers and digital beststreamers in the Storytel platform relate to each other over time. This can be accomplished by means of linear regression, a standard statistical analysis that calculates correlations between two parameters in a dataset.[17] In Figure 2.1, the three regression lines in such an analysis – based on finished streams per day for the whole dataset – show that the beststreamers (dashed line) are gaining ground, while the print bestsellers (solid line) and the titles popular both in print and in book streaming services (dotted line) are decreasing as per finished streams.

The result indicates that book streaming services are starting to find their stride as a portal for reading, and that they are – slowly but steadily – drifting

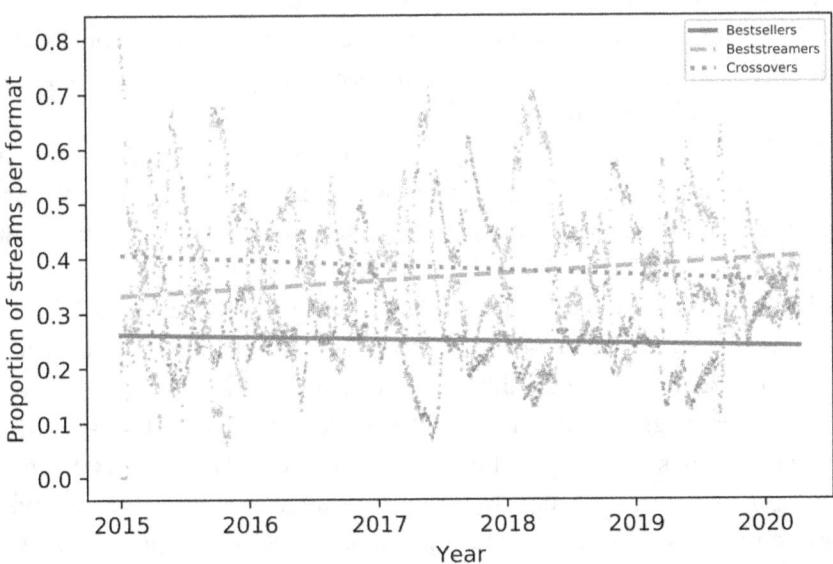

Figure 2.1 Relative frequencies of finished streams: regression lines by subset and day.

---

[17] Linear regression, a standard procedure in applied statistics, is a prediction of the best-fitting interpolation line for all data points (x_n, y_n) according to the formula $y = mx + b$, where m is the slope of the line, and b is the value of the line where it crosses the y-axis (that is, the starting point, in this analysis it equals 1 January 2015). A positive m-value indicates a positive, rising trend (in this case an increased proportion of the streams in the platform), whereas a negative m-value indicates the opposite. In this analysis, the regression lines have been calculated with the Python standard maths library NumPy.

away from the traditional book sales channels in terms of what kinds of fiction are primarily read. In relative numbers, successful beststreaming-only titles are becoming more important on the Storytel platform, while bestsellers in print are becoming less important. The observed textual differences in prose style between popular audiobooks and popular print books found by Berglund and Dahllöf point in a similar direction; audiobook readers in book streaming services seem to favour a certain kind of writing.[18]

What these changes will mean for the book market in the future is yet to be seen. One scenario is that the categories bestsellers and beststreamers will continue to diverge. This could lead to a book trade consisting of two increasingly separated segments, where books are published either in different versions to suit each book format or in one of the segments only, depending on the kind of literature in question (which means: literary fiction will mainly be read as print books, while the genres of popular fiction will mainly be streamed, generally as audio). Another scenario is that the print world will start to adapt to the rules that apply to book streaming. Such an adaptation can take many forms – editing and publishing with audio in mind, experiments with audio-only publishing, well-established print authors turning to born-audio formats, etc. – some of which are already happening.[19]

In the 1950s the leading literary sociologist of his time, Robert Escarpit, launched a model of the book market in which the distribution of books was separated into two main circuits: 'the cultured circuit' and 'the popular circuit'. Although there are 'blockade breakers' in Escarpit's model – that is, individual books and distribution methods that bridge this gap – the dividing line between the circuits is strong and concrete in Escarpit's understanding: literary fiction and popular fiction are sold in different places, by different professional groups and to different groups of readers.[20] The model was launched in the 1950s in France, a book market with little resembles to the contemporary Swedish one. In Sweden, literary fiction and popular genre fiction have for a long time coexisted in most contexts, and the separation between their production and distribution that did exist has diminished over time. Although there are still certain publishers and sales channels specialized in either literary fiction or popular genre fiction, it has in recent decades been unreasonable to speak of the Swedish book market in terms of two clearly separated circuits.

---

[18] Berglund and Dahllöf, 'Audiobook Stylistics'.
[19] See further Tanderup Linkis, 'Reading Spaces'; Tanderup Linkis and Pennlert, 'Episodic Listening'; Steiner and Berglund, *Barnlitterära strömningar*.
[20] Robert Escarpit, *Sociology of Literature*, 2nd edn (1958; London: Cass, 1971).

But the rise of book streaming services – and especially streamed audiobooks – paves the way for a comeback of Escarpit's model. Since popular genre fiction is so dominant in book streaming services, it is possible to consider them as a distributor of primarily popular genre fiction, clearly demarcated from the rest of the book market through its form of distribution (digital apps where literature is streamed), its business model (subscriptions instead of purchasing individual titles) and its dominant medium for book consumption (audiobooks). Of course, it is not possible to speak of the remaining book market as a literary fiction circuit, as popular genre fiction is a central part there as well. But the results in this chapter point to a development where literary fiction and popular genre fiction have once again begun to be separate on the book market.[21] Mark McGurl's investigation of the many thriving micro-genres of popular fiction in Amazon's Kindle Direct Publishing – which, he emphasizes, should be placed 'at the center of scholarly concern rather than at the margins where it usually finds itself' – points in a similar direction, but for ebooks and in the US context.[22] The differences between literary fiction and popular genre fiction in the contemporary book trade have been accentuated by the fact that it has also increasingly become a matter of book medium and distribution, which risks reinforcing the different material conditions that apply for niche literary fiction, on the one hand, and popular genre fiction, on the other.

Mapping nuances in book streaming through completion rates

The patterns of consumption and reading have so far in this chapter been discussed in terms of finished streams, which equates with books that have been completed by the reader in the sense of being read all the way through. Average finishing degree (AFD), on the contrary, measures levels of completion and thereby reader devotion as well as the ability of narratives to keep readers. What immediately stands out when AFDs are investigated are the correlations between popularity on the platform (in terms of finished streams) and high completion rates. This goes for practically all parameters: audiobooks have higher completion rates than ebooks (74 per cent compared to 69 per cent);

---

[21] For a more thorough account of this development, see Määttä, Steiner and Berglund, *Skilda världar*, 58–81.
[22] McGurl, *Everything and Less*, 205.

crime fiction has the highest completion rate among the genres, while prestigious fiction has the lowest (76 per cent for crime fiction, 65 per cent for other popular fiction and 53 per cent for prestigious fiction); Swedish originals have higher completion rates than translated titles (74 per cent compared to 64 per cent); and beststreamers and books popular both in streaming services and in print have higher completion rates than print bestsellers (79 per cent and 75 per cent, respectively, compared to 64 per cent) (see Figures 2.2 to 2.4).

This means, in general, that books read by many users on the Storytel platform (in terms of finished streams) also are the books that readers tend to finish. This result makes sense and can also be tracked down by statistical means. Figure 2.5 shows a scatterplot of all the titles in the dataset, distributed along the x-axis by AFD and along the y-axis by number of finished streams. The rising curve of

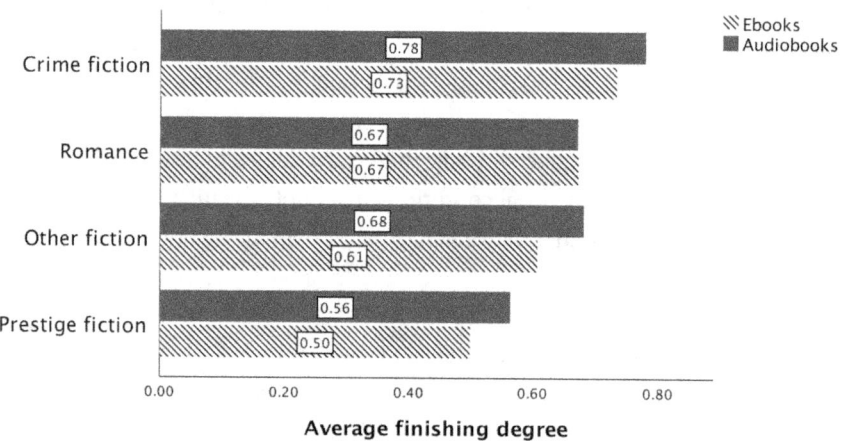

Figure 2.2 Average finishing degrees in the commercial top segment 2015–19 by genre and format.

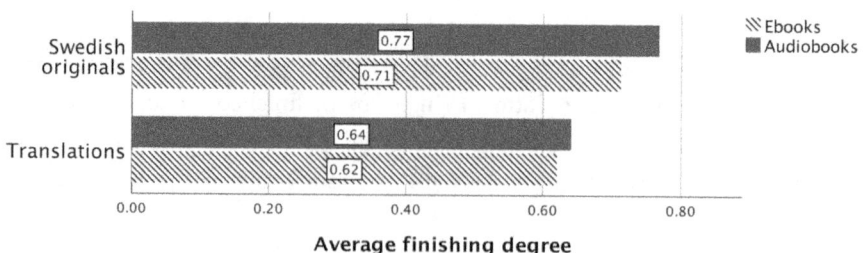

Figure 2.3 Average finishing degrees in the commercial top segment 2015–19 by country of origin and format.

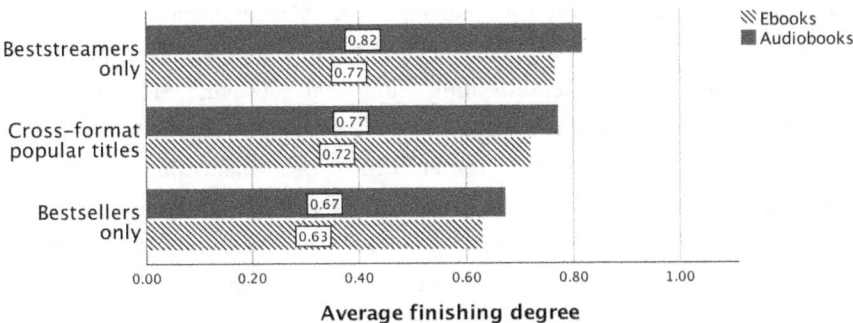

Figure 2.4 Average finishing degrees in the commercial top segment 2015–19 by subset and format.

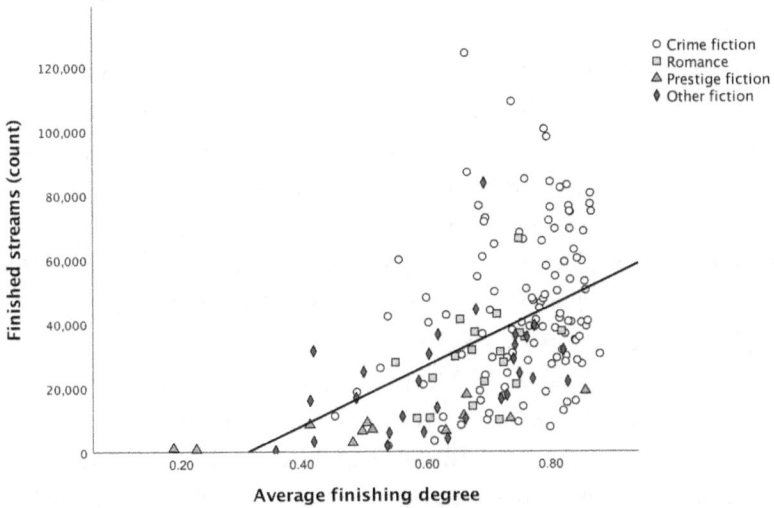

Figure 2.5 Average finishing degree and finished streams in the commercial top segment 2015–19 by genre.

the grey interpolation line indicates the positive correlation between the two variables in statistical terms. The R-value 0.475 from the regression analysis suggests a moderate to weak linear relationship, which can be interpreted as, often, a high AFD follows a high number of finished streams, but there are also several exceptions to this rule.

Taking a close look at Figure 2.5, this seems plausible. In fact, a lot more nuanced information can be drawn from this scatterplot. Almost all books with really high AFDs (over 80 per cent) are works of crime fiction. Indeed, crime fiction seems to be the genre that manages to keep readers and produce page-turning effects. This is not surprising per se, as crime fiction has for a long time had a strong position in the bestselling segment in Sweden.[23] Moreover, it is a genre that contains textual and narrative features with the explicit aim to keep up reader interest all the way to the end. Most prominent, the crime fiction reader knows that a killer will be caught at the end of the story, but the reader also knows that who the killer is will – generally – not be revealed until the final part of the book.[24] To find out the most important point in a crime novel, then, one needs to read it all the way through.

It is important to note that it is not the most popular novels in terms of finished streams that are completed to the highest extent, but rather the segment just below the top. It is not books by, for instance, David Lagercrantz, Lars Kepler or Camilla Läckberg that have AFDs over 80 per cent but lesser-known names such as Carin Gerhardsen and Dag Öhrlund. A probable explanation for this outcome is that the latter category of authors is highly profiled within the crime genre but not so much outside of it. Thus, they mostly attract already engaged crime-fiction readers, whereas writers such as Lagercrantz, Kepler and Läckberg attract a broader audience. But this wider audience is also less faithful as readers, which leads to lower completion rates.

The exceptions to the rule that a high AFD equals a crime fiction novel are interesting to study further. These include Jan Guillou's historical novel *Blå stjärnan* ('Blue Star', author's translation) (2015), Jojo Moyes's romantic novel *Still Me* (2018), and two books in Elena Ferrante's Neapolitan Novels series, *Storia di chi fugge e di chi resta* ('Those Who Leave and Those Who Stay') (2013) and *Storia della bambina perduta* ('The Story of the Lost Child') (2014).[25] What unites these books is not genre, or country of origin, but that they all belong to a series, and that none of them are the first title in their series. On closer inspection, the Neapolitan Novels tell a clear story. All four were bestsellers in Sweden in the period and are thus included in the dataset. The first novel in the series is the one streamed the most, but it is also the one with a significantly lower AFD than the others (see Table 2.5).

---

[23] See Berglund, 'Detectives in the Literary Market'.
[24] This is a simplification of the genre, obviously, and the narrative strategies in crime fiction can be discussed in more elaborate ways. For a famous example, see the 'The Typology of Crime Fiction', in Tzvetan Todorov's *The Poetics of Prose* (1971; Ithaca, NY: Cornell University Press, 1977), 42–52; for a computational approach to the structures of crime fiction narratives, see Karl Berglund, 'Killer Plotting: Typologisk intriganalys utifrån fjärrläsningar av 113 samtida svenska kriminalromaner', *Tidskrift för litteraturvetenskap* 48, no. 3–4 (2017).
[25] The latter is here categorized as prestige fiction as it was shortlisted for the 2016 Booker International Prize.

Table 2.5 Finished Streams and AFDs for Elena Ferrante's Neapolitan Novels

Number in series	Title	Finished streams (index = 100.0)	AFD
1	*My Brilliant Friend*	100.0	0.42
2	*The Story of a New Name*	77.6	0.75
3	*Those Who Leave and Those Who Stay*	69.6	0.83
4	*The Story of the Lost Child*	60.4	0.86

Thus, while there exists a positive correlation in general between reader popularity (a high number of finished streams) and reader devotion (high completion rates), the correlation on the level of *individual series* is likely to be inverted in most cases. As the Ferrante case shows, the first title in a series is often the most widely read – generally, readers start with the first title to see if they like it or not. Those who cling to a series to the end, on the other hand, are the most devoted readers. If you have read the first three Ferrante novels and start to stream the fourth and final one, you are presumably much more motivated to read it through than if you have just embarked on the first book in the series. The Ferrante case exemplifies this reader psychology. The relationship between popularity and reader devotion should therefore be regarded simultaneously on two levels. On the generic level, the number of finished streams and high completion rates have a positive correlation. On the level of the individual book series, the number of finished streams and high completion rates is likely to have a negative correlation.

Conclusion: Aligning publishing studies and reading studies

In this chapter, I have used Storytel reader consumption data on the title level to track how the commercial top segment of fiction has been consumed in the major book streaming service in Sweden over a recent five-year period. In doing this, two new methodological concepts for digital publishing studies are introduced: the *beststreamer*, which equals the most read books in a book streaming service in a particular region and time; and the *completion rate*, a metric to study which books readers tend to finish, and which they tend to abandon half-way through. The reading data paired with these concepts allow for the tracking of reading practices simultaneously at scale and in a far more nuanced way than what is possible by means of traditional measures of book consumption. Furthermore, it aligns publishing studies and reading studies, since book popularity is measured through reading practices.

Empirically, large differences between the bestselling and the beststreaming segments were found. Print bestsellers show a much larger heterogeneity genre-wise than digital beststreamers. Where the former spans prestige fiction to crime fiction, the latter consists mostly of crime fiction, primarily written by domestic Swedish authors. This pattern emerges on the title level but grows stronger when finished streams are analysed. Similarly, crime fiction is by far the most successful genre in terms of completion levels, whereas prestige fiction, on the other hand, is the kind of literature where most readers tend to drop out in the middle of the story.

The results indicate that readers prefer different kinds of fiction when they stream books to when they buy print books and/or that other groups of readers subscribe to book streaming services than those who buy print books. Here, I am studying the Swedish context, where streamed audio and crime fiction are especially prominent, but similar key differences are found also in an Anglophone context, where the explosion of self-published ebooks distributed through Amazon's Kindle Direct Publishing is perhaps the most important recent book-trade intervention, and where a similar favouring of popular genre fiction can be noted.[26]

There are a multitude of reasons for these differences – including platform design, pricing models, supply, marketing, customer base, print book's possession value and media-specific features of the audiobook – of which several are discussed in detail in other chapters of this book. The subscription-based models for selling access to large collections of digital books affects reading practices, but perhaps not in the ways one would immediately assume. For instance, one could imagine that most readers try out lots of books when they have access to 'it all', so to speak, before settling on one to listen to. While there are indeed such readers – I call them 'swappers' and examine them more closely in Chapter 6 – it is a rather uncommon practice in the datasets I have access to. Similarly, one could presume that people who buy print books also tend to read them through, but this is not necessarily the case. While there is no corresponding

---

[26] See, for instance, McGurl, *Everything and Less*, especially 193–210; Wilkins, Driscoll and Fletcher, *Genre Worlds*, especially 28–57.

data available for the reading practices of print books, the reading data in this investigation complicates all such preconceptions.

The completion rates for the most popular titles in this investigation are arguably rather high – if all readers and all books in the dataset are considered, books are on average finished to 71 per cent of the narrative (where 0 per cent is the first word of the book and 100 per cent is the last word). Several titles have average completion rates over 80 per cent, and some are bordering 90 per cent. Thus, most narratives investigated here appear to be rather successful in keeping their readers interested. The clearest exception to this is prestige and literary fiction, which to a large extent fail to attract readers in book streaming services, especially in the audiobook format. As prominent commentators from the Swedish publishing industry frankly have concluded, such genres are 'underachieving' in book streaming services, and they 'do not work in audio'.[27] What is surfacing in the data, then, is that the inherent value in buying, owing and giving away print books of prestige fiction simply disappears in book streaming services, where reading rather than sales is measured. This discrepancy in consumption behaviour between buying books and reading them will become increasingly important as Storytel and other book streaming platforms (Kindle Unlimited, BookBeat) are paying publishers per number of minutes streamed. This is different from getting paid by the number of sold entities, and it will make books that people tend to finish more valuable for publishers henceforth. Books that readers are repeatedly reading will be even more treasured. I investigate such repetitive reading practice in depth in Chapter 6.

Finally, the ability to track and understand how reader devotion works and operates on the level of book trade segments, genres, authorships and individual titles will be a crucial task for both publishers and publishing-studies scholars in the future. As I have tried to demonstrate in this chapter, reading data in terms of completion rates is one way of accomplishing an operative and understandable metric of reader devotion.

---

[27] See further Lenas and Cederskog, 'Konflikt om ljudböcker på Bonniers'; cf. Määttä, Steiner and Berglund, *Skilda världar*, 72–5.

3

The re-emergence of the old: Backlist and frontlist reading

If you walk into a bookstore and have a look around, what do you see? Depending on where you are in the world and which type of bookstore you visit (a major chain, an independent bookshop, a niche store, etc.) the surroundings will vary, obviously, but there are likely to be lots of books in sight. Moreover, what will be placed in the most visible spots for customers of the store are *new books*, the fresh releases from publishers. In publishing lingo, these books at the front are – suitably – called *frontlist*, as opposed to the older titles placed further back, known as the *backlist*. This news-focused logic of the book trade is so taken for granted that no one barely thinks about it: current book releases get reviewed and discussed in the media, attract readers the most and drive sales, end of discussion.

The same logic is transferred to the digital bookselling of internet retailers and book streaming services, where the new titles are highlighted and made most visible on the platforms. In comparison with brick-and-mortar bookstores, however, there is less difference between a newly published book and older titles in both internet retailers and book streaming services. When the frontlist titles are not physically present as piles of books they can be easier to neglect. Even more important, the backlist is potentially endless in digital bookselling and does not come with the same types of costs as it does for physical bookstores. There was a shift towards a wider selection of books already at the advent of internet bookstores, which was observed by Chris Anderson in his concept 'the long tail'.[1] Book streaming services have propelled that change a step further. Their recommendation-based user customization paired with their subscription

---

[1] Chris Anderson, *The Long Tail: How Endless Choice Is Creating Unlimited Demand* (London: Random House, 2006).

logic can, in a novel way, put backlist titles in front of customers when they are to choose their next book.

This has not gone unnoticed from the agents of book streaming. 'Backlist is the new frontlist!' said Lotten Skeppstedt at Storytel, when she was asked to sum up the book trade of 2019.[2] In this chapter, I investigate and critically discuss this statement and the implications of it in the light of the rapid growth of subscription-based book streaming. It is argued that previous ideas of the relationship between frontlist and backlist must be updated in relation to reading patterns in book streaming platforms. The book trade has long been driven by frontlist bestsellers, and while frontlist obviously still retains an important position as the instigator of book consumption, it appears that backlist has become more important, also when it comes to titles in the bestselling segment, namely titles that are not expected to have a long commercial life. This shift in publishing balance between frontlist and backlist is driven by streaming services, and it is particularly visible in the reading practices of bestselling titles. Bestsellers are generally understood to be oriented towards frontlist rather than backlist publishing. In examining backlist patterns of the flagship of frontlist publishing (and not, say, modern classics or prize-winning literature, i.e. fiction that is often associated with a strong backlist), the ambition is to shed light on the ongoing changes.

A publishing house sells two kinds of books: new books and old(er) books. All recently published books are called frontlist, while all other books to which a publisher holds the publishing rights are called backlist. Unfortunately, there is no decisive definition of where the dividing line between those two categories goes. Giles Clark and Angus Phillips state that '[n]ew titles are the frontlist; established titles the blacklist', which is conceptually clarifying but hard to operationalize.[3] In *Merchants of Culture* (2010), John B. Thompson is a bit more precise: '"Frontlist" refers to new and recently published books. A title is commonly treated as frontlist for up to 12 months, after which it becomes a backlist title.'[4] Moreover, Thompson points out that backlist publishing is much more profitable for publishers – it is safe money, whereas frontlist publishing comes with costs and risks. However, it takes time to build a profitable backlist,

---

[2] *Svensk Bokhandel*, 'Årets viktigaste händelser enligt bokbranschen', 27 December 2019, https://www.svb.se/nyheter/arets-viktigaste-handelser-enligt-bokbranschen (accessed 24 November 2022).
[3] Giles Clark and Angus Phillips, *Inside Book Publishing*, 6th edn (London and New York: Routledge, 2020), 165.
[4] Thompson, *Merchants of Culture*, 29.

and frontlist publishing has grown in importance, mainly due to a strong focus in retail chains and supermarkets on bestsellers and new books. Thompson's summation of this development is striking:

> The field of trade publishing as a whole has become increasingly focused on frontlist bestsellers, and the amount of time that any particular title has in order to prove itself in this highly competitive arena has diminished over time.[5]

His argument is backed up with numbers that reveal that around 60–75 per cent of revenue for the major players in the trade comes from frontlist publishing. Thus, a clear majority of the total sales figures emerge from new books, and the period of time for how long a title is considered to be current seems to be shrinking. However, Thompson's figures are more than a decade old and the trade has changed.

The established practice in contemporary publishing is that backlist is everything published previous to the present season or older than twelve months. If in print, a backlist renders safe revenue but also a publisher's out-of-print copyright can be an asset. According to Thompson a backlist provides the counterweight to the frontlist, but they also offer each other constant support. The repeated publication of a book in a series or by a brand-name author makes it possible both to feed the already loyal readers and to attract new readers to the author.[6] During the last decade the business of books has undergone major changes, of which most relate to digital developments. Print sales in retail stores and supermarkets have gone down year on year in most European and North American countries, whereas internet retail sales – both print and digital – have gone up. In addition, lately book streaming, especially of audiobooks, has become a strong trend globally.[7]

---

[5] Thompson, *Merchants of Culture*, 221.
[6] See Thompson, *Merchants of Culture*, 211–18.
[7] See, for instance, Statista, 'US Book Market – Format Market Shares 2011–2019', https://www.statista.com/topics/1474/e-books/ (accessed 13 October 2020); Wischenbart and Fleischhacker, *The Digital Consumer Book Barometer*; Thompson, *Book Wars*, 53–6, 355–61; Anderson, 'AAP StatShot'; Spjeldnæs, 'Platformization and Publishing'. In most English-speaking countries, Amazon is the single dominant player for book selling and distribution, both in general and concerning book streaming and audiobooks, where the company's platforms Kindle Direct Publishing (for primarily ebooks, with large amounts of self-published titles) and Audible (for audiobooks) currently have few competitors. It is hard to give a more precise figure of Amazon's market shares. A study in Canada showed that Amazon Prime, Kindle Unlimited and Audible jointly had 83 per cent of the market share of book subscription services for audiobooks in 2021 (*BookNet Canada*, 'Listening In: Audiobook Use in Canada 2021', https://issuu.com/booknetcanada/docs/listening_in_2021 (accessed 25 November 2022), 7). For more general discussions about the importance of Amazon for contemporary Anglophone book culture, see, for example, McGurl, *Everything and Less*; Wilkins, Driscoll and Fletcher, *Genre Worlds*, 42–57.

In *Sociology of literature*, Robert Escarpit claimed that '[c]ommercially, the only real public is that constituted of book buyers'.[8] For a long time this acted as a law of the trade (if libraries were counted as book buyers), but today it no longer holds true. Although there are differences between models, they all affect the core of what bookselling is about.[9] Rather than books, it is access to books that is the product being sold, which, in turn, affects reading habits. The threshold for starting to read is substantially lower in a subscription model than if the book must be bought in advance and paid for individually.

In this chapter, I investigate the changes in the relationship between backlist and frontlist book reading that surfaces when book sales are transferred into subscription-based book streaming. How are bestsellers consumed as frontlist titles in subscription-based streaming services, and how are they consumed as backlist titles? What can the reader consumption data reveal about the temporal aspects of the frontlist window? How does fidelity to series and author brands manifest? And what does the outcome from such questions say about the relationship between frontlist and backlist in contemporary publishing and for contemporary reading practices?

The dataset used in this chapter is in many respects similar to that in Chapter 2: it is reading data on the level per ISBN and day, covering the period January 2014 to February 2020 (that is: *the first dataset*, as it is described in the introductory chapter). In total, 6.23 million finished streams form the empirical foundation for the analyses in this chapter. On the title level, I investigate how all print bestsellers published in Sweden over a fifteen-year period have been read in the Storytel platform during a five-year period. This set-up enables the study of bestsellers both on the frontlist and backlist.[10] The material is limited in terms of time and regionality, but the patterns can be assumed to shed light on the contemporary book business in a more general sense, beyond Sweden.

In the dataset there are large differences in the number of finished streams for different titles. This depends on several factors: some works exist only as e-books

---

[8] Escarpit, *Sociology of Literature*, 82.
[9] Kindle Unlimited grants access to as much as you can read for a monthly fee; Storytel and BookBeat offer various subscription models depending on how much you want to read, ranging from a maximum of 20 hours per month to unlimited reading; Audible offers one book per month for free and the possibility to buy extras.
[10] The bestseller corpus was defined as all fiction bestsellers in print format (both hardback and paperback) in Sweden in the period 2004–19, altogether 308 titles, of which all but six (302 titles, 98 per cent) were available at Storytel, either as ebooks, audiobooks or both. It is thus resembling the subset 'Bestsellers' in Table 0.1, but without the last year, 2020. The reason why the year 2020 is left out in the study is that the data work was carried out before data on bestsellers for the year 2020 had been published.

on the platform, others only as audiobooks; some have been present on the platform for the whole period, while others have only appeared at a later stage. As bestsellers in general get the most attention in the time around publication, the most important factor is when a book was originally published. The dataset covers complete statistics from Storytel of consumption for the period 2014–19, which means that the bestsellers in the dataset from previous years (2004–13) are here only studied as backlist titles, that is, as *previous bestsellers*. This is important, but it does not mean that the numbers for the previous bestsellers are less useful. On the contrary, in tracking the longer afterlife of contemporary bestsellers older titles are a valuable resource.

It should also be noted that the number of users of the Storytel platform has grown during the time period. In December 2015, 200,000 registered users were reported by the company, a figure that in June 2016 had grown to 300,000 and in August 2017 to 500,000.[11] Thus, the statistics of finished streams are somewhat disproportionately distributed over time. Although it does not affect the relation between frontlist and backlist in any substantial way, all data should be considered with this in mind.

Bestseller frontlist patterns in streaming services

Bestselling fiction generally receives attention during a short time span. Even a successful title might not sell well after a year. A way to approach different kinds of bestsellers is by defining their pace of sales. In *The Book Revolution*, Robert Escarpit conceptualizes sales curves in three formats: 'fast sellers', 'steady sellers' and 'bestsellers'.[12] Fast sellers – or as Escarpit calls them in French 'les livres de choc', books that shock – are books that quickly reach high sales but that sell for only a short period of time, are soon forgotten and go out of print.[13] Steady sellers, on the other hand, never achieve high sales at a specific time and will therefore never end up on any bestseller list. Escarpit names them 'livres des fond', books in the background, as a way of describing titles that are there for a

[11] Storytel, 'Bokslutskommuniké 2015', press release, 26 February 2016, https://investors.storytel.com/sv/bokslutskommunike-2015/ (accessed 5 January 2023); Storytel, 'Passerar 300 000 betalande abonnenter', press release, 27 June 2016, https://investors.storytel.com/sv/passerar-300-000-betalande-abonnenter/ (accessed 5 January 2023); Storytel, 'Storytel passerar 500 000 betalande abonnenter', press release, 17 August 2017, https://investors.storytel.com/sv/storytel-passerar-500-000-betalande-abonnenter/ (accessed 5 January 2023).
[12] Robert Escarpit, *The Book Revolution* (1965; London: Harrap, 1966), 115–17.
[13] Robert Escarpit, *La révolution du livre* (Paris: United Nations Educational, Scientific and Cultural Organization, 1965), 119–25.

long time but are given little attention.[14] In publishing terms, these books will be regarded as bestsellers as the sales numbers will be high over time. Steady sellers are often nonfiction works on cooking or gardening, but also other kinds of books such as fiction classics. Thirdly, a *bestseller* in Escarpit's terminology is a title that will combine the first two sales trends. They start out as fast sellers but then continue as steady sellers.

Previous research has stated that most print bestsellers are Escarpit's fast sellers.[15] The reader consumption data from Storytel both confirms and departs from such a pattern. Most of the books show short and distinct peaks of reading streams, centred around the publication date and the following months, with the absolute peak being the month of release or the following month. Thereafter, the number of readers sinks to significantly lower levels.

This pattern holds for all types of genres in the study. Figures 3.1 to 3.3 show similar graphs for authors of crime fiction (David Lagercrantz), historical novels (Jan Guillou) and romance (Jenny Colgan). The graphs for the two domestic writers, Guillou and Lagercrantz, show the regular pace of publishing that characterizes many bestselling authors – for Guillou a new title each autumn, for Lagercrantz every second year. The graph for Colgan is trickier to interpret as it relates to when the titles have been published in Sweden, while the years in the legend in Figure 3.3 show the original year of publication. But it can be noted that all her titles have been launched in the summertime in Sweden and thus have their respective streaming peaks in May to July, with one noteworthy example: *Christmas at Bakery Street*, which was published in Sweden in December 2016. Colgan as a frontlist author is thus matched with the seasonal shifts depicted in her novels.

Newly published bestsellers thus seem to be streamed at a much higher rate during the first four months; that is approximately how long the time window of topicality of new titles is in digital book streaming. These frontlist reading habits of bestsellers correspond quite well with print bestsellers. But there is also another pattern visible in Figures 3.1 to 3.3 – smaller but still significant bumps of streaming rates for backlist titles when there is a new title published by the same author. For instance, when David Lagercrantz' second book in the Millennium series, *Det som inte dödar oss* (The Girl Who Takes an Eye for an Eye), was published in October 2017, it led to a significant increase of streams

---

[14] Escarpit, *La révolution du livre*, 119–25.
[15] Escarpit, *The Book Revolution*; cf. John Sutherland, *Bestsellers: Popular Fiction of the 1970s* (London: Routledge and Kegan Paul, 1981), 8; Helgason, Kärrholm and Steiner, *Hype*, 10.

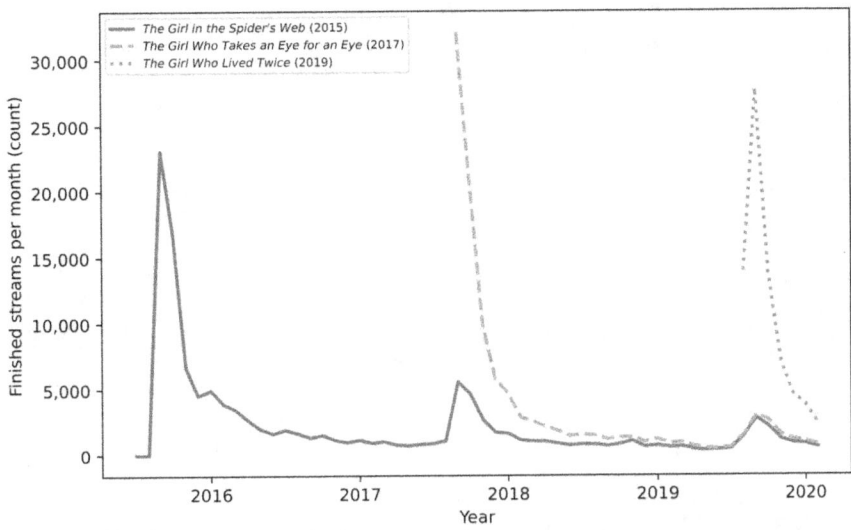

Figure 3.1 Finished streams per month for three crime novels by the Swedish writer David Lagercrantz.

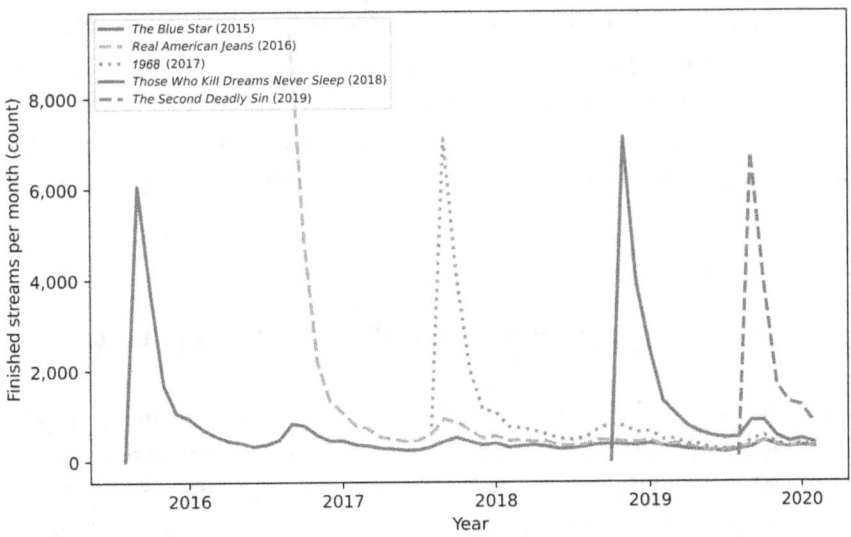

Figure 3.2 Finished streams per month for five historical novels by the Swedish writer Jan Guillou.

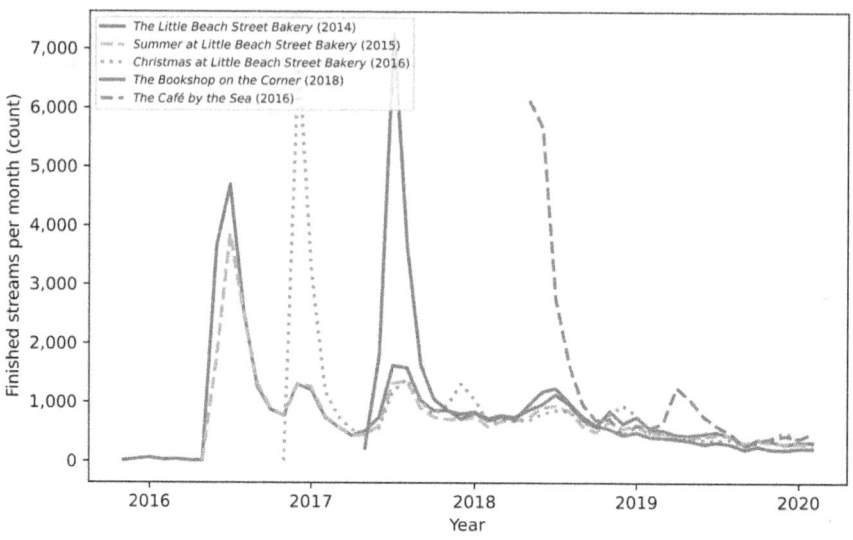

Figure 3.3 Finished streams per month for five romance novels by the British writer Jenny Colgan.

for the previous book in the series, the by then two-year-old backlist bestseller *Mannen som sökte sin skugga* (The Girl in the Spider's Web). And when the third book, *Hon som måste dö* (The Girl Who Lived Twice), was published in October 2019, both previous books in the series saw an increase in streams. While the frontlist reading patterns of bestsellers seem to stay more or less the same when book sales are transformed to book streams, the backlist reading patterns work differently.

The rule of topicality: Bestseller backlist in practice

Unlike the brick-and-mortar bookstore, most older titles in streaming apps are readily available at the click of a button. In one respect, book streaming services have similarities with internet retailers and their large backlists, prompting the possibility to sell 'less of more'.[16] But there are also large differences. Access to backlist titles is easier and more rapid in subscription-based book streaming platforms, and there is a sense that books are available for free (while obviously

---

[16] Anderson, *The Long Tail*.

that is not the case as the subscriber pays a monthly fee). The system as a whole – where the reader can instantly start streaming any book – places the backlist at the forefront, which has led commentators in the business to note the increasing value of the backlist and long series.[17]

The pattern of a strong backlist emerges clearly in the data for bestselling authors that are topical in the period studied, that is, with new frontlist titles being published continuously. Swedish crime writer Mons Kallentoft, for instance, started his Malin Fors series in 2007 and published a new title every autumn up until 2018. Each time a new book was published in the series, the streamed reading of the whole backlist set rose significantly, and the series' first title, *Midvinterblod* (Midwinter Sacrifice) (2007), saw the highest peak (see Figure 3.4).

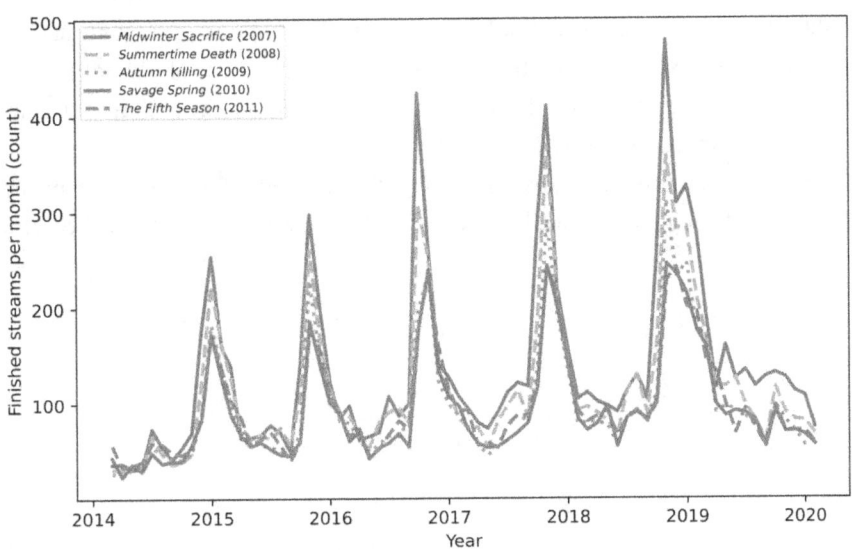

Figure 3.4 Backlist streaming pattern of previous bestsellers in the Malin Fors series by Swedish crime writer Mons Kallentoft.

---

[17] See Sölve Dahlgren, 'JK Rowling mest lyssnad på Storytel men Laila Brendan visar värdet av långa bokserier', *Boktugg*, 2 December 2019, https://www.boktugg.se/2019/12/02/jk-rowling-mest-lyssnad-pa-storytel-men-laila-brenden-visar-vardet-av-langa-bokserier-2019/ (accessed 25 November 2022); Mark Williams, 'Spotify's Move Into Audiobooks Is a Seismic Shift in the Publishing Landscape, but the Ripples Will Take Time to be Felt', *The New Publishing Standard*, 18 August 2020, https://thenewpublishingstandard.com/2020/08/18/spotifys-move-into-audiobooks-is-a-seismic-shift-in-the-publishing-landscape-but-the-ripples-will-take-time-to-be-felt/ (accessed 25 November 2022).

A similar reading pattern is discernible for Camilla Läckberg, one of the most popular authors in Sweden in the twenty-first century. When *Lejontämjaren* (The Ice Child) was released in late 2014, the number of streams for all backlist titles in her Fjällbacka series grew significantly, and three years later, when Läckberg published *Häxan* (The Girl in the Woods) (2017), the backlist reading pattern was about four times stronger – probably much due to the general growth of streaming services and audiobooks in Sweden during the period. Also the release of a book in a new series in 2019 affected streaming rates for her previous bestsellers published around fifteen years earlier (see Figure 3.5).

Thus, the single most important factor for older bestsellers' continuous popularity among readers in streaming services is an unabating publishing of new books: *frontlist pulls backlist*. If there is a steady pace and/or a brand series, the enhanced backlist effects are greater and more predictable. When a book is published the older ones in the series receive attention, and many readers choose to start with one of the earlier books. In this way the whole series is continuously kept up to date. New titles are the driving force, but it is their ability to increase streaming numbers for older titles that creates high numbers of reading streams as a whole and makes the backlist concept advantageous.

It is a given that readers consume plenty of other kinds of media, which means that frontlist topicality is not limited to books but all kinds of topicality. One

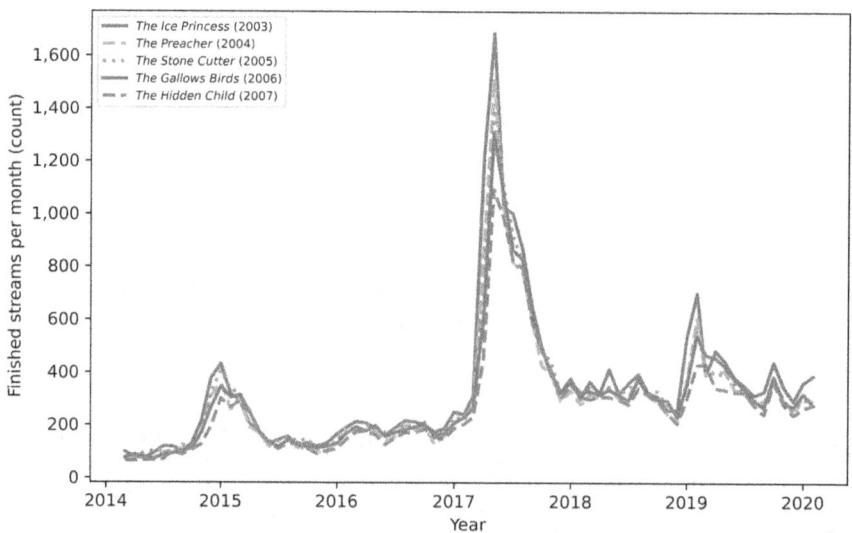

Figure 3.5 Backlist streaming pattern of previous bestsellers in the Fjällbacka series by Swedish crime writer Camilla Läckberg.

example of how the backlist is affected by other factors is the British romance writer Jojo Moyes's Me Before You series. The number of finished streams of her backlist titles rise when new books are released in Sweden (January 2016, August 2018), which is perfectly in line with the discussion above. But there is also a significant bump in streams in July and August 2016 (see Figure 3.6). The latter is undoubtedly due to the movie adaptation of the first title in the series, *Me Before You*, which was released in June 2016. Reading behaviour in digital streaming services is thus highly sensitive to all kinds of author and/or serial topicality. The same goes for print book retailing, at least to some extent (books with covers showing pictures from the adaptation are an obvious example of ways to boost synergetic sales), but these patterns get amplified in streaming services. The instant access of streamed books eliminates the threshold for reading and makes the flow of synergetic consumption behaviour between different media much more seamless.

All of the above have concerned backlist titles with active authors that release new books. If this is not the case, the presumptive gains of the accessibility do not matter that much. Books by Afghan American writer Khaled Hosseini, for instance, were truly global bestsellers in the 2000s and the early 2010s, including in Sweden, where his three titles showed up on the bestseller lists. Nonetheless, since *And the Mountains Echoed* was published in 2013, Hosseini has not published any

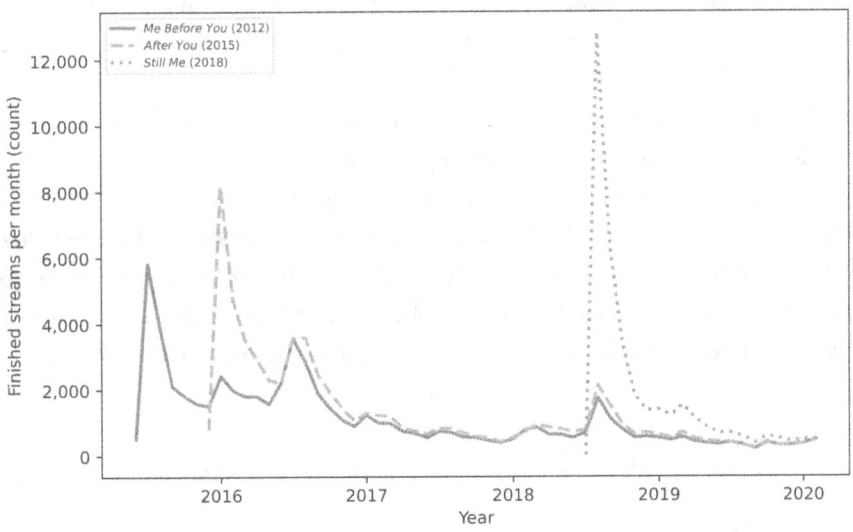

Figure 3.6 Streaming patterns of the Me Before You series by British romance writer Jojo Moyes.

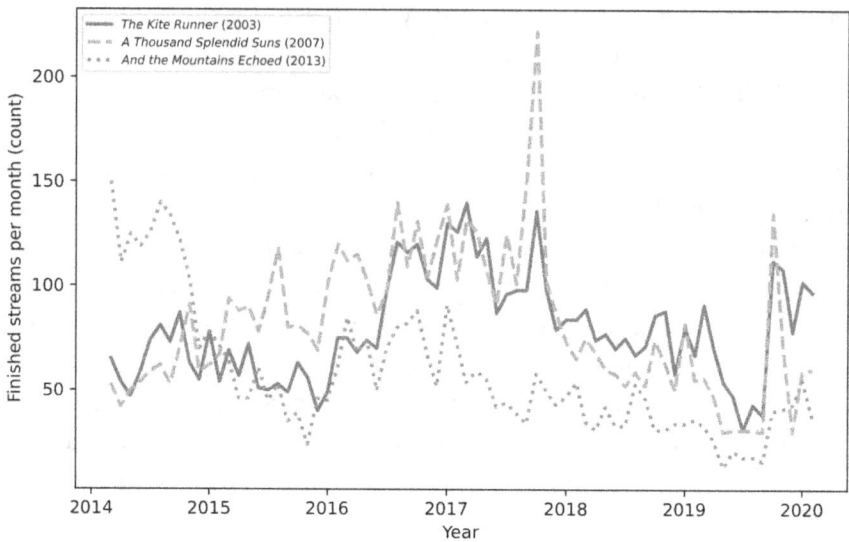

Figure 3.7 Finished streams for three previous bestsellers by Afghan American writer Khaled Hosseini.

more bestselling novels. Even though he is accessible in the streaming services in the sense that the three previous books are available, both as audiobooks and e-books, he is consumed to a rather low extent. Despite the fact that Hosseini was hugely popular in print not so long ago, he has a very low number of readers and there is no obvious temporal pattern (see Figure 3.7). Since Hosseini lacked frontlist publishing during this period, his backlist was forgotten by readers.

The reading patterns for previous bestsellers in book streaming services seem to follow the *rule of topicality*: if a writer publishes new books or is topical in other ways, their backlist is apparently consumed to a higher extent than in print; if not, there is no strong pattern of differentiation between digital and traditional forms of book consumption. The instant access provided in streaming services turns out to be remarkably valuable for publishers only when combined with media coverage. If not, accessible authors risk drowning in the large digital library.

Alterations in the backlist–frontlist power balance

The combination of a new book and a backlist creates a strong brand that generates many streams, but mostly of the new book. For example, Camilla Läckberg's *Häxan* (The Girl in the Woods) peaked at approximately 19,200 streams in May

2017. This can be compared with her older book *Isprinsessan* (The Ice Princess) (2003), which received less than 1,700 streams. Counted together, though, the backlist is a substantial part of many bestselling authors' digital reader base. In Läckberg's case, the nine previous titles in her series had 12,000 streams in total during May 2017. During the peak month, then, the streams of the new title constituted 61 per cent of all streams of the series, and already in the following month the backlist surpassed the frontlist title (51 per cent backlist, 49 per cent new book, see Figure 3.8).

The figures from Läckberg's series show the position of the backlist in the streaming services when there is a cohesive series with continuing titles. In other cases, it is instead the author that is the brand, where a new title will attract readers to older non-linked books. A number of authors of different genres and cases, but all bestselling in print, show the same pattern: Jojo Moyes's *Still Me* (2018) was surpassed by her backlist after four months (see Figure 3.9); Norwegian crime writer Jo Nesbø's *Tørst* (Thirst) (2017) after five months (see Figure 3.10); Jan Guillou's *De som dödar drömmar sover aldrig* ('Those Who Kill Dreams Never Sleep', author's translation) (2018) after three months; Jenny Colgan's *The Café by the Sea* (2016) in 2018 after three months.

While some authors and books have a somewhat longer time span – for example, Håkan Nesser's *De vänsterhäntas förening* ('The Association of the

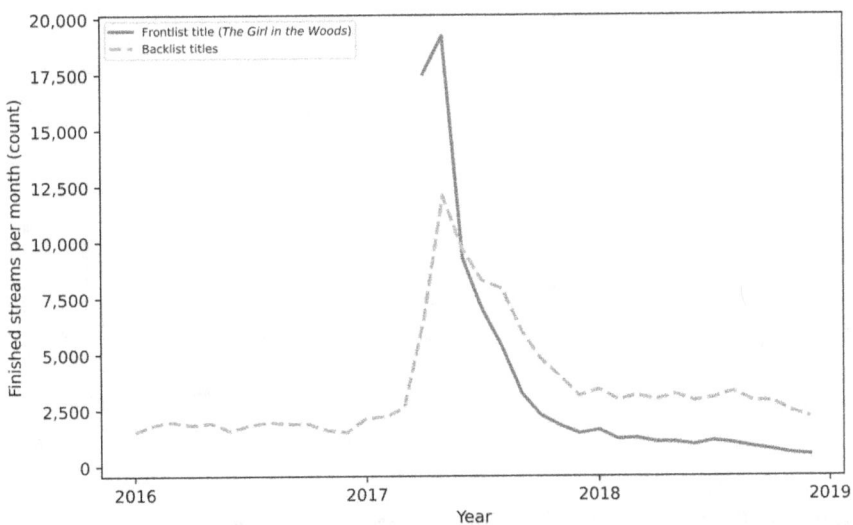

Figure 3.8 Frontlist and backlist power balance for Camilla Läckberg's Fjällbacka series.

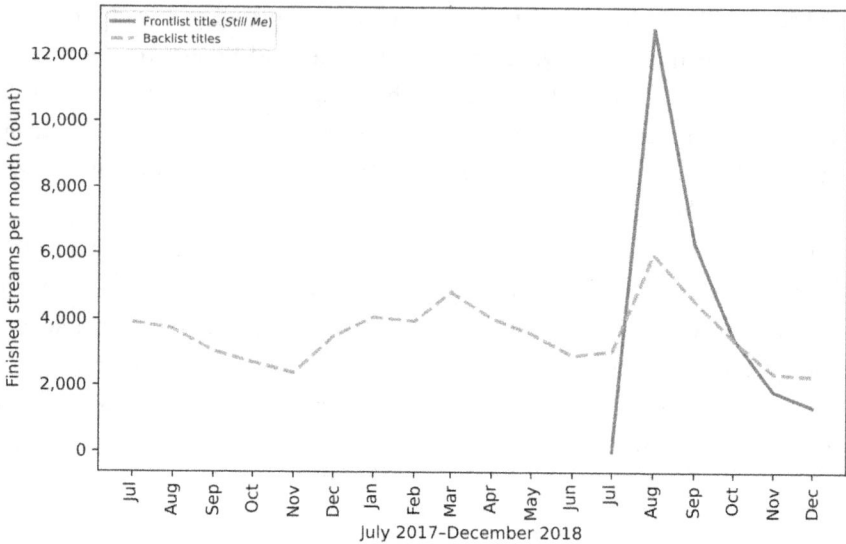

Figure 3.9 Frontlist and backlist power balance for British romance writer Jojo Moyes.

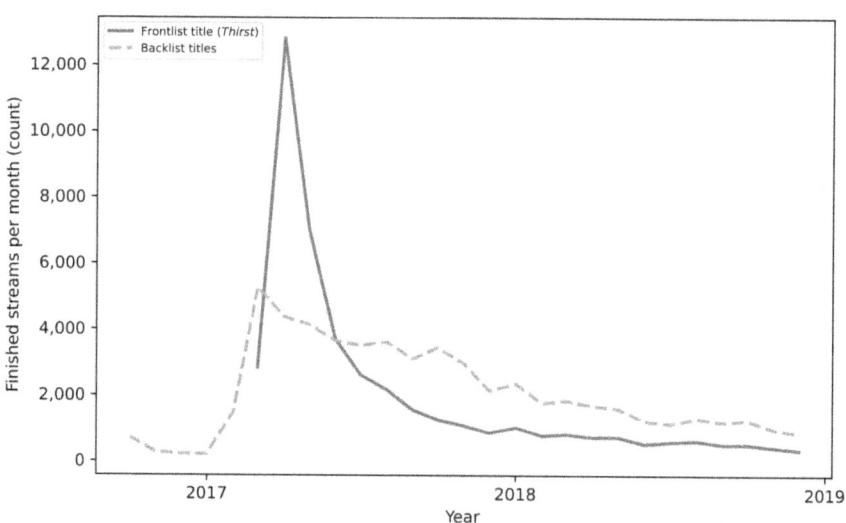

Figure 3.10 Frontlist and backlist power balance for Norwegian crime writer Jo Nesbø.

Lefthanded', author's translation) (2018) that was surpassed by the backlist after eight months – the generic pattern is strong. All in all, the backlists of previous years' bestsellers seem to be, relatively speaking, far more popular among readers in the Storytel data than in traditional book retailing. Considering John Thompson's numbers from 2010 that frontlist titles constitute around 60–75 per cent of the revenues for the major publishing houses, the shift in the book trade is distinct. Importantly, these figures cover all titles at these publishing houses and not just bestsellers, a clearly frontlist-oriented kind of publishing.[18]

In the Storytel reading data, the balance between new and old is altered. When the number of frontlist streams is compared with the number of backlist streams, it is clear that the backlist constitutes the majority of the streams. With data noise removed, the frontlist–backlist relationship is 44–56 per cent with frontlist calculated as streams up to twelve months after publication, and 36–64 per cent when calculated as up to six months after publication (see Table 3.1).[19]

Hence, the backlist is crucial in subscription-based book streaming services as well as to the most recent and frontlist-driven kind of publishing. These numbers are not immediately comparable with Thompson's, since I track streams where he tracks revenues, and I map only bestsellers where he considers all kinds of titles from major publishing houses. Nevertheless, it is indisputable that

Table 3.1 Frontlist and Backlist Titles: Number of Finished Streams

	Threshold 1: Frontlist 0–6 months after publication (000s rounded (%))	Threshold 2: Frontlist 0–12 months after publication (000s rounded (%))
Frontlist	2,150 (35)	2,661 (43)
Backlist	3,891 (62)	3,380 (54)
Noise/not relevant	192 (3)	192 (3)
Total	6,232 (100)	6,232 (100)

[18] Thompson, *Merchants of Culture*, 221.
[19] The frontlist and backlist numbers have been calculated in a two-step process, where: (1) all titles on bestseller lists 2004–13 have been counted as backlist, and (2) all streams for titles on bestseller lists 2014–19 have been calculated as frontlist when the streaming dates for each title are earlier than its publication date plus the chosen frontlist threshold, here either six months or twelve months; if the opposite holds true (i.e. a later streaming date than threshold date), the streams has been counted as backlists. Streams considered as noise are the few cases where data points concern titles not in the dataset studied. Important to note is that publication date in this context is the earliest date for publication in the Storytel platform, which is almost always very close to or the same as the titles publication date in print.

the book streaming services make a significant difference to book consumption. Rather than two-thirds frontlist and one-third backlist, here it is closer to the other way around. It is likely that the instant access provided by these platforms will affect future publishing patterns in ways that favour popular authors with large backlists. Backlist rights will increasingly be regarded as treasure troves.

Digital steady sellers? Seriality, brand names and algorithms

There are several aspects that affect the patterns of reading in the subscription-based book streaming services. The most obvious one is instant access: when older titles are readily available for reading or listening one click away, the threshold for consumption shrinks. This pattern can in part be explained by reader psychology. If one seeks a new read after completion of a book it is easy to continue reading works by the same author, either by discovering old titles or rereading them. As earlier studies have shown, an author is the single most important factor when people choose which book to read or buy.[20] In book streaming services, this consumption behaviour gets amplified. The browsing functions of an app are not as functional as walking along shelves in a brick-and-mortar bookstore. Instead, it is previous reading, recommendations and algorithms that will influence the reader's choice. It is evermore easy to continue with the already known.

Apart from this, there are also more app-specific reasons for the increased focus on seriality and backlist. Once a reader has finished a book on the Storytel platform, different kinds of suggestions to 'Find your next book' ('Hitta din nästa bok') appear (see Figures 3.11 and 3.12). If the completed book is part of a series, and not the final book in it, the next book in the series will be pushed as the main suggestion in the app – it is placed at the top of the scrolling list, highlighted in pink and presented with both the book cover and the 'back-cover blurb' (see Figure 3.11).

The app thus urges the reader to go on to the next book in the series. As this is the prime option, it is extremely easy to follow the path recommended by the app; all other choices require more active work by the reader. The system shapes the almost symmetrical pattern of streams across backlist bestseller

---

[20] Angus Phillips, 'How Books Are Positioned in the Market: Reading the Cover', in *Judging a Book by Its Cover: Fans, Publishers, Designers and the Marketing of Fiction*, edited by Nicole Matthews and Nickianne Moody (Aldershot: Ashgate, 2007), 21; Squires, *Marketing Literature*, 87.

Figure 3.11 'Find your next book' in the Storytel app: seriality and similar books.

Figure 3.12 The Fjällbacka series by Camilla Läckberg, as presented in the Storytel app.

series that emerges in Figures 3.4 and 3.5. After completion of a book within a series, the choice pushed forward by the app is to continue to the next one, which – as the data shows – most users do; the dropout rate within the series is astonishingly low.

Readers of print books have for a long time formed the habit of completing book series in bulk, and the series format is highlighted equally in physical bookstores, where titles are presented together in various ways. Moreover, serialization was already before the rise of book streaming one of the strongest trends in bestselling fiction in the twenty-first century.[21] However, book streaming platforms enhance and therefore foster this kind of bulk reading in a new way. Besides the 'next book in the same series'-suggestion, the Storytel platform groups and presents books not only by author and genre, but also by series (see Figure 3.12). The suggestion 'More books from the same series', starting with the first, is also recommended when a book has been completed, although a bit further down in the scrolling list. Iben Have and Mille Raaby Jensen argue that Storytel Originals – namely, books produced by Storytel as audio-first – is a merging of books and TV series, which emphasizes seriality.[22] Although there is a point to their argument, the same emphasis on series is true for all serialized fiction in Storytel; in fact, the series is a crucial kind of metadata parameter in the app, comparable to genre and author. Hence, the invention in book streaming services is not so much a new kind of serialized storytelling format as a new kind of reading platform guided by instant access and the law of least resistance.

Below the suggestion for reading the next book in the series (if there is such a possibility), the app presents the reader with five ways of finding their next book to read, in the following descending order based on how they appear in the scrolling list:

1. *Similar books*
2. *Popular books by this author*
3. *Popular books by this performing narrator*
4. *More from this series*
5. *More from this category*

---

[21] On serialization and bestsellers, see Ann Steiner, 'Serendipity, Promotion, and Literature: The Contemporary Book Trade and International Megasellers', in *Hype: Bestsellers and Literary Culture*, edited by Jon Helgason, Sara Kärrholm and Ann Steiner (Lund: Nordic Academic Press, 2015), 48–50.
[22] Have and Raaby Jensen, 'Audio-bingeing'.

The last four of these options are all straight-forward to understand. Each is based on a key metadata parameter of the finished work in question, which is paired with some kind of ranking algorithm, often based on popularity on the platform. Thus, 'popular books by this author' lists books by the same *author*, ranked by popularity. The metadata parameters *performing narrator*, *series* and *genre* works in a similar fashion. What is worth noting is the fact that both the *performing narrator* and the *series* are listed as suggestions for further reading above *genre* in the scrolling list, which indicates the importance of these parameters for audiobook readers.[23]

Even more interesting is the first category of recommended books, the slightly more cryptic 'similar books'. As this is placed at the top in the Storytel platform (again, besides the 'next book in the same series' suggestion), it is likely regarded by the book streaming service as the best way to provide readers with new suggestions of books to keep them reading. Although the list of suggested 'similar books' is compiled by an algorithm which I do not know the exact construction of, it is likely that it is a statistical recommendation system based on reading patterns by (1) *the user who gets the recommendation* (in this case me) and (2) *other users who have read the same book*. What is recommended as similar books to a particular reader is thus based both on what the particular reader prefers and what other readers with somewhat similar reading tastes prefer.

For instance, when I (from a Swedish account in November 2022) finished Camilla Läckberg's *Häxan* (The Girl in the Woods), other contemporary works of Swedish crime fiction by female authors appeared as the highest ranked suggestions by the app (see Figure 3.11 under 'Liknande böcker', 'Similar books'). The recommendations presented make both commercial and literary sense. The two top recommendations – Lisa Bjurwald's *Tills bara aska återstår* ('Until Only Ashes Remains', author's translation) (2016) and Susan Casserfelt's *Prästens lilla flicka* ('The Priest's Little Daughter', author's translation) (2013) – are both the first titles in series in the same genre (or even sub-segment of a genre: contemporary female Swedish crime writers). Lots of Storytel users who read Läckberg's Fjällbacka series apparently also read Bjurwald's Rebecka Born series and Casserfelt's Höga kusten series, hence the recommendation. But my own reading history plays in as well. All suggested books in the 'similar titles' category are books that I have not yet read but that the platform's underlying

---

[23] The importance of series was discussed above, and performing narrators are discussed further in Chapter 4.

algorithms have predicted are the most likely to interest me to continue reading. Because this is the goal: to make the reader keep reading on the platform. Exactly how elaborate these algorithms are (in terms of how many factors of my own and other readers' reading practices they are weighting into their predictions) is impossible to know, but their basic logic is evident.

Accordingly, bookstore and library shelf browsing has in the book streaming services been replaced by recommendations based on yours and others' previous reading patterns. The subscription-model makes it possible for the reader to choose among an almost infinite collection of books. But, ironically, in this place of constant and never-ending possibilities for reading, do readers really have that much of a choice after all? Research on algorithms, books and literary culture has shown that algorithmic-based interfaces in themselves create cultural hierarchies and construct the idea of choice as less free. While on the other hand, there is an inherent risk in underestimating human free will in a digital environment. Simone Murray notes that 'because such algorithms operate in a digital environment of manifest cultural plenitude, their rhetorical positioning is always as a helpful guide through over-abundance – allaying consumer "choice paralysis" by promising to individually customise cultural selection'.[24] In the Storytel app, the balance between individually driven choice and algorithmically helpful suggestions is constantly present. Discoverability has become a number one asset in the contemporary book trade of metadata, algorithmically driven systems and digital flows.[25] Ted Striphas suggests that 'what is at stake in algorithmic culture is the privatisation of process', namely, the struggle over decision-making and ideas of value, cultural practices and art.[26] If this argument is transferred to book streaming specifically, what is at stake is the personalization of book distribution and book advertising.[27] While the subscription-based book streaming services only offer one example of how the dynamics is changing in the book business, it is clearly part of a larger pattern.

Conclusion: The universal and the personalized

In this chapter I have argued that previous ideas of the relationship between frontlist and backlist must be updated in relation to book streaming platforms.

---

[24] Murray, 'Secret Agents', 973.
[25] See further Steiner, 'The Global Book'.
[26] Striphas, 'Algorithmic Culture', 407.
[27] See further Chapter 1; Steiner, 'The Global Book'; Murray, 'Secret Agents'; Thompson, *Book Wars*, 176–94.

The contemporary book business is still a frontlist-driven market of 'big books' and bestsellers, but backlist titles are becoming increasingly important, built on instant access to large collections of digital books. Streaming services are knowingly pursuing and developing the technology and media of book streaming. Their general goal is to attract more subscribers to their platform and keep the ones they have, and therefore they try to foster systems for habitual reading. In turn, these platforms create patterns among readers, which affect reading practices also on a larger scale. Thus, book streaming services are changing the relation between the frontlist and backlist due to a combination of technology, media, reading habits and social change. As these platforms grow in importance, it is likely that these effects will be accentuated.

The main conclusion is that the dynamics between the backlist and frontlist in the bestselling segment have changed, but not to the extent that they have traded places. Instead, they have become interdependent in the book streaming services. Backlist titles will increase their readership if there is a frontlist book that brings renewed attention to the book series or an author's older titles. On the other hand – and this is the major difference from traditional book retailing – if the backlist is made relevant it soon has more streams than the new frontlist title, which makes backlist titles simultaneously more visible and commercially significant. I label this correlation between a new book coming out and a rise in streams of older books the *rule of topicality*. It is particularly visible for titles published in book series or by strong brand-name authors, albeit there are other factors that can create renewed interest in backlist titles, for example adaptations of books into a film or TV series. It should also be noted that the systems for recommendations in the streaming services strengthen this repetitive character of reader's choice as it almost always has a similar title in a series, by an author or in the same genre.

This book concerns Swedish readers and the Swedish book trade, and in some respects Sweden and the Nordic countries differ from other parts of the world as the book streaming services have had such a strong impact. However, the changes identified in this chapter are by no means an exception or a separate regional case. Instead, it reflects a general and ongoing alteration in the book business that is founded in a technological and social transformation, and that will have major effects on what people read and what is being published. This reshaping of sale systems can be compared with previous historical changes in book sales and book distribution – the periodical and newspaper feuilletons of the nineteenth century, the paperback revolution and the book clubs of the twentieth century, the internet bookstores of the late 1990s and so on. Similarly, historically, new sale systems have quickly affected how people access books, their reading choices and by extension what is being published. Streaming services thus follow a path where book access, reading habits and media change.

Is the backlist the new frontlist? No, but book streaming will fundamentally alter how, when and why older titles are read, as well as how the concept of the backlist can be understood. When older books are constantly and instantly available for reading, they have the potential to be as present in the digital bookshelf as any other book. What lies ahead is therefore perhaps not primarily backlist versus frontlist, but instead topical versus non-topical books. A situation where book topicality, then, at least to some extent, follows author topicality. And book streaming service topicality, I should add, because what will emerge as interesting for readers is up to the supply, curation, interface and reader behaviour-generated recommendations that lead the reading patterns in these platforms. This ties back to the consumption-feedback loop described in Chapter 1. The topicality of books in the age of streamed audio is at the same time universal and highly personalized. But the 'personalization' ironically risks leading to more generic reading practices overall, since recommendations are steered by quantitative means. What will matter is not so much the original publication dates as each title's degree of immediate relevance and appeal. When everything is always there for us, the ability to stand out in the vast digital library is what will guide reading patterns.

4

Voices leading the streams? Narrated reading

When reading audiobooks, a special kind of mediation comes between the reader and the text, namely the voice of the *performing narrator*.[1] This voice – or these voices – is fundamental to the reading experience of any audiobook and the aspect that most evidently separates audiobooks from text-based book media. The central position of the performing narrator applies to the whole spectrum of narration practices in the audiobook format. Think of a book narrated in a straightforward way by an unknown female voice. Compare this to the narration made by a dramatizing famous actor, such as the Harry Potter series 'brilliantly brought to life by Stephen Fry', as the publishing house Bloomsbury's sales text for the audiobook version reads.[2] Or to an audiobook production taking advantage of what multiple voices can add to a narrative, such as Taylor Jenkins Reid's *Daisy Jones & the Six* (2019), narrated by a full cast of twenty-one (!) different narrators, who in the rock mockumentary format enacts the band members, managers, sound technicians, roadies and so forth.[3] In all these cases, the narration affects the reading experience, albeit in various ways.[4] Audiobooks are intimately tied to their voices. Without performing narrators there are no audiobooks. Consequently, the performing narrator is

---

[1]   Have and Stougaard Pedersen use the term *performing narrator* for audiobook narrators to avoid confusion with the literary narrator in books (*Digital Audiobooks*, 17). I do make use of their term, but at times I also speak only of narrators, since this is the term used in the book industry. Unless explicitly stated otherwise, 'narrator' in this chapter always refers to the person reading aloud the text in an audiobook recording.
[2]   Bloomsbury, 'Harry Potter The Complete Audio Collection', https://www.bloomsbury.com/uk/harry-potter-the-complete-audio-collection-9781408882290/ (accessed 30 November 2022).
[3]   Penguin Random House Audio Publishing, 'Daisy Jones & The Six (TV Tie-in Edition)', https://www.penguinrandomhouseaudio.com/book/577211/daisy-jones-and-the-six/ (accessed 30 November 2022).
[4]   A difference between performing narrators and literary narrators is that the latter only narrates the parts of the prose where literary characters are not speaking directly themselves. Thus, dialogue is, strictly speaking, not narrated by the literary narrator, whereas the performing narrator of audiobooks naturally narrates all text in a novel. The audiobook adaptation of *Daisy Jones & the Six*, then, can be said to follow the inner narratological logic of the novel, where each character is allowed to speak to the reader in their own voice.

central also in most audiobook definitions. Iben Have and Birgitte Stougaard Pedersen define an audiobook as 'a sound recording of a book read aloud by a performing narrator'.[5] Matthew Rubery, slightly different, as 'a single speaker's word-for-word recording of a book originally published in print'.[6]

As I tried to show with my introductory examples, no narrators are neutral readers. What would a 'neutral reader' even mean, and how could such a subject position even exist? Who they are, furthermore, matters a lot, both in terms of how they perform and if the listener recognizes them from elsewhere, for example, from other books or if they are actors or other celebrities. This matters for the reading experience, naturally, but also influences readers' choice of books. Following from this, the most popular performing narrators have become increasingly requested by both publishers and audiobook readers. Some of them – such as Katarina Ewerlöf and Jonas Malmsjö in a Swedish context – are becoming audiobook narration superstars, a kind of hidden power player in the contemporary book trade. It is even reported that the performing narrator might steer the choice of audiobook for some readers.[7]

The publishing industry understands the significance of performing narrators and therefore has created awards and galas for audiobooks, where the narrators are one of the categories of recipients of prestige. Importantly, these prizes measure qualities in distinctly different ways than traditional literary prizes. What is rewarded is not literary works, written by authors, but audiobook productions, written by authors, yes, but first and foremost narrated and dramatized by a performing narrator, and furthermore produced by an audiobook publisher. It is thus the complete audiobook production that receives

---

[5] Have and Stougaard Pedersen, *Digital Audiobooks*, 154.
[6] Rubery, *The Untold Story of the Talking Book*, 3. Rubery does, however, note and discuss examples for audiobooks with multiple narrators. His highlighting of a *single* speaker should be understood in relation to his historicist approach. Single narrators have for long been a very strong norm for audiobooks, at least when it comes to book publishing. In radio drama, multiple voices and other kinds of oral dramatization have on the contrary been commonplace for long. Today, in the emerging 'audio boom', multiple narrators, or even full casts as in the Jenkins Reid example above, are becoming more common. See, for example, Tattersall Wallin, 'Reading by Listening'; Steiner and Berglund, *Barnlitterära strömningar*.
[7] For an historical account that frequently discusses the importance of the performing narrators, see Rubery, *The Untold Story of the Talking Book*. For empirical case studies of the importance of performing narrators, see Elizabet Knip-Häggqvist, *Den talande bokens poetik: En studie med fokus på olika unga vuxnas reception av tre fiktiva texter inlästa på band* (Åbo: Åbo Akademi University Press, 2010); Cecilia Björkén-Nyberg, 'Vocalising Motherhood: The Metaphorical Conceptualisation of Voice in Listener Responses to *The Girl on the Train* by Paula Hawkins', *International Journal of Language Studies* 12, no. 4 (2018); and Cecilia Björkén-Nyberg, 'Hearing, Seeing, Experiencing: Perspective Taking and Emotional Engagement Through the Vocalisation of *Jane Eyre*, *Heart of Darkness* and *Things Fall Apart*', *International Journal of Language Studies* 14, no. 1 (2020). For theoretical approaches uniting narratives and audio, see further in Jarmila Mildorf and Till Kinzel, editors, *Audionarratology: Interfaces of Sound and Narrative* (Berlin: De Gruyter, 2016).

an award. In this respect, the audiobook prize culture more closely resembles film awards than literary awards. Manuscripts and scriptwriters (text producers) are celebrated also in the world of Oscar statuettes, but it is directors and actors (enactors of text) that get most of the spotlight.

In the United States, the Audio Publishers' Association hosts the Audie Awards, an event that started in 1996, but that has gotten more media attention in recent years, following the audiobook boom. For 2023, the Audie Awards has no less than twenty-three categories, covering text-based categories such as 'fiction', 'mystery' and 'young adult' as well as narration-based categories such as 'best female narrator', 'best male narrator' and best 'narration by the author(s)'. And the text-based Audie categories are awarded to audiobooks that show 'excellence in narration, production, and content' in these three categories.[8] Note the order of these qualities. That narration comes first becomes apparent when one of the judges of the awards in 2022, Gayle Forman, commented upon the winner in the most prestigious category, 'Audiobook of the year', in 2021: 'The audio of Project Hail Mary did exactly what I want an audiobook to do, which is to *use the medium to expand the story*' (my emphasis).[9] In what way the medium did expand the story is not explained further, but the praise implies that it is due to the narration by Ray Porter. In the world of US audiobooks, he is well known. Among other things, he was dubbed Audible's Narrator of the Year 2015, and described by the company in the following words: 'Porter's commanding voice allows him great versatility, which he showcases across a wide range of genres from epic nonfiction to groundbreaking sci-fi.'[10]

A survey conducted of Swedish audiobook readers indicates that the voice and the need for human company are central to many audiobook users.[11]

---

[8] Audio Publishers Association, '2023 Audie Awards Categories', https://audieawards.secure-platform.com/a/page/Submit/categories (accessed 27 June 2022).

[9] Audio Publishers Association, '2022 Audie Awards', https://www.audiopub.org/2022audieawards (accessed 30 November 2022). The award-winning audiobook, *Project Hail Mary* (2021), was written by Andy Weir, narrated by Ray Porter and published by Audible Studios. In Sweden, the biggest audiobook prize is administered by Storytel. It is called the 'Storytel Awards', and in a similar fashion it highlights the importance of narrators and production when it comes to audiobooks: 'The Storytel Awards, the grand audiobook prize, is awarded in order to draw attention to the audiobook as an independent format in the entertainment industry. [...] An audiobook is a large production where both publishers, editors and audio technicians are involved. The interplay between the author's text and the reader's interpretation is absolutely crucial to what actually becomes a good audiobook' (my translation) (Storytel, 'Om Storytel Awards', https://awards.storytel.com/se/sv/storytel-awards-4/ (accessed 27 June 2022)).

[10] Audible, 'Ray Porter: Narrators' Greatest Hits. Volume 4', https://www.audible.com/ep/NarratorsGreatestHitsVol4_Porter (accessed 30 November 2022).

[11] See, for instance, Hedda Hanner, Alice O'Connor and Erik Wikberg, *Ljudboken: Hur den digitala logiken påverkar marknaden, konsumtionen och framtiden* (Stockholm: Svenska Förläggareföreningen, 2019), 29.

Several scholars have likewise claimed the importance of the oral aspects and the performing narrator for audiobook readers. Matthew Rubery suggests that reading aloud is an intimate type of interaction that can generate feelings of security, comfort and socializing, and even replace face-to-face interactions.[12] Iben Have and Birgitte Stougaard Nielsen claim that the 'enunciation of the performing narrator and his or her voice seem absolutely crucial to the audiobook listening situation', and that the 'performing narrator becomes a competitor to the author'.[13] Lutz Koepnick, in a passage about Audible product reviews, concludes:

> When selecting versions of texts, users of audiobooks are picky about the grain, dramatic registers, speed, and energy of the reader's voice. Often they *appear drawn more to the performer than to the author*, to the dramatic aspects of the interpretation than to the novel's place in the canon of critics, scholars, or talk show hosts.[14] (My emphasis.)

It seems beyond doubt that performing narrators are of high importance when it comes to audiobook reading. But can we be sure? And what does it mean, more specifically? Is it true that narrators are as important as authors in the age of streamed audiobooks, as both Have and Stougaard Pedersen and Koepnick suggest? The aim of this chapter is to draw from the data to answer such questions and to discuss the complexities and nuances of the role of the performing narrator in the age of streamed audio.

For this task, I use three sources covering audiobooks in the commercial top segment in Sweden in the twenty-first century. Firstly, metadata information about performing narrators paired with other parameters such as author, author gender and genre. This enables me to track production aspects on a structural level when it comes to the role of performing narrators. Secondly, reader consumption data on the ISBN level, which helps me map consumption patterns for performing narrators compared to other parameters. Thirdly, reader consumption data on the individual level for audiobooks. This provides answers to how important certain performing narrators are for specific audiobook readers.

Drawing from these sources, this chapter discusses the rising stars of performing narration and their role as increasingly important stakeholders in contemporary literary culture, as well as the role of self-narrated audiobooks,

---

[12] Rubery, 'Introduction', 1–17.
[13] Have and Stougaard Pedersen, *Digital Audiobooks*, 83.
[14] Koepnick, 'Reading on the Move', 235.

and the strong correlation between author gender and performing narrator gender. Reading patterns are used to problematize the claim foregrounded above that voices are the leading reason for choice of audiobook stream. It seems to be true for some readers, but certainly not for all. The special case of the crime novel *Spegelmannen* (henceforth *The Mirror Man*, its title in English translation) (2020) by Lars Kepler is discussed in detail, since it was simultaneously released in two different audiobook versions, with the only difference being the performing narrator (one male, one female). The example of *The Mirror Man* enables the isolation of the performing narrator as a parameter by studying reading practices where the text and author are the same but the narrator is not.

Mapping performing narrators

The audiobooks in the commercial top segment are read by a large number of performing narrators and constellations of performing narrators, in the ten cases where there are more than one.[15] In total, 136 narrators are used for the 481 books in the selection. This gives 3.5 books per narrator on average, but the distribution of narrated titles among these persons is extremely varied. Eighty-two narrators have only performed a single title in the selection. At the other end of the spectrum, eight persons have narrated over ten titles, six over twenty titles and the by far most popular narrator – the Swedish actress Katarina Ewerlöf – has narrated sixty-two titles, or almost 13 per cent of the audiobooks in the commercial top segment. This is a rather astonishing market share for a single individual.

All top narrators but one are actors (see Table 4.1), and the same goes for the vast majority of the narrators in the selection. There is reason to speak about an *actor praxis* amongst performing narrators: at least for commercially strong titles, professional actors from stage, TV and film are by default hired to do the narration jobs. When their readings become popular, they get more requests, which in some cases leads to a change of profession. Some of the top narrators in Table 4.1 are today arguably more known in Sweden as performing narrators of audiobooks than actors; they are transforming into professional audiobook narrators. Furthermore, quantity and quality go hand in hand in the world of

---

[15] In total, ten of the 481 books have multiple performing narrators (2.1 per cent), which indicates that a single performing narrator is still a very strong norm in the audiobook segment.

Table 4.1 Performing Narrators with More Than Fifteen Narrated Audiobooks in the Selection

Performing narrator	Gender	Year of birth	Profession	Number of titles	Number of authors	Well-known authors narrated
Katarina Ewerlöf	Female	1959	Actress	62	19	Camilla Läckberg, Liza Marklund
Stefan Sauk	Male	1955	Actor	25	9	David Lagercrantz, Jussi Adler-Olsen
Gunilla Leining	Female	1968	TV producer	24	12	Jojo Moyes, Lucinda Riley
Jonas Malmsjö	Male	1971	Actor	22	4	Dan Brown, Lars Kepler, Jo Nesbø
Marie Richardson	Female	1959	Actress	20	7	Fredrik Backman, Anna Jansson
Anna Maria Käll	Female	1966	Actress	20	13	Gillian Flynn, Delia Owens
Tomas Bolme	Male	1945	Actor	18	3	Peter Robinson, Jan Guillou
Torsten Wahlund	Male	1938	Actor	16	8	Conn Iggulden, Mons Kallentoft

audiobook narration. The five top performing narrators have all received the prize for best audiobook in Sweden. Narrators who are liked by many readers are liked by the publishing industry, which creates a positive spin where audiobook awards and a large amount of narration assignments correlate.

The actor praxis also tells another story: self-narrated books are uncommon, at least for commercially strong fiction. Iben Have and Birgitte Stougaard Pedersen claim that self-narration is common in the audiobook format, which they suggest strengthens the bonds between authors and their readers.[16] But of the 481 titles in the selection, only thirty-five (7.3 per cent) are self-narrated. To

---

[16] Have and Stougaard Pedersen, *Digital Audiobooks*, 81; cf. Have and Stougaard Pedersen, 'The Audiobook Circuit in Digital Publishing', 417–18.

put things in perspective, books in this dataset narrated by Katarina Ewerlöf are almost twice as common.

The results concur with how the book trade professionals interviewed in John B. Thompson's *Book Wars* describe audiobook production, where professional actors are preferred, 'especially actors who have chosen to focus on audiobook narration as part of their portfolio activities', and authors are used only in special cases:

> [O]nly rarely are authors involved in doing the actual narration; the only times when authors will narrate their own books are when they are public speakers or actors and their voice is so well known that you couldn't imagine anyone else reading the book, and this is especially the case when it's a personal story.[17]

A closer inspection of the self-narrated audiobooks reveals that it is certain popular books that share this characteristic. For crime fiction, self-narration is rare – only seven titles (2.5 per cent) have the author as performing narrator. Romances are more often self-narrated (7.4 per cent),[18] but it is most common in prestige fiction (19.2 per cent) and in the 'other' category (16.7 per cent).

Based on these figures, it appears that literary fiction to a larger extent than popular genre fiction uses the author's own voice for creating bonds between authors and readers. This applies to autofictive accounts, which makes sense and ties in to Have and Stougaard Pedersen's argumentation.[19] Should memoirs and the like have been included in my selection they would likely have shown an overrepresentation of self-narrated titles. But also, non-autofictive, 'pure' literary fiction is overrepresented when it comes to self-narration. While well-known and celebrated Swedish literary authors such as Torgny Lindgren, Johannes Anyuru, Nina Wähä and Jonas Gardell all narrate their own audiobooks, their well-known popular genre fiction author counterparts such as Camilla Läckberg, Jan Guillou, Mari Jungstedt and Fredrik Backman do not.[20]

One explanation of this pattern might be that writing literary fiction is often a more personal investment for authors than writing popular genre fiction, which

---

[17] Thompson, *Book Wars*, 380.
[18] Five romance audiobooks are self-narrated in total, of which the Swedish queen of chick lit Kajsa Ingemarsson has the lion's share (four).
[19] See Have and Stougaard Pedersen, *Digital Audiobooks*, 83–4. The self-narrated autofictive audiobooks in my dataset include works by Alex Schulman, Klas Östergren and Ulf Lundell.
[20] The only major exception in popular genre fiction is Håkan Nesser, who regularly narrates his own books. Of Nessers six audiobooks in the selection, four are self-narrated. Since Nesser has a high status and rather special place in the contemporary Swedish crime fiction genre, in some respects bordering literary fiction and middlebrow, that he is the outlier actually points in the same direction as the results in general: the more literary the audiobook, the more likely it is to be self-narrated.

could increase the willingness to also narrate it. Another reason connects to prestige. For literary fiction, the author's position is traditionally aesthetically autonomous, while popular genre fiction writers have a more pragmatic standpoint and often see their writing as 'a work', which can be and is being improved by others.[21] With such pragmatism, it makes more sense to hire the best person for the job. A third explanation has to do with money and material conditions. Since popular genre fiction is so dominant and commercially important in the audiobook format, these books are given the best conditions available by their publishers. That is, the star narrators who the publishers know are appreciated by large groups of audiobook readers.

Table 4.1 also highlights patterns regarding preferred audiobook voices and age. All the top narrators are over fifty years old. Several are much older, with the oldest being well over eighty years old. Generally, the narrators are older than the authors of the books they narrate, and the authors, in turn, are older than their protagonists. This creates a significant age gap between the narrating voices and the characters depicted. It seems, then, that audiobook readers prefer to listen to the voices of the elderly; for sure, young voices are absent.[22] The reason for this can only be speculated about without conducting interview studies. The parent reading us to sleep or the cliché of the elderly storyteller around the campfire telling stories to future generations might still be present in the minds of audiobook readers (and audiobook producers). Older and already established actors may more easily attract larger crowds of dedicated listeners. The comfort and company provided by audiobooks, as suggested by previous research,[23] might be more important than the self-reflexive use of voices, either in relation to the author, the protagonist or the reader. Still, the choice of voices is clearly related to the authors. This becomes perhaps most evident when looking at gender patterns.

---

[21] See Karl Berglund, *Mordförpackningar: Omslag, titlar och kringmaterial till svenska pocketdeckare 1998-2011* (Uppsala: Uppsala University, 2016), 132–36; cf. Johan Svedjedal, 'Författare och förläggare', in *Författare och förläggare och andra litteratursociologiska studier* (Hedemora: Gidlunds, 1994), 18–19.

[22] It should be noted that young adult (YA) books widely popular among adult readers are underweighted in the datasets studied here in relation to global fiction sales, since they are generally counted in the category 'YA and children's literature' in Sweden and therefore excluded. The division between adult and YA fiction in Swedish book trade categorizations is however not clear cut. For instance, Suzanne Collins's Hunger Games series is included among adult fiction bestsellers, while Veronica Roth's Divergent series and Stephenie Meyer's Twilight series are not. Such YA series often have younger performing narrators. The Hunger Games in Swedish is performed by the actress Rebecka Hemse (b.1975).

[23] See, for instance, Rubery, 'Introduction'; Hanner, O'Connor and Wikberg, *Ljudboken*.

The gender dimension in the choice of voices

When investigating audiobook narrators more closely, what is immediately striking is the gendered pattern: male actors appear to be narrating audiobooks written by male authors, while female actors narrate audiobooks written by female authors. This correlation between the gender of authors and narrators holds true also on a general level.[24] While the overall gender distribution among performing narrators is quite balanced in the selection (51 per cent female narrators), 90 per cent of the audiobooks written by female authors have female narrators, while, correspondingly, 80 per cent of the audiobooks written by male authors have male narrators (see Table 4.2). An investigation of the exceptions to this pattern – that is, audiobooks by female authors narrated by men, or audiobooks by male authors narrated by women, sixty-three in total and in bold in Table 4.2 – shows that almost all of these titles instead have a protagonist with the same gender as the performing narrator (see Table 4.3).[25]

What emerges out of Tables 4.2 and 4.3 is another industry praxis for audiobooks: *narrator gender follows author and/or protagonist gender*. Of the vast majority of the audiobooks in the selection that have single authors and narrators (454 titles, 94 per cent), only four (0.9 per cent) break this rule.[26]

---

[24] A note on method, and binary and non-binary gender categorizations is needed here. The gender information regarding both authors and performing narrators was derived from gendered pronouns and first names in the presentations of the authors and narrators in the publishers' marketing materials and/or on other official webpages. Constellations of two or more men have been counted as male, and the same for women, while teams of authors or performing narrators consisting of both men and women are counted as 'F/M teams'. The binary gender categorization used here is crude, obviously, and fails to account for all non-binary and queer gender positions. The binary distinction of male-female should therefore be regarded as an operative and simplified gender categorization. With that said: it works unproblematically for the material investigated. All authors and performing narrators investigated are, based on their public personas, possible to categorize as either male or female without difficulties, although there might be discrepancies between their public personas and private identities that are unknown to me.

[25] Protagonist gender has been identified by means of manual reading of introductory parts of these sixty-three books as well as their paratexts. The few cases where there are arguably two equally important protagonists of different gender have been counted as following the protagonist gender praxis. Narratologically, a related parameter is of course the *narrator*, which can theoretically be of a different gender than the protagonist. In the kind of popular genre fiction investigated here, though, the narrator in most cases plays no active role. It is either objective third-person narration (by far most common) or subjective first-person narration. Where analyses of the former would not bring anything to the discussion, the latter gender-wise always corresponds with the protagonist. For these reasons, I do not explicitly discuss narrators.

[26] There is no obvious pattern or interpretation ready for these four exceptions. Christina Larsson's crime novel *5:e Moseboken* ('Deuteronomy', 2018) has a female detective but is narrated by Kjell Bengtsson. The same goes with Anne Holt's crime novel *Bortom sanningen* ('Beyond the truth', 2003), narrated by Torsten Wahlund. Catharina Ingelman-Sundberg's crime fiction comedy *Kaffe med rån* ('Coffee with robbery', 2012) stars a group of mostly female senior citizens and is narrated by the well-known Swedish comedian Helge Skoog. The other way around, Fredrik Backman's easy-read comedy *Folk med ångest* ('People with anxiety', 2019) has two male police officers as the main protagonists, but is narrated by Anna Maria Käll.

Table 4.2 Gender Correlations between Authors and Performing Narrators

	Male narrator	Female narrator	F/M narrator teams
Male author	171 (80%)	22 (9%)	11 (52%)
Female author	41 (19%)	220 (90%)	10 (48%)
F/M author teams	3 (1%)	3 (1%)	0 (0%)
Total	215 (100%)	245 (100%)	21 (100%)

Table 4.3 Gender Correlations between Protagonists and Performing Narrators for Audiobooks with Gender Opposite Author–Narrator

	Male author, female narrator	Female author, male narrator
Male protagonist	1 (2%)	19 (86%)
Female protagonist	40 (98%)	3 (14%)
Total	41 (100%)	22 (100%)

In one sense, this outcome is as expected. Of course, male authors more often write about male protagonists, and it goes without saying that male protagonists should be given the voice of a male performing narrator when published in the audiobook format, and the same for female authors of female protagonists and female performing narrators. Cecilia Björkén-Nyberg points out that it can be rather strange to listen to a narrative where mostly male characters are focalized, but where the performing narrator is a woman.[27] Still, the consequences for such an industry-praxis-taken-as-axiom approach possibly have quite a large impact for literary culture in the longer run. If it is true that the performing narrator is crucial for the audiobook medium and deeply affects text interpretation and aesthetic experiences for the reader, then the gendered narrator–author/protagonist praxis will increase the gendered dimensions of literature, when consumed in the audiobook format.[28] This might be true also for other stratifying parameters (age, accents, dialects, sociolects, etc.),[29] but the gender dimension is the most apparent and far-reaching one.[30]

---

[27] Cecilia Björkén-Nyberg, 'Tolkning, tydlighet och tolkande tydlighet', in *Från Strindberg till Storytel: Korskopplingar mellan ljud och litteratur*, eds. Julia Pennlert and Lars Ilshammar (Gothenburg: Daidalos, 2021), 152–6.
[28] For such claims, see, for example, Rubery, 'Introduction'; Koepnick, 'Reading on the Move'; Have and Stougaard Pedersen, *Digital Audiobooks*, 79–94.
[29] See further Rubery, 'Introduction', 13–14; Have and Stougaard Pedersen, *Digital Audiobooks*, 86–7.
[30] The willingness to let the gender of the performing narrator follow the gender of the author also increasingly seems to apply to non-binary gender categorizations. For an example of trans narrators reading audiobooks by trans authors, see Gabrielle Bondi, 'How Trans and Nonbinary Actors are Revolutionizing Audiobooks', *BuzzFeed News*, 6 May 2021, https://www.buzzfeednews.com/article/gabriellebondi/ya-trans-nonbinary-fiction-ownvoice-writers-actors (accessed 2 December 2022).

As pointed out by others, audiobooks provide an interpretation of a literary work that is fixed as a recorded staging of a text. The performing narrator adds a lot of things to the reader's understanding of the text, but they still offer only one possible version among others.[31] Matthew Rubery notes:

> Audiobooks are set apart from other literary formats by the presence of a literal rather than metaphoric voice. Whereas printed texts possess a voice in a figurative sense, as a metaphor for the illusion of authorial presence available through the printed word, the situation is very different in the case of literature made audible by an actual speaking voice. The spoken delivery of the audiobook is a departure from the familiar conception of the narrator as an imagined voice in the reader's mind.[32]

Transferred to the empirical results discussed here, it means that when these audiobook interpretations are gendered in praxis, they will result in audiobooks that are systematically favouring an authorial voice that acts as a stand-in for the author/protagonist of the same gender. The narrator of works by female authors and/or with female protagonists literally becomes a woman, and the narrator of works by male authors and/or with male protagonists becomes a man, which binds the interpretation stronger to an already gendered dimension.

One should not exaggerate the importance of this, but it has consequences. Star narrators become closely connected to books by either male or female authors and/or protagonists. In my dataset, this is true for many of the most popular narrators, for instance the top names Katarina Ewerlöf (who has narrated books by female authors to a share of 92 per cent, containing solely female protagonists) and Stefan Sauk (92 and 100 per cent male, respectively). Although I have not engaged in any systematic analyses of these audiobooks as audio, it is apparent that they perform very differently, with Ewerlöf's voice being gentle and soft, where Sauk's instead is more assertive and dramatic, sometimes even shouting the lines of certain characters. To put it in an oversimplified way, then, it means that the books (of the mostly female authors and all-female protagonists) read by Ewerlöf are interpreted in a gentle and soft manner, whereas the books (of the mostly male authors and all-male protagonists) read by Sauk are interpreted in a more action-packed way. Obviously, this means that the character traits of

---

[31] For further discussions regarding audiobook recordings as fixed stagings of literary works, see Rubery, 'Introduction', 13–14; Mats Malm, 'Ljudlig läsning – ett historiskt perspektiv', in *Från Strindberg till Storytel: Korskopplingar mellan ljud och litteratur*, ed. Julia Pennlert and Lars Ilshammar (Gothenburg: Daidalos, 2021), 38–41.
[32] Rubery, 'Introduction', 13.

these voices are rather stereotypically female and male. Gender biases in certain genres furthermore become intensified, with romance being the most apparent example.[33]

What it comes down to, I guess, is that already existing gendered reading preferences might be cemented further in the audiobook format. In *Uses of Literature*, Rita Felski suggests that *recognition* is one of the more important aspects of why readers engage in books: 'our aesthetic engagement cannot be quarantined from the desire to know and to be acknowledged. We all seek in various ways to have our particularity recognized, to find echoes of ourselves in the world around us.'[34] If this is true, one could speculate that male readers will increasingly recognize themselves in narratives with male protagonists, and female readers with female protagonists. Expanding the argument to audiobook reading, male voices might appeal to male readers more than female voices when it comes to aspects of reading involving recognition, and female voices to female readers more than male voices.

The only empirical study that explicitly deals with audiobook reading and narrator gender preferences points in this direction. Elizabet Knip-Häggkvist found a clear gender pattern among the informants in her study, where men and women had almost opposite narrator preferences: the male informants appreciated the voice of the male performing narrator, whereas the female informants instead appreciated the voice of the female narrator.[35] This can be connected to Felski's argument about recognition, which, and here I am building

---

[33] The reason for the stronger correlation between female authors–narrators than for their male counterparts, which is visible in Table 4.2, is explained completely by the romance genre, which has a strong bias of female authors (87 per cent) as well as female narrators (94 per cent). All other genres investigated are well balanced when it comes to gender. The share of female narrators is 51 per cent in crime fiction, 57 per cent in prestige fiction and 47 per cent in the category 'other fiction'. Again, these results are not surprising but in line with romance being a genre targeted towards women readers, and where the majority of both authors and readers are female. Romance studies is a whole research area focused on discussing these attributes. For a starting point, see Radway, *Reading the Romance*. To have male performing narrators reading standard romance narratives with female protagonists would probably not be appreciated by most female readers, which would make it into a commercially bad decision. Accordingly, the few exceptions to the female narrator praxis among the romance titles in the selection all have male protagonists. There are four such examples in the selection: *Drömmen om Tom* ('The Dream of Tom', 2020), a gay romance between two men written by Sara Dalengren and narrated by Viktor Åkerblom; *En annan strand* ('Another beach', 2017), a romantic travel story with a male protagonist written by Klas Lundström and narrated by Anastasios Soulis; *Härifrån till dig* ('From here to you', 2017), a heterosexual romance with a male protagonist written by Albert Lindemalm and narrated by Viktor Åkerblom; and *I krig och kärlek* ('In war and love', 2016), a romantic story about a married couple with one male and one female protagonist, written by Caroline Grimwalker and Leffe Grimwalker, and narrated by Anton Körberg.

[34] Felski, *Uses of Literature*, 43.

[35] Knip-Häggkvist, *Den talande bokens poetik*, 241.

on Björkén-Nyberg, makes the narrator's voice of audiobooks into an 'important component part of in a reader's or listener's identification process'.[36]

Readers following voices?

To answer how important performing narrators are for audiobook readers is tricky. How do you isolate the narrator parameter from all other aspects involved in reading? One possible approach that offers at least some clues is to depart from completion rates. As described in Chapter 2, the average finishing degree (AFD) metric measures the mean point in a narrative where readers have stopped listening on a scale between 0 (start of book) and 1 (end of book). In contrast to statistics of finished streams, the AFD measures reader devotion (in the meaning of audiobooks people are likely to read all the way through), which is arguably key for understanding digital reading behaviour, and it does so without any absolute numbers involved. The last feature enables comparative analyses between books with very different-sized reader bases. Furthermore, since many narrators have performed audiobooks by more than one author in the selection, and since many authors with several books in the selection have had their audiobooks performed by different narrators, it is possible to comparatively analyse AFD scores and spans for authors, performing narrators and genres.[37] The result from such an analysis will indicate how important these three parameters are for reading behaviour.

To concretize this, I will start with an example. The Swedish cosy crime writer Viveca Sten has written ten books in the selection. They have been performed by three different narrators, but the vast majority (eight) by Katarina Ewerlöf. A calculation of completion rates for Sten's audiobooks divided per performing narrator gives the following result: Anna Maria Käll (0.92); Katarina Ewerlöf (mean 0.89); Gunilla Leining (0.87). Thus, the Sten title performed by Käll is finished by readers to a slightly higher degree than the titles performed by

---

[36] Björkén-Nyberg, 'Vocalising Motherhood', 8; cf. Björkén-Nyberg, 'Tolkning, tydlighet och tolkande tydlighet', 154–56.
[37] Unfortunately, the AFD metric is not possible to use for the 105 Storytel Originals in the selection, since most of these were published as seasons, consisting of ten or more episodes. I have access to AFD scores for each individual episode, but this information cannot in any straightforward way be compared to the AFD for whole narratives. Therefore, the analysis below departs from the remaining 376 print bestsellers and digital beststreamers in the dataset, minus one title where there were no data points at all (Karin Alvtegen's *Skam* from 2005), leaving 375 titles. These books have been narrated by ninety-seven different performing narrators or narrator constellations, of which sixty-two have narrated only one book each.

Ewerlöf on average, which in turn are finished to a slightly higher degree than the title performed by Leining.

A hasty and incorrect conclusion would be that Käll is the narrator of Sten's audiobook that makes readers complete the entire narrative.[38] What seems to affect completion rates the most is where the books are positioned within her series, whereas the choice of narrator does not seem to be that important at all. Introductory books in Sten's series attract a lot of interest in absolute numbers, but also several undedicated readers, which diminishes the AFD score a bit for all narrators.[39] Similarly, the final books in her long Sandhamn series might have become tiring to some of her previously devoted readers, which leaves the first half of an already established series as the point of largest interest – no matter the narrator.[40]

It should also be noted that the AFD span 0.84–0.93 for Sten's ten novels in context is not that high. The nineteen books performed by one of Sten's narrators, Anna Maria Käll, can be used to give these numbers some perspective. Her narrated book with the highest completion rate is a cosy crime novel by the Swedish author Denise Rudberg (0.93), and then there is a descending scale down to the Polish writer Olga Tokarczuk's *Bieguni* (Flights) (2007) (0.32), which gives an AFD span of about six times the size of Sten's. In the case of Käll, the correlation discussed in Chapter 2 between genre and completion rate is prominent. All her narrated books with top AFD scores are works of crime fiction, and the all-time low is a Nobel Prize laureate. In between, we find romance and middlebrow books. Käll as a narrator, then, seems to have little effect on reader AFD. At least not when compared to parameters such as author and genre.

The example of author Viveca Sten and performing narrator Anna Maria Käll can be expanded to discuss the importance of the parameters related to text (author, genre) and audio (narrator), respectively. In Figure 4.1, all narrators, authors and genres with at least five books present in the selection are plotted in relation to their AFD mean and standard deviation.[41] A low standard variation

---

[38] In fact, the single Sten title with the highest AFD is narrated by Ewerlöf: *I natt är du död* (Tonight You're Dead), with an AFD of 0.93.

[39] The books with the lowest completion rates are the final three titles in her Sandhamn Murder series (narrated by Ewerlöf), and the first book in her new series The Åre Murders, *Offermakaren* ('The maker of sacrifices', author's translation) (2021), narrated by Leining.

[40] The books with the highest completion rates are found in the first half of the Sandhamn Murder series (books three to five), of which two are narrated by Ewerlöf and one by Käll.

[41] Mean and standard deviation (SD) are commonly used metrics in statistics. SD measures variation within a set of values. A low SD indicates that the values in the set tend to be close to the mean, while a high SD indicates that the values are spread out over a wider range. Mathematically, the SD is the square root of the variance of the set.

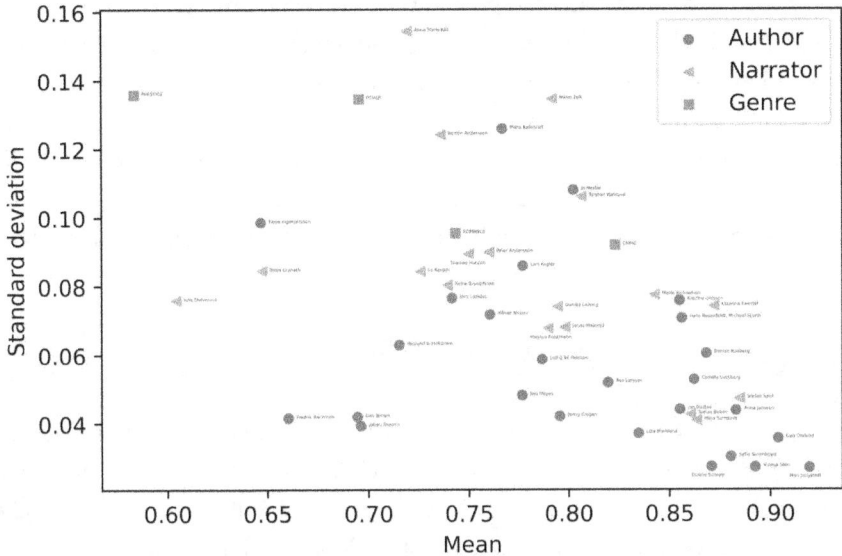

Figure 4.1 Average finishing degree for readers with at least five books in the selection: mean and standard deviation per author, narrator and genre.

indicates that the individual books' AFDs are close to the mean, while a high figure indicates the opposite – books that are diverse in terms of completion. Figure 4.1 shows that books by the same author are generally read in a more similar way on the Storytel platform than books performed by the same narrator or than books within the same genre. This is an indicator that authors and book series are more important for audiobook readers than narrators or genres when choosing books, since dissimilar reading patterns point towards more heterogeneous reader bases. The Sten–Käll case thus appears to be valid also when expanded to the whole dataset, although not as evidently as in the example.

It is also crucial to contextualize the results. For instance, what does it mean that Katarina Ewerlöf is the narrator with among the highest AFD mean in the selection? Is it because she is a narrator that makes readers stick to the narrative until the end, or because she is narrating books by authors with very dedicated readers (Jungstedt, Sten and Sarenbrant, amongst others). Most likely it is a combination, but the results point towards authors being the most important parameter of the two.[42]

---

[42] Both Käll and Sten are outliers, where the former has the highest SD in the selection and the latter amongst the lowest. Furthermore, narrators and especially genres are parameters with more books attached to them in the selection (a mean of 14.5 and 93.8, respectively) compared to authors (7.4). Differences in the size of the set of values might cause biased effects also on the SD, although it is

Distinct reading patterns for entire authorships are especially notable for the group of Swedish crime writers found in the lower right corner of Figure 4.1, who all have high completion rates paired with low AFD standard deviations. These authors have abundantly dedicated audiobook readers.[43] There is no similar pattern among books by any performing narrator in the selection. In the few cases where it appears to be so, it is due to an overlap with the author and genre category, that is, a false pattern, depending not on the narrator after all.[44]

The special case of *The Mirror Man*

There is one special case in the dataset that enables the possibility to isolate the narrator parameter: Lars Kepler's crime novel *The Mirror Man*. When the book was released in autumn 2020, their Swedish publisher Bonniers decided to make an experiment with the audiobook version. Jonas Malmsjö, one of the most popular audiobook narrators in Sweden, had narrated all previous books in Kepler's Joona Linna crime series. Since they all had been very successful, he was chosen as the narrator also for *The Mirror Man*, the eighth novel in the series. In addition, Bonniers published a second audiobook version of the novel, narrated by Gunilla Leining, another one of Sweden's most popular audiobook narrators. The only difference between the two audiobook versions was the narrator and the mirrored book cover of the latter (see Figure 4.2) – the text and date of publication was exactly the same. The publisher explained the experiment with the willingness to create 'a mirror effect' for audio readers, resembling the title

---

hard to say in which way. There are also outliers from the general patterns both in the author category and in the narrator category. When zooming in on these exceptions, they can often be explained by either contextual factors or parametric overlapping. The narrator outliers can all be explained quite easily: Stefan Sauk and Mirja Turestedt have both narrated only crime fiction in similar sub-genres, and Tomas Bolme mostly works for one author with a dedicated readership (Jan Guillou). In these three cases, then, it is not merely the narrator that unites the books in question but also to a large extent similar authors and sub-genres. The three author-exceptions are trickier to explain. The high SD of Mons Kallentoft is due to the low AFD of *Midvinterblod* (Midwinter Sacrifice), his debut crime novel, but apart from it being the first title in a long series (which regularly attracts also many undevoted readers who leave the title unfinished), I cannot explain why he stands out. Jo Nesbø is an outlier mainly because his six crime novels in the Harry Hole series all have high completion rates, while his two standalone crime novels have rather low ones. Kajsa Ingemarsson has low completion rates generally, as well as a low number of listeners, being represented only by backlist titles in the selection. The explanation for her status as an outlier is that her two most well-known novels have distinctly higher completion rates than the rest of her titles in the selection.

[43] See further the discussion in Chapter 2.
[44] It should also be emphasized that I only have access to books in the commercial top segment and not all books performed by the narrators investigated. If all books would have been taken into account, also less successful ones, it is likely that both completion rates and AFD SD would decrease slightly for many narrators.

Voices Leading the Streams?

Figure 4.2 Marketing campaign picture from the publication of *The Mirror Man* as an audiobook.

of the novel as well as that Lars Kepler is an author duo consisting of a married couple (Alexander Ahndoril and Alexandra Coelho Ahndoril).⁴⁵ A more crass explanation is that the publisher wanted to create attention for one of their most successful authors in the audiobook format, and, perhaps, also as a publisher to figure out the importance of performing narrators.

So what happened? The version narrated by Malmsjö, the established narrator familiar to Kepler's previous readers, outperformed the newcomer version narrated by Leining, both in terms of finished streams on the Storytel platform and completion rates. In fact, the Leining version of *The Mirror Man* became the least successful of all Kepler's audiobooks in terms of completion rates – also when compared to the first title in the Joona Linna series, *Hypnotisören* (The Hypnotist), and the standalone novel *Playground* (see Table 4.4).⁴⁶ The results indicate that performing narrators established within a series are important

---

⁴⁵ Albert Bonniers förlag, 'Lars Keplers Spegelmannen – en bok, två röster', https://www.albertbonniersforlag.se/nyheter/lars-keplers-spegelmannen-en-bok-tva-roster/ (accessed 17 August 2022).

⁴⁶ Remember that the first book in a series regularly attracts a large audience in terms of streams but for the same reason gets a lower completion rate (see further Chapter 2).

Table 4.4 AFDs for Lars Kepler's Crime Novels

Title	Year	Narrator	Part in series	AFD
Hypnotisören (The Hypnotist)	2009	Jonas Malmsjö	Joona Linna #1	0.70
Paganinikontraktet (The Nightmare)	2010	Jonas Malmsjö	Joona Linna #2	0.82
Eldvittnet (The Fire Witness)	2011	Jonas Malmsjö	Joona Linna #3	0.86
Sandmannen (The Sandman)	2012	Jonas Malmsjö	Joona Linna #4	0.82
Stalker	2014	Jonas Malmsjö	Joona Linna #5	0.80
Playground	2015	Angela Kovács	Standalone novel	0.65
Kaninjägaren (The Rabbit Hunter)	2016	Jonas Malmsjö	Joona Linna #6	0.86
Lazarus	2018	Jonas Malmsjö	Joona Linna #7	0.84
Spegelmannen (The Mirror Man)	2020	Jonas Malmsjö	Joona Linna #8	0.79
Spegelmannen (The Mirror Man)	2020	Gunilla Leining	Joona Linna #8	0.63

for its audiobook readership, which comes as no surprise. If you would have listened to seven books in a series all performed by the same narrator, liked it, and were eager to read the new one, then it requires quite a lot of curiosity by you as a reader to make the decision to swap narrator to another one, with a different gender. And even if you did decide to try out the new narrator, it is easy to imagine being disappointed and returning to 'the original' narrator.

The audial differences between the two readings come through in the fact that Leining's version is notably shorter than Malmsjö's, thirteen hours and thirty-one minutes compared to seventeen hours and thirty-five minutes – a decrease by just over four hours, or over 20 per cent of the total running time. Again, they are reading the same text. Leining's and Malmsjö's styles of narration in terms of pitch, speed and level of dramatization create aural audiobook experiences that are distinctly different.[47] In the publisher's experiment with two different narrated versions it turned out that most readers appreciated the already established narrator. And since publishers do not want to mess with established concepts that are commercially successful, there have not been any more trials in this vein, at least not in Sweden.

---

[47] For examples of 'close listenings' of certain audiobooks, see, for instance, Have and Stougaard Pedersen, *Digital Audiobooks*, 87–92; Björkén-Nyberg, 'Tolkning, tydlighet och tolkande tydlighet'.

The case of *The Mirror Man* can be used to zoom in even further on reading patterns connected to performing narrators, if turning to the streaming data of individuals.[48] Roughly 36,800 readers started to listen to the Leining version of the audiobook during the year studied. Of them, 57 per cent listened to the book all the way through. These figures can be compared to the audiobook version narrated by Malmsjö, which 90,100 started to listen to and 73 per cent completed. More interestingly, readers who before the publication of *The Mirror Man* were already invested in Kepler's Joona Linna series clearly preferred the version narrated by Malmsjö. Almost half (47 per cent) of the readers who had completed at least one novel in the series in advance on the Storytel platform, and almost a third (31 per cent) of those who had finished at least three novels also finished *The Mirror Man* with the same narrator, Jonas Malmsjö. This can be

Table 4.5 Reading Patterns for the Two Audiobook Versions of Lars Kepler's *The Mirror Man*

	Leining, start (%)	Leining, start but not finish (%)	Leining, finish (%)	Malmsjö, start (%)	Malmsjö, start but not finish (%)	Malmsjö, finish (%)
Leining, start		43	57	37	11	26
Leining, start but not finish				65	13	52
Leining, finish				17	10	7
Malmsjö, start	15	11	4			73
Malmsjö, start but not finish	16	8	8			
Malmsjö, finish	15	12	2			
Invested series reader, ≥1	23	9	14	55	9	47
Invested series reader, ≥3	15	6	9	36	5	31

---

[48] The dataset I use in the rest of this chapter comprises the start date, the finishing date (if such a date exists) and the finishing degree per ISBN and user from 1 January 2016 until 30 April 2021. This period covers the important frontlist window for *The Mirror Man* – the book was published in October 2020. (For a further discussion on frontlist windows and how they can be categorized, see Chapter 3.) In total, the data covers 10.55 million started streams by 480,000 unique users distributed over the 375 audiobooks (Storytel Originals excluded) in the selection of commercially strong audiobooks. 'Finishes' is a metric that book streaming services use to categorize a book as finished by a user. This is an arbitrary threshold, where 90 per cent finished is the current business standard in Sweden for categorizing a book as finished; this is what is reported by Storytel as finished titles in the official book statistics. In the data, I have access to two thresholds, 75 per cent and 90 per cent. When I talk about finished titles I always talk about the 90 per cent threshold unless explicitly stated otherwise.

compared to the corresponding and significantly lower numbers for the Gunilla Leining version for the same category of readers (14 and 9 per cent, respectively). There is also, relatively speaking, a larger drop of invested readers who started and finished the Leining version, compared to the Malmsjö one.

These results – compiled in Table 4.5 – confirm that most readers already invested in the Kepler universe chose to stick with the narrator they were used to. There is indeed a pattern where readers tried out the Leining version only to abandon it for the Malmsjö one, and this to a much higher extent than the other way around. More than half (52 per cent) of the readers that started listening to but did not finish the Leining version went on to instead finish the Malmsjö version. The corresponding figure for the opposite patterns is around 8 per cent of the readers. Hence, quite a few readers familiar with the Kepler universe before starting *The Mirror Man* were indeed curious of the new performing narrator and decided to give it a try. But few liked it enough to finish it, and many instead went back to listening to the already familiar narrator.

Tracing readers who follow voices

The special case of Lars Kepler's *The Mirror Man* clearly shows the importance of the narrator for serialized fiction, as well as the usefulness of reader data on the user level for investigating audiobook reading practices. But *The Mirror Man* is still only one book. Perhaps Lars Kepler, or Jonas Malmsjö or Gunilla Leining, are outliers in some less obvious respect?

One way of accomplishing an expanded analysis is to trace readers who follow narrators to a high extent. As stated, most audiobook scholars invoke narrators to be crucial for audiobook readers. As Matthew Rubery phrases it, 'Audiences develop passionate attachment to the voices of audiobook narrators even when they know nothing else about them.'[49] If such claims are correct, then quite a group of passionate readers following the voices of particular narrators should exist in the Storytel dataset.

To study readers who follow narrators, the dataset needs to be narrowed down to subsets of users who have started or finished a certain amount of books on the Storytel platform.[50] This can be done in various ways. In the following, I

---

[49] Rubery, *The Untold Story of the Audiobook*, 10–11. See also Koepnick, 'Reading on the Move', 235; Have and Stougaard Pedersen, *Digital Audiobooks*, 83.
[50] Remember that the dataset is limited to audiobook reading practices covering 375 books in the commercial top segment. This means that what is accessed is only partial information per reader – most readers in the dataset have likely read a lot of books on the Storytel platform in addition to

work only with audiobooks read all the way through, not books that people have started reading but not completed. The reason for this is that finished books are a better measurement for reader investment. People can start reading a book for various reasons, but if one completes an entire novel, it is more probable that the reader likes the novel – or the performing narrator, which is the point of interest here. Onto the dataset of completed books (8.1 million finished audiobooks in total), two thresholds were applied to single out two levels of more frequent readers:

- Readers with *at least ten finished audiobooks* (~202,000 readers, or 42 per cent).
- Readers with *at least twenty-five finished audiobooks* (~117,000 readers, or 24 per cent).

Naturally, readers in the former subset overlap entirely with readers in the latter. The thresholds can be discussed, but my hope is that they together give a reasonable view of two levels of the more frequent users in the dataset.[51]

So, are these users following certain narrators? The short answer is no. Most of them swap quite frequently between narrators, as they do between authors.[52] To find the readers dedicated to certain narrators that Rubery and others are speaking of, one possibility is to create additional subsets of readers, with a lower threshold of completed books, but with an additional threshold of a maximum number of narrators. For instance:

---

these 375 titles. For instance, roughly 77,000 of the 480,000 users had only started one book during the entire period (16 per cent), and roughly half of the users (49 per cent) had started less than ten books. These users are not very useful for identifying readers dedicated to certain narrators. What is needed is thresholds for singling-out only the readers who are frequent readers of the titles in our dataset, that is, users with a certain kind of taste who during the period studied read commercially successful fiction recurrently on the Storytel platform.

[51] This is a certain group of readers, naturally, but a group of large interest here. They are readers who are frequently consuming audiobooks in the commercial top segment, and whose reading practices accordingly are hit with the selection used in this study. Following from this, they are the readers that I have the most information about. For instance, the roughly 117,000 readers who finished at least twenty-five books constitute 24 per cent of the readers in the dataset, but consumed 75 per cent of the finished books.

[52] The mean of different narrators among the books read are 12.2 for the group of readers who finished at least ten books and 15.6 for the smaller group who finished at least twenty-five books. The corresponding means for numbers of authors listened to within these groups are larger (17.6 and 23.8, respectively), but if adjusted for the fact there are more authors than narrators in the selection, then this difference is insignificant. One way of weighting that there are more authors than narrators in the selection is by calculating the ratio between mean scores of books by narrators/authors read divided by the total number of narrators/authors. For the ten or more finishes group, this gives an adjusted mean of 12.0 authors, which is very close to the group's mean for narrators (12.2). For the twenty-five or more finishes group, the adjusted mean of authors is 16.2, which is very close to this group's mean for narrators (15.6).

- Readers with *at least five finished audiobooks and a maximum of three unique performing narrators* (~45,000 readers, or 9.4 per cent).
- Readers with *at least five finished audiobooks and a maximum of one unique performing narrator* (2,770 readers, or 1.1 per cent).

The most distinct narrator presence is obviously found among the readers in the latter group. However, two-thirds of these readers (1,848, 67 per cent) only listened to one single author, which makes it unlikely that they are actually following a narrator. Rather, they are invested in certain authorships and series. The remaining 922 readers are indeed examples of audiobook readers that seem to be dedicated to books performed by certain narrators. While the bigger subset is significantly larger, the thresholds used for defining it (maximum three narrators, at least five finished titles) make it not a very precise tool for tracing readers dedicated to certain narrators. For instance, it includes readers who have read three books by one of their favourite authors (which generally have the same narrator), and then two other books (with different narrators). If a third threshold is inserted onto this group of readers (at least six different authors, two books per narrator on average), the subset shrinks to 926 readers, and if it is raised to at least nine (at least three books per narrator on average) only ninety-three readers remain.

To sum up, among all these numbers, what can be said for sure is that I have identified less than 2,000 readers who seem to be dedicated to specific performing narrators, and just over 1,000 readers who are more apparently dedicated to certain performing narrators. Hence, audiobook readers following voices do exist, but they are rare. Given the size of the subset of all users who have finished at least five books in the selection, they make up only 0.4–0.7 per cent of the population. With this empirical background, then, it seems to be an exaggeration to claim that narrators are the single most important thing for audiobook readers.[53]

---

[53] The gender of the narrator does not seem to be that important for most readers. Few readers among the most frequent users listen only to narrators of one gender. Of the readers with at least five finished books, 10.0 per cent do so, while the corresponding figures among readers with at least ten finished books is 5.4 per cent, and among readers with at least twenty-five finished books 1.1 per cent. Importantly, these figures include all readers who prefer authors of a certain gender, which above correlated with narrator gender to a large extent. The group of readers that actively follow narrator gender, rather than author gender, is probably smaller than these figures indicate, which makes the behaviour of choosing books primarily by the gender of the narrator rare.

Conclusion: The elusive significance of the voice

In this chapter, I have investigated the role of the performing narrator in audiobook publishing and for audiobook readers. There are strong industry praxises for choosing narrators that highlight their importance – they are chosen carefully by publishers. This is in line with previous audiobook research. 'Casting is the single most important decision made by an audio publisher', as Matthew Rubery claims.[54] Also audiobook readers themselves believe the performing narrator to be key for their audiobook experience. In a survey study of dedicated audiobook readers by Sara Tanderup Linkis and Julia Pennlert, around two-thirds of the respondents claim that the performing narrator is an important factor when they choose which audiobook to read.[55]

Yet, in the rather rigorous empirical investigations of the reader consumption data I have carried out in this chapter this importance does not really show; at least, it is not that evident on a general note. Most readers in my selection are swapping frequently between narrators, and readers who follow certain narrators are rare. The data points investigated speak of authors, genre and literary series being far more important for readers' choices of audiobooks than narrators. I therefore believe that Rubery's claim needs to be rephrased: it is textual factors (authors, genres, series) that are the most important decisions also for audiobook publishers, whereas casting is the single most important *media-specific* decision.

This can be considered a detail, but I think it is important. The focus on narrators and aural aspects of audiobooks in previous research is understandable since it has the media-specific aspects of audiobooks as its main interest. In the words of Iben Have and Stougaard Pedersen, 'the sonification of written text offers radically different affordances', why audiobooks 'can and should be studied as an alternative way of experiencing literature'.[56] I basically agree with this, but my mission is different. Rather than the aesthetic experiences involved in reading audiobooks, I am interested in how people make use of the medium. And it turns out that however important narrators and aural aspects of audiobooks are for the reading experience, the perception, and the aesthetics of audiobooks, it is the authors, series and genres that appear to be key when people are choosing audiobooks.

---

[54] Rubery, *The Untold Story of the Talking Book*, 10.
[55] Tanderup Linkis and Pennlert, '"En helt annan upplevelse"', 48.
[56] Have and Stougaard Pedersen, *Digital Audiobooks*, 8.

I argue for an increasing awareness in audiobook research of the differences between aesthetics/perceptions of audiobooks, on the one hand, and audiobook use/reading practices, on the other. Media-oriented literary scholars might often be most interested in the unique media aspects of audiobooks, but it is far from certain that readers care as much about this. Rather, and in line with the results in this chapter, it appears that also readers of audiobooks – just like any book readers – are mostly interested in narratives and stories. That is, textual content, albeit transferred to another medium. Equally important, at least regarding the Nordic context, are the material aspects surrounding audiobook reading, which is now a notably accessible and cheap way of consuming literature.[57] Perhaps most audio readers are first and foremost practical readers?

With that said, narrators are by no means unimportant for reading practices. As *The Mirror Man* example shows, they can matter a lot. Narrators are key when readers are already invested in a series where a certain narrator is tied to it. To swap narrator in the middle of a series – or even to swap narrator between an author's books in general – is not popular among readers as it alters the presentation of the fictional world. There is likely also a 'negative importance' at play connected to the performing narrators of audiobooks. While most users do not have narrators that they like so much that they choose audiobooks after them, many probably have narrators that they dislike to the extent that they avoid books narrated by them; there are several reports that point in this direction.[58] One can similarly imagine readers who favour certain 'kinds' of narrators, for instance more or less dramatizing performances. Unfortunately, patterns of avoidance and narration style are hard to trace. As Cecilia Björkén-Nyberg points out, readers perceive voices differently; dramatization means different things to different audiobook readers.[59] This brings me back to the elusive role of the performing narrator. They are important for the audiobook, yet in many respects second to the author and the text. They affect the reading experience a lot. They are important for some audiobook readers, but not for all.

The role of the narrator also needs to be related to the probable next shift in the world of audiobooks: speech synthesis. As Matthew Rubery noted in 2016,

---

[57] See further the discussion in Chapter 1.
[58] See, for instance, the Goodreads discussion thread 'Love It or Leave It: What To Do When You Can't Stand the Narrator', Goodreads.com, https://www.goodreads.com/topic/show/1954770-love-it-or-leave-it-what-to-do-when-you-can-t-stand-the-narrator (accessed 26 August 2022). See further also Rubery, *The Untold Story of the Talking Book*, 10–11; Have and Stougaard Pedersen, *Digital Audiobooks*, 108–15.
[59] Björkén-Nyberg, 'Tolkning, tydlighet och tolkande tydlighet', 156.

synthetic voices have seen a rapid technical development in the last decades.⁶⁰ This has not slowed down since then. Already, audiobook readers using Storytel and similar platforms can choose to alter the recorded voice by speeding up or down the pace of the narration without any substantial loss of quality. (In Storytel, the possible speeding span is 0.75–2 times the recorded speed.) In June 2022, Storytel announced that they will soon be starting to implement synthetic voices on their platform, which they expect to lower production costs and increase user flexibility.⁶¹ Apple Books offer synthetic audiobook narration services targeted towards small presses and self-publishing authors, with the promise to offer rapid and cheap audiobook productions of a high quality from an ebook file. Such voices – trained on large amounts of voice data – do not resemble one single existing narrator, but rather a 'type', like the fiction/romance soprano 'Madison' or the nonfiction/self-development baritone 'Mitchell'.⁶² This and similar commercial services will likely rapidly expand the number of self-published audiobooks available on the market, resembling how Kindle Direct Publishing changed the conditions for ebook publishing some fifteen years ago. As Apple Books say in the promotional text for the service:

> More and more book lovers are listening to audiobooks, yet only a fraction of books are converted to audio – leaving millions of titles unheard. Many authors – especially independent authors and those associated with small publishers – aren't able to create audiobooks due to the cost and complexity of production. Apple Books digital narration makes the creation of audiobooks more accessible to all, helping you meet the growing demand by making more books available for listeners to enjoy.⁶³

This technical development will make the competition for work between performing narrators far tougher. A probable development is that humans will be used for the more commercially important titles, while the long tail of audiobooks will be increasingly synthetic.⁶⁴

---

[60] Rubery, *The Untold History of the Talking Book*, 271–4.
[61] Storytel, 'Storytel Enters Strategic Partnership with ElevenLabs and Announces Upcoming Launch of New VoiceSwitcher Feature', press release, June 13, 2023, https://investors.storytel.com/en/storytel-enters-strategic-partnership-with-elevenlabs-and-announces-upcoming-launch-of-new-voiceswitcher-feature/ (accessed 29 June 2029).
[62] Apple Books, 'Every Book Deserves To Be Heard', https://authors.apple.com/support/4519-digital-narration-audiobooks (accessed 25 April 2023).
[63] Apple Books, 'Every Book Deserves To Be Heard', https://authors.apple.com/support/4519-digital-narration-audiobooks (accessed 25 April 2023).
[64] See Leyland Cecco, 'Death of the Narrator? Apple Unveils Suite of AI-Voiced Audiobooks', *The Guardian*, 4 January 2023.

In the not-so-distant future, it will furthermore be possible to generate speech of good quality reminiscent of any known voice. This will have transformative power for audiobook production and reading. If readers become free to choose which voice they prefer to narrate their audiobooks, the role of the narrator will simultaneously be emphasized but unimportant. Emphasized, because readers will make active choices and to a higher extent think about the narration. It represents the next level of personalization in book streaming platforms, where the reader's own fiction bubble – created by streaming patterns feeding recommendation algorithms – is enhanced further by the option to choose the narrating voice. Unimportant, because if 'all' (or at least a large span of) voices are available for each book, cases where a specific narrator (or indeed narration) brings readers to a specific book will disappear.

It will also cause ethical and copyright discussions. Let's make an AI-based synthetic voice somewhat reminiscent of Stephen Fry narrate *Fifty Shades of Grey*. Or perhaps the voice of Reese Witherspoon, or Benedict Cumberbatch, or Meryl Streep, or … Who owns the rights to a voice? Deliberate deep fakes of well-known voice actors will most probably be considered illegal, but what about voices that only sound like a famous voice? This vocal grey area paired with the commercial incentives involved will likely cause heated debates and court cases in the future.

5

The reading hours of the day and night: Temporal reading

The most common question to ask any reader is probably: *what* are you reading? This question might be followed by more in-depth questions, such as *why* are you reading this particular book, and what do you think of it? A more odd question, however, is this: *when* do you read? Yet, when books are read is not at all an unimportant aspect of what reading is and what it means for people. It can reveal a lot about reading practices and the 'uses of literature', to connect to Rita Felski's terminology.[1]

Robert Escarpit once claimed that there are three major categories of reading time available for most people: 'those unrecoverable slack moments (traveling, eating, etc.), regular free time (after the day's work), periods of non-activity (Sunday, holiday, illness, retirement)'.[2] The audiobook medium alters these temporal aspects of reading. Since you don't have to sit down (or at least not be on the move), and you don't have to have your hands and eyes occupied, audiobooks enable reading in many more daily situations – while working out, cleaning, cooking, walking the dog, driving and so on. Of course, people also pair reading of print books with their daily routines. As Janice Radway notes in *Reading the Romance*, the 'reading habits and preferences of the Smithton women are complexly tied to their daily routines, which are themselves a function of education, social role, and class position'.[3] With streamed audiobooks, such ties are made less complex, enabling more daily reading time. Audiobooks extend and prolong 'those unrecoverable slack moments', to use Escarpit's phrasing.

This is an important aspect of the medium and an explanation of its newly gained popularity, and it has accordingly been highlighted in most previous

---

[1] Felski, *Uses of Literature*.
[2] Escarpit, *Sociology of Literature*, 93.
[3] Radway, *Reading the Romance*, 50.

audiobook research. Such work often addresses another important question: *where* are people reading? Lutz Koepnick emphasizes this in the very title of his essay, 'Reading on the Move'.[4] Iben Have and Birgitte Stougaard Pedersen point out how the portability of the audiobook medium 'change[s] the act of reading, moving it into fields of social practices such as exercising, commuting, and housework in which reading has not previously been common'.[5] In an interview study of young adults, Elisa Tattersall Wallin conceptualized what she calls 'audiobook routines', where the informants' audiobook reading is described in terms of routinized practices distributed over the twenty-four hours of the day.[6]

In this chapter, I make use of the temporal information in the reading consumption data provided by Storytel to discuss questions concerning when people are reading audiobooks. Time is an aspect of reading that book history has had little insights into previously. There has been little reliable material available that enables the mapping of temporal reading patterns. Taking a computational perspective with the Storytel data changes this situation, rather dramatically. In the datasets supporting this book, reading sessions are clocked by the hour, which allow new questions to be answered: When are people reading audiobooks, and how does it differ from ebook reading? Are there temporal differences in reading between genres, authors or titles? What kinds of temporal reader profiles are visible in the datasets – are there, for instance, typical 'night readers'? And what about longer time axes – what do the weekly or yearly audiobook reading practices tell us of the contemporary book trade and reading? These and similar kinds of questions are thoroughly discussed in this chapter. The overarching purpose is to understand what the various temporal layers of reading mean for contemporary digital audiobook culture.

Comparing ebook and audiobook reading

Let's start by comparing book formats. According to the data, audiobooks are read during all hours of the day. This is a truism, obviously, but it is worth mentioning since audiobook reading in this respect differs from ebook reading on the Storytel platform. Audiobook reading peaks in the afternoon, has higher

---

[4] Koepnick, 'Reading on the Move'.
[5] Have and Stougaard Pedersen, *Digital Audiobooks*, 8.
[6] Elisa Tattersall Wallin, 'Audiobook Routines: Identifying Everyday Reading by Listening Practices Amongst Young Adults', *Journal of Documentation* 78, no. 7 (2022).

consumption rates during mornings than evenings and remains steady at night. Ebooks, on the contrary, have a distinct peak of consumption in the evening hours, especially between 8 pm and 10 pm when almost a fifth of the total consumption takes place. If the hours of the day are grouped into four six-hour segments – *night time, morning, afternoon, evening* – the temporal spread in listening habits clearly emerges: audiobook reading is most frequent in the mornings (28.2 per cent) and afternoons (31.2 per cent), whilst ebook reading instead is most frequent in the evenings (36.1 per cent) (see Figure 5.1).

Ebook consumption furthermore rises on the weekends – Saturdays and especially Sundays are the two days of the week when people read ebooks in the Storytel platform the most. For audiobooks, the pattern is different. Sundays are an important day also for audiobook reading, but it is surpassed by Mondays, when people read the most audiobooks during the week. Saturday is the day of the week with the lowest audiobook reading (see Figure 5.2).

Thus, while ebooks are read mostly in traditional leisure time (evenings, weekends), audiobooks are read at any time, not least during traditional working hours. If we use the temporal patterns for ebook reading as a proxy for print reading (assuming that reading with your eyes in different formats are at least fairly similar practices), audiobook reading clearly diverges from other

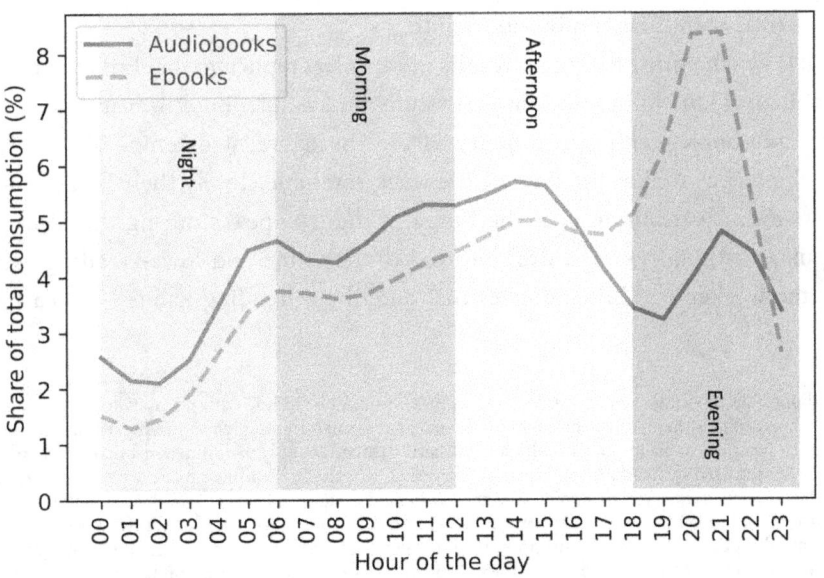

Figure 5.1 Audiobook and ebook reading: percentage per hour of the day.

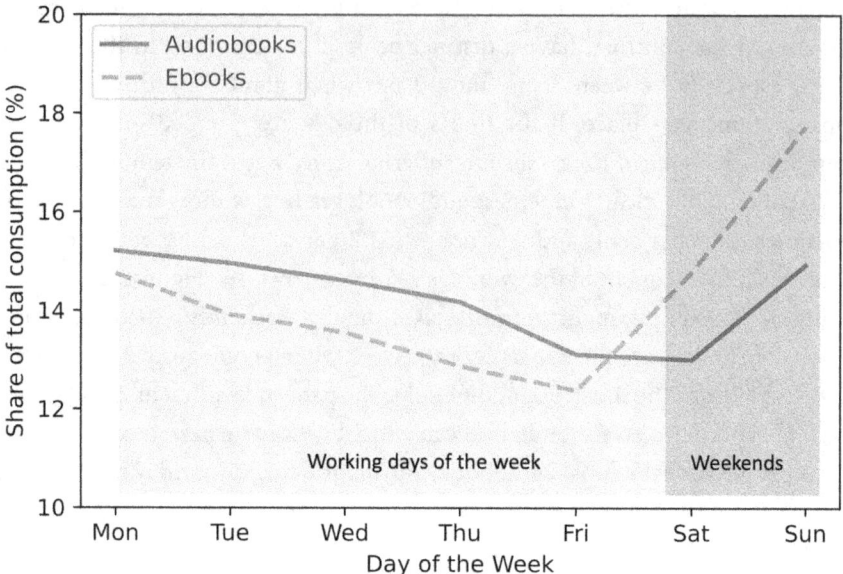

Figure 5.2 Audiobook and ebook reading: percentage per day of the week.

kinds of reading.[7] I find the drop in audiobook listening around dinner time especially telling as it highlights the unsocial part of book reading. It seems that audiobooks can be combined with work, studies and other daytime activities, but when people eat dinner, they need to unplug for a couple of hours to spend some time with their family and friends.

It is worth noting that these results more or less replicate what Elisa Tattersall Wallin and Jan Nolin found in their study on Swedish BookBeat user activity for audiobook reading in January 2018. The aggregated temporal patterns for the day as well as the days of the week resemble closely their findings – a quite even distribution over the hours of the day, peaks during the daytime regular working hours, a drop around dinner time and lower reading rates on the weekends.[8] This indicates that audiobook reading habits – at least in

---

[7] Ebooks are obviously not the same thing as print books, but in line with previous research I think it is safe to assume that text-based book formats have much more in common regarding how they are consumed than audiobooks, which is a different thing, not only medium-wise but also regarding the senses used for reading (ears instead of eyes; cf. Koepnick, 'Reading on the Move'; Rubery, *The Untold Story of the Talking Book*; Have and Stougaard Pedersen, *Digital Audiobooks*). What should also be noted is that ebooks are consumed far less than audiobooks in the Storytel platform; only around 8 per cent of the consumption in the datasets emanate from ebook reading. It might thus be risky to break this consumption down into smaller subsets, but the general temporal pattern for ebook consumption makes it a solid comparative data point.

[8] See Tattersall Wallin and Nolin, 'Time to Read', especially figures 1 and 2, 481–2.

the Swedish context – are consistent and not a result of factors particular to this study, such as time (pandemic), platform (Storytel) or types of books (commercial top segment).

Reading what when?

Interestingly, all categories of books in the dataset share these temporal reading patterns. I somewhat anticipated finding differences between genres, but there were none (or at least close to none). The same goes with all parameters I have access to. Regardless of subset, author gender, narrator gender and publisher, the pattern remains the same. Books are read in a similar way across the hours of the day (see Figures 5.3 and 5.4).

If I had access to data on all books and peripheral titles, there would likely be larger discrepancies. Still, the result at least indicates that *what people read does not seem to affect immensely when they read*. One explanation for this is the length of novels. Audiobooks regularly exceed ten hours of running time, sometimes twenty hours. You most often need more than one day to complete

Figure 5.3 Audiobook reading divided by genre: percentage per hour.

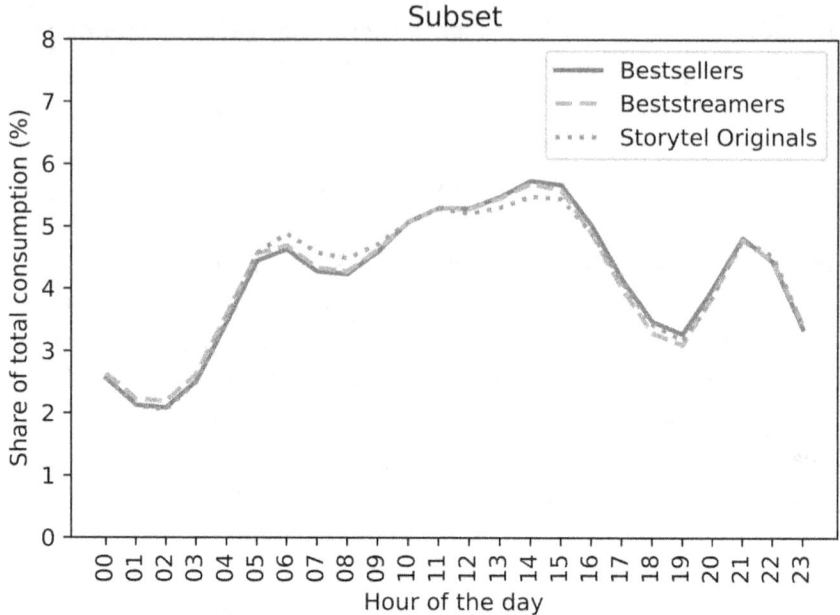

Figure 5.4 Audiobook reading divided by subset: percentage per hour.

a full-length novel, which smooths effects on the title-level and makes temporal reading habits most prominent.

The similar temporal reading pattern holds true also on the title level, whether it be high-pace thrillers or Nobel Prize laureates. Although there are naturally larger differences between single titles than categories, all titles in the datasets investigated here adhere to the same basic consumption pattern – there are thus no books in the commercial top segment that are primarily consumed at night, for instance, or only in the daytime.

With that said, there are always outliers on the title level. One way to identify them is to measure the *diversity in temporal listening* for each title, here defined as the difference between the hour with the highest share of consumption and the hour with the lowest share.[9] The books with the smallest temporal differences across the twenty-four hours of the day include several previous megasellers, for instance the entire Millennium Trilogy by Stieg Larsson as well as books by Jonas Jonasson and Dan Brown. The single book with the least diversity is

---

[9] In practice, this means that if a title hypothetically has a peak in reading between 4 pm and 5 pm, an hour accounting for 6 per cent of the total consumption, and a bottom between 4 am and 5 am, accounting for 2 per cent, then the temporal diversity for this particular title is 6 – 2 = 4 per cent.

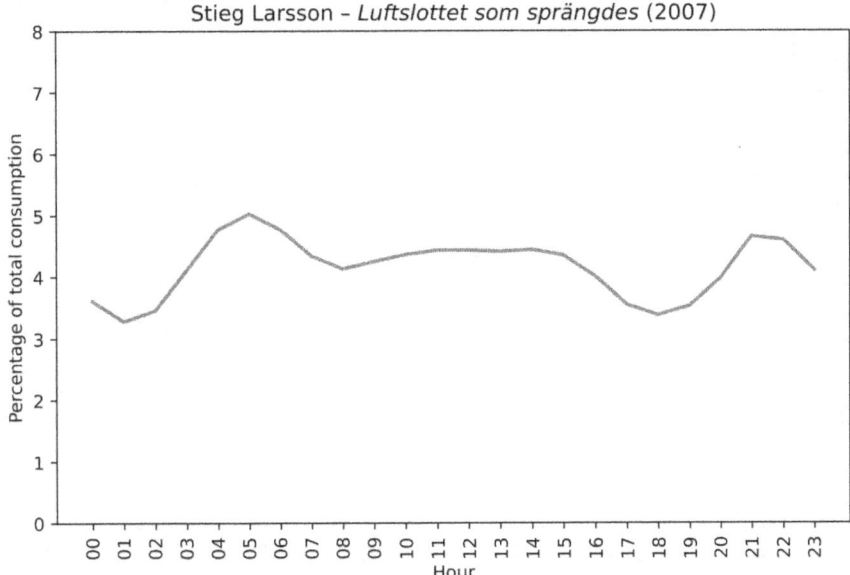

Figure 5.5 The book in the dataset with the lowest temporal diversity: percentage per hour.

the finale in Larsson's trilogy, *Luftslottet som sprängdes* (The Girl Who Kicked the Hornet's Nest) (2007) (see Figure 5.5).

At the other end of the spectrum are those that have been consumed little in the Storytel platform as audiobooks during the year studied, mostly works of prestige fiction that were in previous years popular in print. The title with the highest temporal diversity is Susanna Alakoski's *Svinalängorna* ('The Swine Rows', author's translation) (2006), an autobiographical account of growing up with alcoholic parents that became a major hit in Sweden (see Figure 5.6). Rather than drawing on the content or theme of this novel, I believe data sparsity to be the best explanation of the jumpy graph. But what is perhaps most interesting with Figures 5.5 and 5.6 is that also these outlier titles still show reading patterns that are reminiscent of the generic one – one flattened curve (emphasizing that audiobooks are read during all hours of the day) and one dramatized (emphasizing that audiobooks are primarily read during traditional working hours). Not even the outliers on the title level, then, exhibit different kinds of aggregated reading patterns but versions of the generic curve drawn in two different directions.

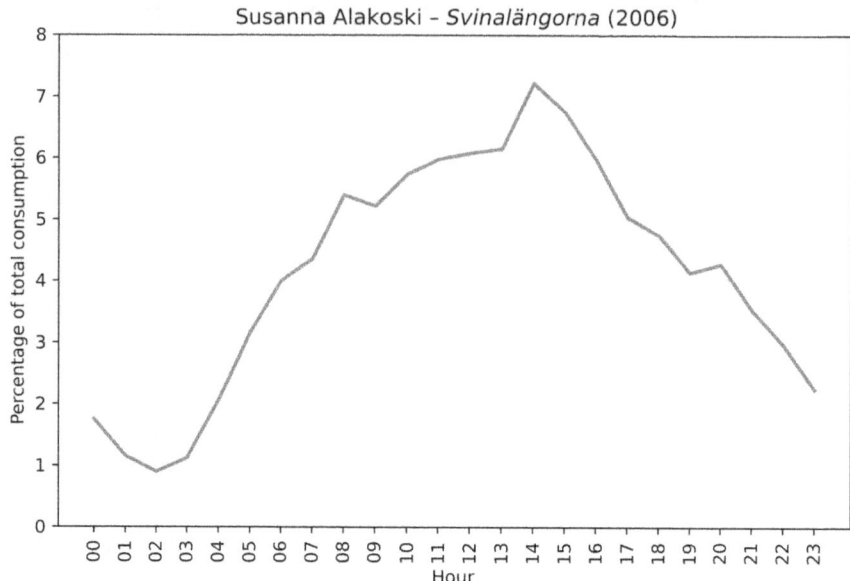

Figure 5.6 The book in the dataset with the highest temporal diversity: percentage per hour.

Kinds of readers

Concerning reading time, then, the choice of book medium matters, but so does the type of audiobook reader. Many readers seem to have integrated certain audiobook reading practices into their lives – 'audiobook routines', to use Tattersall Wallin's term.[10] Some read audiobooks in the daytime, others at night and yet others anytime. The first thing I noted was that there is a strong correlation between the amount that a user reads audiobooks and when they read them. To put it succinctly, heavy readers are often night readers. Or the other way around: night readers are often heavy readers. When I adjusted various thresholds regarding minimum consumption for users (250 hours, 500 hours, 750 hours), the pattern was clear: the higher the consumption, the more users were biased towards reading late in the evening and at night.

To study this further, I divided the dataset into subsets based on *when* individual users read. In doing this, I only included users who spent at least

---

[10] Tattersall Wallin, 'Audiobook Routines'.

100 hours reading on the platform during the year studied. This equals approximately 128,000 unique users, or just over a quarter (26.5 per cent) of the users in the dataset. These users together listened to audiobooks during approximately 27.8 million hours in the year studied, which is a share of almost three-quarters (73.9 per cent) of the total time spent by all users in the dataset. The threshold thus manages to keep only the more active readers of the books in the selection (100 hours are roughly ten completed books of an average length), whilst at the same time maintains a broad picture of generic audiobook reading practices.[11]

There are two basic parameters to adjust in clustering subsets of readers by temporal reading patterns. The first regards the hours of the day. My starting point was the division into the four six-hour temporal time spaces that are visualized in Figure 5.1. Since most readers who read a lot in the morning also read a lot in the afternoon, I group these two together. In the following, I consequently use three broad segments of temporal readers: *night readers* (12–6 am), *day readers* (6 am–6 pm) and *evening readers* (6 pm–12 am). The second parameter regards how large a share of each individual's reading time falls within each group of hours to be counted into one of the subsets – night, day, evening. Since such threshold values are arbitrary, I make use of multiple thresholds to identify both extremes and larger groups of readers within each temporal subset.

A majority of the average audiobook reading in the group takes place during the daytime (60 per cent), but a lot of reading is going on also in the evening (23 per cent) and night (17 per cent). As noted in Figure 5.1, audiobook reading is distributed quite evenly over the hours of the day. Among individuals, however, many readers have rather elaborated temporal reading practices. There is a large group of readers who read mostly during the daytime, and little in the evening and night. Somewhere between 7–28 per cent of the readers in the subset can be categorized as distinctive day readers (see Figure 5.7). In fact, just over 11 per cent of the frequent users *never* stream audiobooks during the night. At the other end of the spectrum, there is a smaller but still significant group of readers who read mostly in the night and late evenings, and little during the daytime. Somewhere between 4–13 per cent of the frequent readers can be categorized as distinctive night readers (see Figure 5.8). Finally, there is a significant group of readers who read mostly in the evenings, and little during the day as well as during the night.

---

[11] It can be added that I experimented with lots of various thresholds before settling with this, both regarding limits of lowest total consumption (twenty hours, fifty hours) and lowest number of titles (five, ten), and combinations of the two. None of the other thresholds changed the results in any dramatic way.

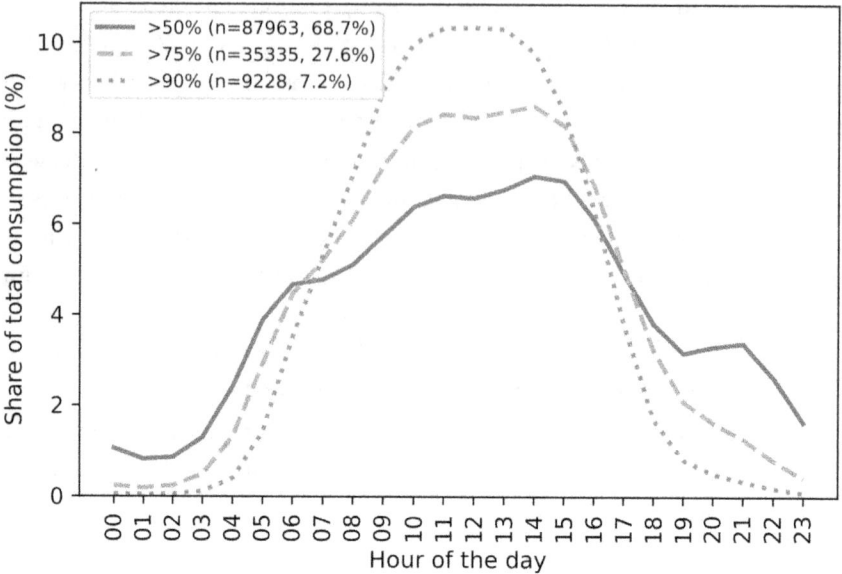

Figure 5.7 Three subsets of day readers (6 am–6 pm): average consumption per hour.

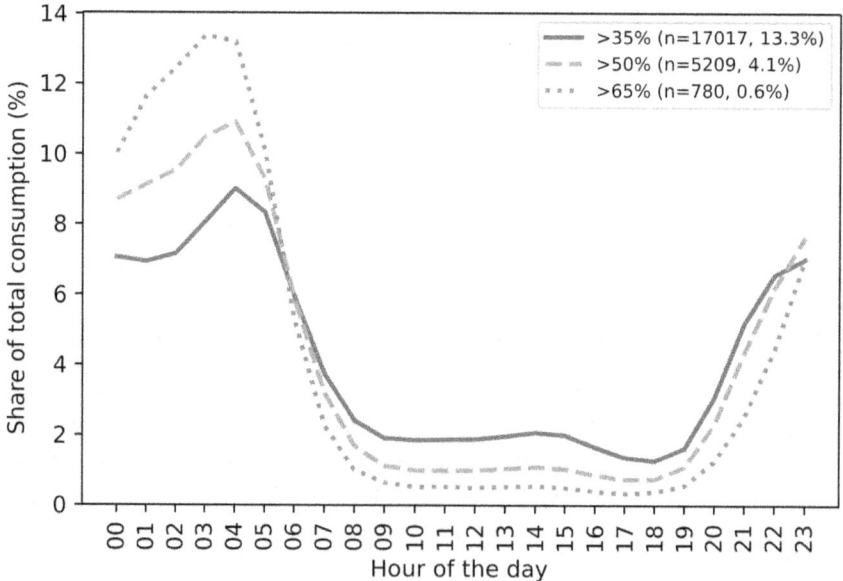

Figure 5.8 Three subsets of night readers (12–6 am): average consumption per hour.

Somewhere between 4–18 per cent of the frequent readers can be categorized as distinctive evening readers (see Figure 5.9).

These numbers are revealing in themselves as they give a sense of the proportions of how audiobook readers are divided over the days, evenings and nights. Even though the rates are uncertain and dependent on several thresholds they provide a basic understanding of when various groups of people interact with audiobooks. At least, it can act as a foundation for future studies of audiobook reading time.

They also show that a significant proportion of the frequent readers have rather elaborate temporal audiobook practices. Although there is still a large group of readers who show no distinct temporal reading patterns, the three kinds of readers I have visualized make up an important part of the frequent readers. It is hard to point at a specific number or percentage of readers, but judging by the patterns in Figures 5.7 to 5.9 it seems that around half of the frequent readers (give or take 10 per cent) are reading audiobooks mostly during specific hours. That is, they are readers with specific audiobook practices reflected on a temporal level.[12]

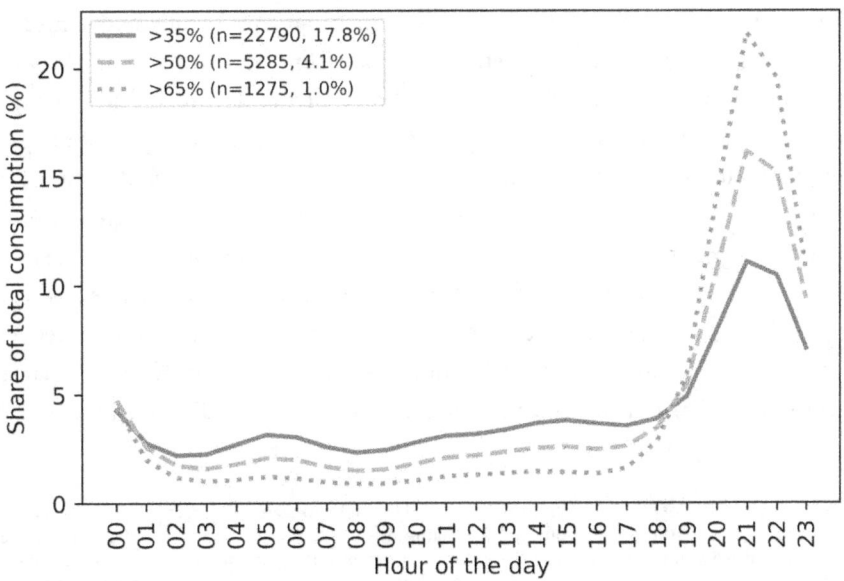

Figure 5.9 Three subsets of evening readers (6 pm–12 am): average consumption per hour.

[12] It should also be remembered that what is tracked here is reading patterns per user account. Readers who are sharing accounts might therefore hide additional actual readers with distinct temporal reading practices. The numbers and shares of readers in Figures 5.8 to 5.10 should therefore be considered as possibly a bit too low.

The common perception that audiobooks are read during all hours of the day thus needs to be nuanced. It holds true on an aggregated level, but it is not true for all readers at the individual level. Instead, large groups of readers seem to use audiobooks in certain kinds of situations, connected to certain kinds of practices or daily routines. The evening readers are the ones who most closely resemble reading practices of print books and ebooks, with peaks in reading hours when most people have some time off from work and their daily chores, as well as in relation to going to bed. The night readers are likely both users who read audiobooks while trying to sleep or in dealing with sleep trouble, and readers who are working night shifts and are reading simultaneously. The day readers are the ones who listen to audiobooks in all the daily situations where reading in other media formats is harder to accomplish – while driving, commuting, working, exercising and so on. The day readers tie in well with previous qualitative audiobook research, which has emphasized such situations as a new arena for reading.[13]

To get a better understanding of these temporally distinct subsets of audiobook readers, one needs to dig deeper into the data points. One way of doing this is to zoom in on a small selection of users in each category by qualitative means. Such an approach enables a better understanding of what people do with audiobooks, and how it differs over the hours of the day. In the following, I draw from a *randomized selection of ten individual users per category* of distinct temporal audiobook readers. Methodologically, I use the strictest thresholds to track down the audiobook use for readers who are strongly connected to each temporal segment.[14] In one way, it is therefore a study of outliers, but if one pays close attention to these readers' status as outliers I believe they enable a way of extrapolating the poles of reading practices within the larger group. Moreover, it is a very small randomized sample of readers that I investigate, so any claims regarding readers in general cannot be drawn from their audiobook practices. It

---

[13] See, for example, Koepnick, 'Reading on the Move'; Have and Stougaard Pedersen, *Digital Audiobooks*; Tattersall Wallin, 'Audiobook Routines'. It is naturally hard to narrow down such practices further only by investigating temporal data since, for instance, exercising and doing the dishes are done at various times. The only such daytime behaviour clearly connected to specific hours is commuting, but when I experimented with more narrow temporal segments for typical commuting hours (6–9 am, 3–6 pm), I could not identify many readers whose audiobook consumption peaked clearly at these hours. Only somewhere between 0.1 and 1 per cent of the readers read audiobooks clearly the most during commuting hours, whereas most readers who read a lot in these hours also read a lot during the rest of the hours of the working day in between.

[14] In practice, this means thirty individual user profiles during the year studied: ten (randomized, individual) users who have done at least 65 per cent of their audiobook reading during the night, ten users who have done at least 90 per cent of the reading during the day and ten users who have done at least 65 per cent of their reading during evenings.

can be thought of as a glimpse into how some readers within specific temporal strata make use of audiobooks.

Night readers – sleep trouble or graveyard shifts?

Starting with the distinct night readers, what emerges clearly is that several of the investigated readers in the group seem to use audiobooks to try to sleep or when having sleep trouble. A strong indication in this direction is recurring patterns with streaming sessions during the night, which are all a certain length. This points towards the use of the Storytel sleep timer. In the Storytel app, users can access a sleep timer by pressing a little 'moon button' just to the right of the main play/pause button (see Figure 5.10). There are four default options for the sleep timer – the player stops automatically after 15, 30 or 45 minutes, or when a chapter ends. Users can also set their own sleep timer to any number of minutes they prefer. For one night reader, over three-quarters (77 per cent) of their streaming sessions lasted exactly either fifteen, thirty or forty-five minutes, with fifteen minutes being the most common (48 per cent of the sessions). A typical night pattern for this reader is a first fifteen-minute session between 12–1 am, followed by one thirty-minute session between 1–2 am (or, perhaps more likely, two fifteen-minute sessions during the same hour; remember that I have access to data of the granularity per hour). Then this person has a listening break before two additional fifteen-minute sessions occur, one between 3–4 am, and one between 4–5 am. Then there is no more audiobook reading carried out until the next night. A likely interpretation of this behaviour is that someone is using audiobooks with a sleep timer to try to get back to sleep, and then finally succeeds. Another reader prefers the thirty-minute sleep timer, which accounts for 29 per cent of all their sessions. Yet another reader seems to prefer a longer sleep timer, with around a third (32 per cent) of their sessions lasting exactly sixty minutes. Of the ten night readers investigated, seven have these kinds of audiobook streaming patterns.

A related pattern is recurring 180-minute sessions. Since the Storytel app automatically stops playing after three hours if there has been no interaction from the user, such sessions during the night indicate that the user has fallen asleep – the player keeps playing the book until it automatically stops after three hours. This can be understood as a similar practice as the use of the sleep timer (listening to audiobooks while trying to sleep, while falling asleep or while

Figure 5.10 Screen dump of the Storytel app in reading mode.

sleeping), but without the timer. Such sessions are found more frequently among two of the investigated night readers.

Most of the night readers in the sample seem to use audiobooks in relation to sleep and sleep trouble. Since the sample of readers is small, too much should not be drawn out of these numbers, but it at least indicates that the sleeping timer is frequently being used by people who listen a lot to audiobooks at night.

This is not surprising per se, but it points towards a kind of audiobook use that has been relatively absent in previous discussions. While nearly all research emphasizes the mobility of the audiobook medium as well as its potential for reading without the need of occupying your hands and eyes with a book, much less attention has been drawn to the possibilities to engage with audiobooks in the dark, when trying to sleep or when de facto sleeping. Tattersall Wallin approaches these practices when discussing audiobooks used for falling asleep as a part of her informants 'bedtime routines', but she does not relate it to sleep trouble during the night.[15] Still, the behaviour makes perfect sense in relation to the audiobook medium. Of course, also print books and ebooks have for long been and are still read by people when going to sleep or when having trouble sleeping. But the audiobook has the advantage that you can read in complete darkness and with your eyes closed, which are two key factors for falling asleep.

Although it is impossible to say how common this way of 'reading' audiobooks is, there are several indicators that point towards it being at least not very uncommon. One is the data points investigated here: a lot of reading during the night and several individual readers who use the sleep timer. Another one is the sleep timer itself and its salient appearance in the app, on Storytel as well as similar audiobook platforms. These streaming services would of course not introduce and highlight such a feature in their apps if it was not appreciated by their customers. As a comparison, there is no similar sleep timer in streaming platforms for TV and film such as Netflix. In the music and podcast streaming service Spotify there is, however, although it is not visible in the main interface and thus less apparent to the users.[16] These differences make it plausible to believe that it is specifically audiobook reading and sleeping that are closely related activities, while music and podcast listening is somewhat related, and TV series and film watching is less related.

---

[15] Tattersall Wallin, 'Audiobook Routines'.
[16] To access the sleep timer in Spotify, you need to push the 'three dots' in the upper right corner in the player view, and then scroll down in a menu to find the sleep timer, where the option is number nine out of ten possible options.

A third indication is that there are audiobooks that are specifically dedicated to sleeping matters and insomnia. For example, author and psychologist Helena Kubicek Boyes's *Somna* series ('Fall asleep', author's translation, 2020), narrated by the Swedish actor Mikael Persbrandt, are books designed to help people to fall asleep. As the cover text reads: 'These are soothing texts based on scientific methods that help you let go of your thoughts and feelings and relax your body to fall asleep faster' (author's translation). Such books would not be published if there was no audience for them.[17] Relatedly, Ann Steiner and Karl Berglund show in a study of repetitive reading practices of audiobooks for children that a special segment of 'falling-asleep-books' – for example Carl-Johan Forssén Ehrlin's *Kaninen som så gärna ville somna* (The Rabbit Who Wants to Fall Asleep) (2010) – are among the most frequently repeated books by Swedish audiobook readers.[18] This very instrumental use of fiction – to get your kid to sleep – points in the same direction.

One reason why this highly practical use of audiobooks has not been highlighted in previous scholarship might relate to the level of pragmatism involved. It is a use of literature that seems to have little to do with reading in the sense of engaging in the literature involved. And when one falls asleep, the reading – at least in any cognitively aware sense – stops, albeit not the book consumption since the audiobook player goes on. What the audiobook night readers above show is a use of literature as a means to an end. They seek to achieve something very concrete with their reading, namely, to fall asleep.

Not all night readers appear to be reading for sleeping, however. There are streaming patterns for individual users that point towards people reading audiobooks while working night shifts or engaging in other kinds of periodized nightly undertakings. One reader has streamed audiobooks consistently during the nights for two longer periods in the year studied, covering roughly one and a half months each. During these periods, the sessions are of irregular length and include lots of shorter breaks. Their typical pattern is to start between 11 pm and 12 am and go on during the entire night up until around 5–6 am. Most such nights, the total reading time adds up to somewhere between two and five hours in total. Another reader has a similar pattern, though it is broken up into several shorter periods of night reading, most often spanning between two and five days, with a total reading time of between three and six hours per night. One

---

[17] It can also be noted that there exist several podcasts based on the same idea. The phenomenon of getting to sleep via sound is thus not exclusive to audiobooks but available in general in other oral voice media.
[18] Steiner and Berglund, *Barnlitterära strömningar*, 48–51.

could easily imagine these reading patterns aligning with working night shifts, breast-feeding an infant or night activities of other sorts.

Regarding what kinds of literature the group of night readers are reading, the results point in no certain direction at all. Most of them complete roughly ten to twenty books during the year studied, written by roughly five to ten different authors. They regularly stream a book all the way through and then move on to the next, and most of them read in various genres, though crime fiction is the most common genre overall. There are no obvious preferences for performing narrators either. Again, what people read does not seem to be decisive for when they read.[19]

Day and evening readers – periodical reading

Turning to the distinct day readers, most of the ten individuals in the group have rather irregular patterns, with no apparent recurring reading hours during the day. They listen in the daytime in general, some more in the morning and some more in the afternoon, but most of them during all hours related to the traditional working day (6 am–6 pm). One reader is an exception and appears to be a morning commuter, where the majority of their sessions take place between 5 am and 9 am, and most of the others in the afternoons between 3 pm and 5 pm, which could indicate reading while commuting back from work. Reading at other times during the day is uncommon for this reader, and reading during the evening and night is rare. Neither do the day readers' choices of books stand out. They all read in mixed genres but prefer popular fiction and especially crime fiction, just like audiobook readers in general. Moreover, none of them seem to be particularly bound to certain authors or performing narrators, and they all read authors whose genders are evenly distributed.

What is striking among the group of distinct day readers is that they read a lot but only during certain periods of the year. In between these periods of reading, they read nothing – or other books than the ones in the selection. In Figure 5.11a–d, the reading patterns of four of the individual distinct day

[19] The distinct night readers appear to read more or less the same titles as most users in the dataset: bestsellers, popular genre fiction and especially crime fiction, and lots of domestic Swedish authors. Some of the most common authors for night reading include authors such as Anna Bågstam, Rolf and Cilla Börjlind, Jan Guillou, Stina Jackson, Anna Jansson, Mari Jungstedt, Lars Kepler, Peter Nyström and Peter Mohlin, Delia Owens, Lucinda Riley, Hans Rosenfeldt, Sofie Sarenbrant and Emilie Schepp. These are all popular authors in the audiobook segment, and they do not stand out in any way from the patterns on the aggregated level.

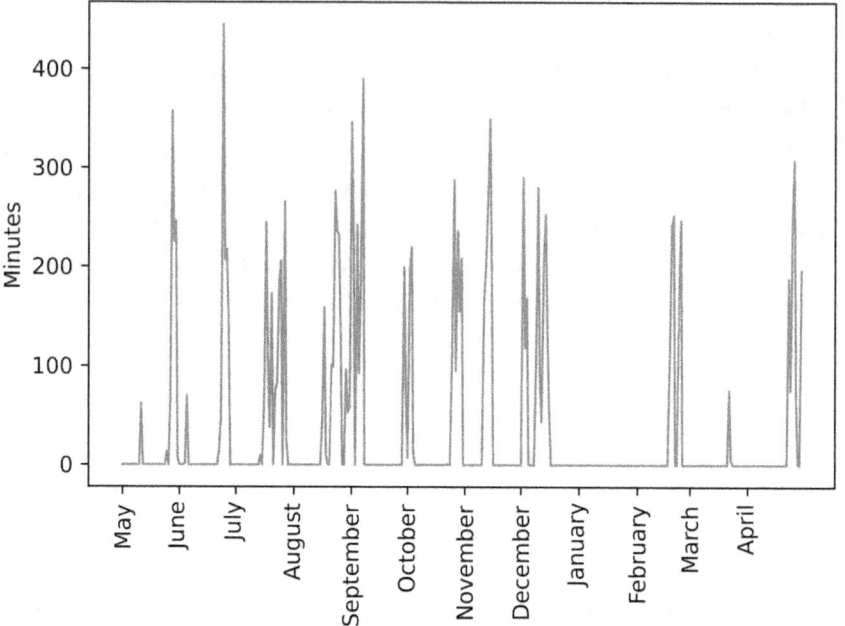

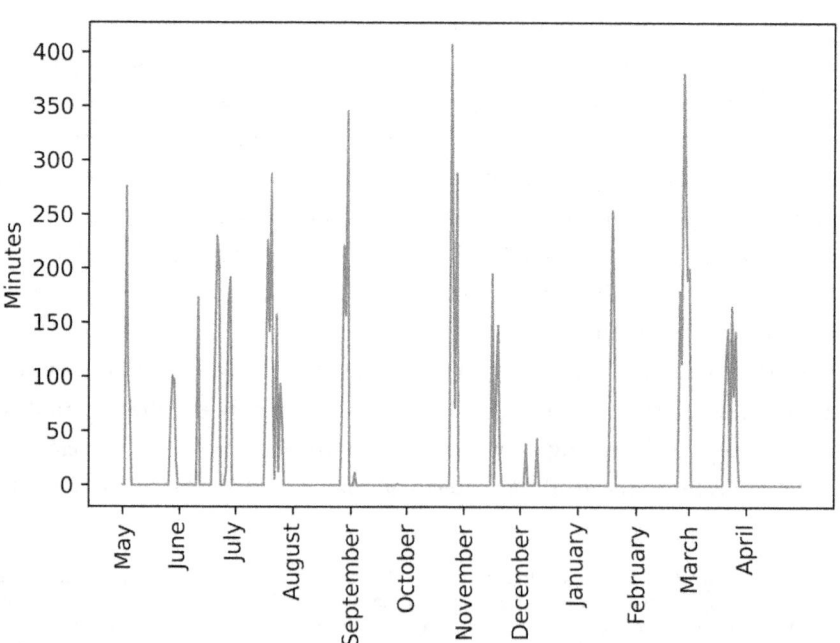

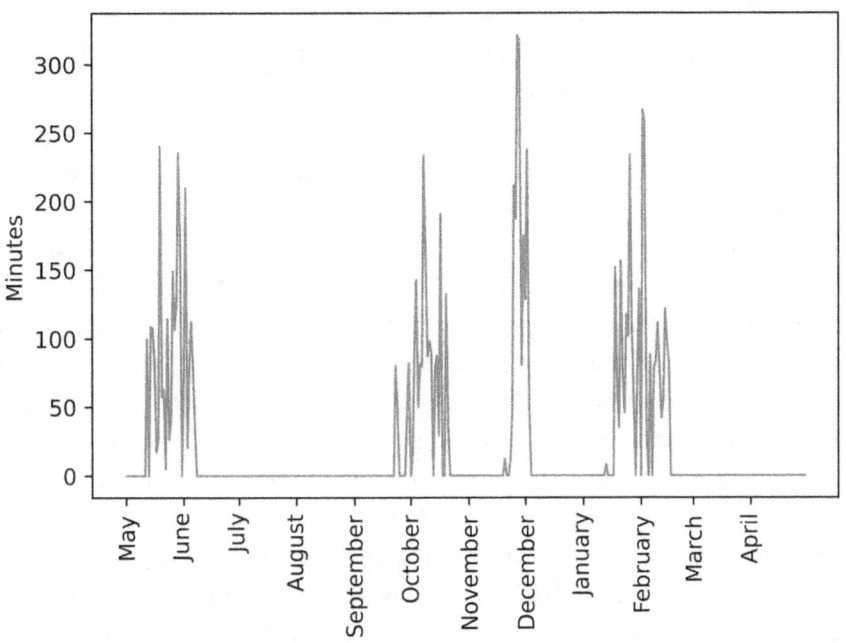

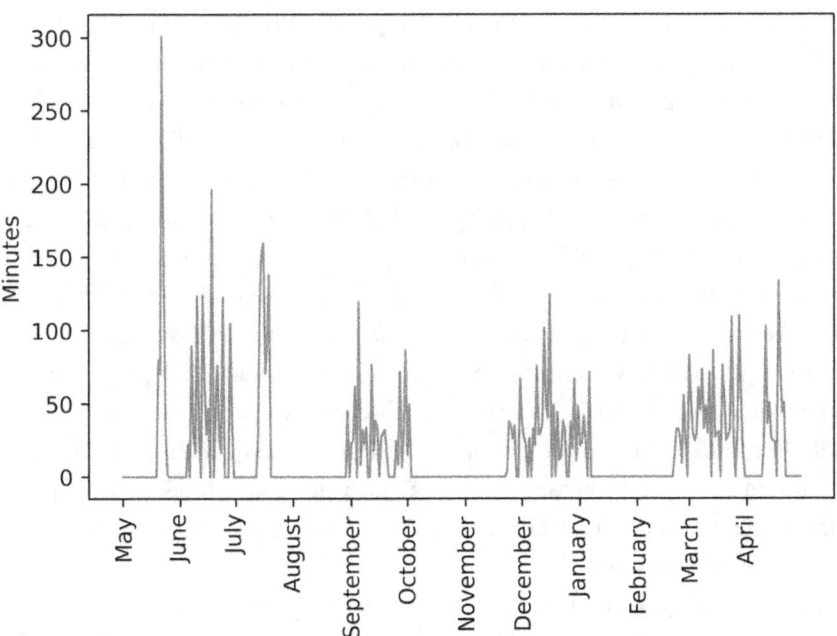

Figures 5.11a–d Four individual distinct day readers: minutes read per day distributed over the year.

readers in the group are plotted over the entire year studied. Two of them (Figure 5.11a–b) read books in the commercial top segment extensively during several shorter periods, in most cases somewhere between one to five days each. The other two (Figure 5.11c–d) instead read during four longer periods, roughly between one to two months each, followed by longer periods of non-reading of the titles in the selection in between.

I can only speculate on why these reading practices are so periodized. One answer is that they are reading other kinds of more niche audiobooks, outside of the dataset, in the 'silent' periods in between. A related explanation is that they read outside of the Storytel platform in between – print books as well as audiobooks and ebooks from other sources than Storytel. But these are unlikely to explain the pattern in full. Another guess is that the irregularities are work related. People might be long-distance remote workers, who read audiobooks primarily when they commute back and forth (which could explain the patterns in Figure 5.11a–b), or they could work periodically under circumstances that allow them to read audiobooks during work in these periods (which could explain the patterns in Figure 5.11c–d). A less media-specific explanation is that these patterns reflect how many people read, no matter the book format. You read a lot when you have a good book going, but when it is finished, you might fall out of your current reading loop and prioritize other things for a while, before you start with the new one. The reader shown in Figure 5.11d, for instance, might indicate such a reading practice. One book is started and completed in the May period, then two books in a row are started and completed in the June period. Then comes a break for a couple of weeks before a new book is started and completed in the July period. What triggers the decision to start to read is of course impossible to say in any generalizable way, but for this reader, freshly released titles seem to be a reason. The June period starts with reading of Sofie Sarenbrant's crime novel *Mytomanen* ('The Mythomaniac', author's translation), which was released only two weeks earlier in late May 2020. The same holds true for the July period, which consists solely of reading Cilla and Rolf Börjlind's crime novel *Fruset guld* ('Frozen Gold', author's translation), published some weeks before. For this reader, then, new titles at the centre of media attention appear to boost audiobook reading, at times leading also to reading of backlist titles.

When looking at the group of distinct evening readers, they diverge from the group of day readers in primarily three ways (apart, of course, from when the reading takes place during the day). First, they have comparatively more regularized reading patterns. Many readers in the group read audiobooks nearly every evening during the period studied, and they often repeatedly started at the same time and for a similar amount of time, with common streaming peaks between 9 pm and 11 pm. These are likely reading practices connected to reading while going to bed, sometimes also when falling asleep, and most of the readers in the group *only* use audiobooks during these hours. Both the day readers and the night readers investigated are more flexible and irregular in their audiobook reading than evening readers, which is interesting since evening reading is the temporal reading practice most similar to print and ebook reading. Perhaps these evening readers have switched book medium but stuck with their old and well-established temporal reading habits, while the day and night readers, on the other hand, are using streamed audiobooks in ways that give them new and extended reading hours.

Second, while the readers in the evening group appear to be daily users, there are also several examples of readers who have a daily pattern for a longer period, followed by an equally long period with no reading at all of the books in the selection. And both the periods of heavy audiobook reading and the periods with silence are apparently regular in length and reading behaviour, in contrast to the periodical reading among the day readers noted above. One reader, for instance, read between thirty minutes and two hours almost every evening during the three months from August to October. Then comes a period of no reading of books in the commercial top segment for two months, followed by another period of three months from January to March with a reading pattern closely matching the first one. A possible explanation of this behaviour is that these readers are following certain subscription offers. For instance, as of this writing, Storytel is offering new subscribers in Sweden a reduced fee of 50 per cent for a period of four months, while their main competitor BookBeat offers a one-month free subscription to new customers.[20] The pattern of alternating heavy and regular audiobook reading with periods of non-reading might indicate that users are jumping between subscriptions to keep down their own costs.

Third, the group of evening readers shows the most distinct literary preferences when it comes to choices of authors and books. Most of the readers in the selection read only Nordic Noir, and several read only female Swedish crime writers. The most frequently recurring names include Susan Casserfelt, Anna Jansson, Camilla Läckberg, Sofie Sarenbrant and Viveca Sten. Furthermore, several readers followed series in this genre dedicatedly, finishing book after book by the same author. One reader repeats the *same two books* evening

---

[20] See Storytel, 'Storytel'; BookBeat, 'BookBeat'.

after evening. In other words, this reader continuously reads, in this case, Dan Brown's *The Da Vinci Code* and *Angels and Demons* while going to sleep for the entire year studied. Such repetitive audiobook practices are analysed further in Chapter 6.

When discussing audiobook practices henceforth it is crucial to keep in mind that there are several different temporal layers at play simultaneously – the hours of the day, the days of the week, the months of the year and perhaps even the years of the decade (although the latter lies beyond what I can study with the datasets investigated in this book). What I have also emphasized in this chapter is that the aggregate level is crucial in understanding audiobook reading, but that it tells us less about individual reading practices. A similar point, but stressed from the opposite perspective, is made by Hoyt Long in *The Values in Numbers* (2021). He challenges the norm of 'the case study' in literary scholarship as a way to infer knowledge about the whole from a part (i.e. 'the case'). As Long rightly points out, such practices are risky and can lead to wrong conclusions, since – and here he is building on Andrew Piper – there is an 'evidence gap' between the part and the whole; one cannot presuppose that the part is representative of the whole.[21] I argue that it is important to recognize that this also works the other way around. One cannot presuppose that most readers (the individual 'parts') read in ways resembling the average ('the whole'). The aggregates show mean figures composed of a large number of individual audiobook reading practices. Aggregate averages do not imply that most readers read in ways that lie close to the mean, but rather that various quite distinctly different reading practices together form the aggregate.

Coda: The aggregated literary year

To illustrate the importance of being able to move between different temporal layers and between individual readers and aggregates, I end this chapter by looking at the yearly audiobook reading patterns on an aggregated level. From a publishing perspective, there are certain periods where more books are published and where more books are sold. For the regular book trade, these

---

[21] See the chapter 'Archive and Sample' in Hoyt Long, *The Value in Numbers: Reading Japanese Literature in a Global Information Age* (New York: Columbia University Press, 2021), especially 69–77; see further Andrew Piper, *Enumerations: Data and Literary History* (Chicago: University of Chicago Press, 2018), 6–12.

cyclical patterns of publishing have developed over a long period of time. Torbjörn Forslid and colleagues give a precise description of this year cycle of the Swedish book trade:

> There is a year-cycle in the book trade which can be followed in publishing seasons, sales peaks, and periods where certain kinds of books are easier or harder to sell. In January, the book trade is calm, with few new releases. February is characterised mainly by the Swedish book sale, with plenty of re-publications of previous bestsellers in cheaper bindings. In March the new titles of the spring season are launched. In the summertime it is easy to sell paperbacks, which is reflected in retailer campaigns, i.e. 'buy four, pay only for three'. The summer is dominated by popular fiction, especially crime fiction, which is understood to be suitable reading during lazy days of vacation. The fall is traditionally the time when 'big' books and authors are launched. To get media attention around the [Gothenburg] book fair in September and the following months is harder than in any other time during the year, and most publishers plan their publishing schedules accordingly. *The Christmas sales finishes the year and is the single most important period for everyone in the book trade – retailers, publishers, and authors. An expensive hardback published during the fall, fiction or non-fiction, is a common Christmas gift, and at no other time during the year is it easier to sell books.*[22] (My translation and emphasis.)

This cycle is visible in book sales statistics, where sales during the first and last quarter of the year are significantly higher than during the second and third quarters, and where December is the single month with the highest book sales.[23] But this data concerns sales of books sold as entities, mainly print books. For book streaming, the trends are connected to the description made by Forslid

---

[22] Torbjörn Forslid, Jon Helgason, Lisbeth Larsson, Christian Lenemark, Anders Ohlsson and Ann Steiner, *Höstens böcker: Litterära värdeförhandlingar 2013* (Gothenburg and Stockholm: Makadam, 2015), 104. The quote in original Swedish reads: 'Det finns en årscykel på bokmarknaden som går att följa i utgivningssäsonger, försäljningstoppar och perioder där vissa typer av böcker är lättare eller svårare att sälja. I januari är det i huvudsak stiltje i bokbranschen med få nya titlar. Februari präglas av bokrean med en stor återutgivning av gamla succéer i billigt kartonnage. I mars lanseras vårens nyheter. På sommaren är det lättast att sälja pocketböcker och återförsäljarnas kampanjer, till exempel "köp fyra betala för tre", återspeglar detta faktum. Sommaren domineras också av populärlitteraturen, främst deckare som anses vara läsning för hängmatta och semester. Hösten har traditionellt varit den tid på året då de "stora" författarskapen och böckerna lanseras. Att få medial uppmärksamhet kring bokmässan i september och under månaderna fram till julen är svårare än under någon annan tid på året och de flesta förlag planerar sina publiceringslistor därefter. Julförsäljningen som avslutar året är den enskilt viktigaste perioden för alla på bokmarknaden – för återförsäljare, förläggare och författare. En dyr inbunden nyutkommen bok, skönlitterär eller facklitterär, är en vanlig julklapp och ingen tid på året är det lättare att sälja böcker än då.'

[23] Forslid et al., *Höstens böcker*, 104–05; cf. Wikberg, *Bokförsäljningsstatistiken: Helåret 2021*, 37–40.

and colleagues above, but due to the nature of the format and distribution, they are also different.[24]

The Storytel streaming data enables a rather detailed look (on a day-by-day basis) at the yearly trends as it regards audiobook streaming in Sweden. In Figure 5.12, the total number of starts per day of the year for the 376 bestsellers and beststreamers in audiobook format have been aggregated over the four complete years that the data covers – 1 January 2017 to 31 December 2020.[25]

There are three distinct peaks in consumption: late May/early June, late August/early September and late October/early November. All these periods

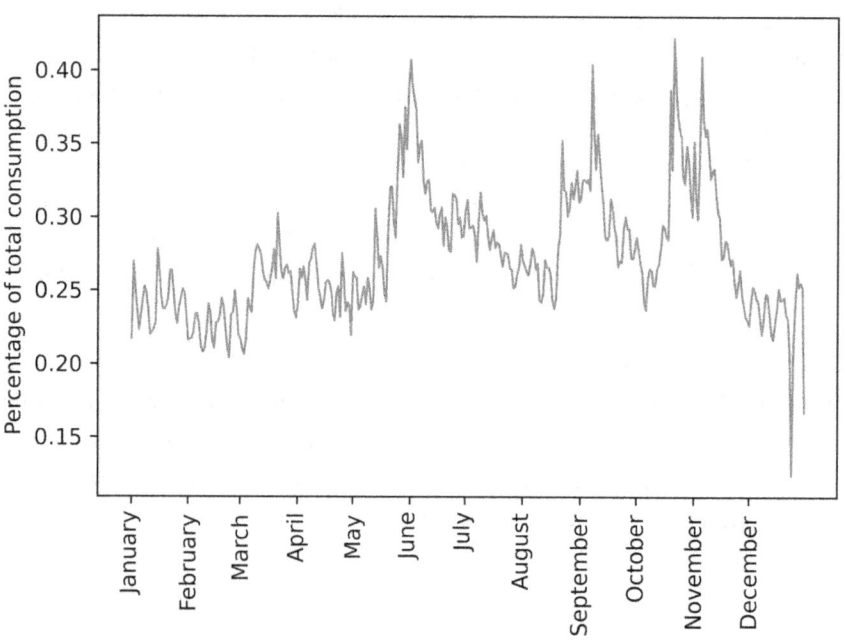

Figure 5.12 Started streams of bestsellers and beststreamers in audiobook format (n=376) aggregated over four whole years, 2017–20: average percentage of total consumption per day.

---

[24] In the Swedish Publishers' Associations statistics for 2021, the difference between the quarter with the highest revenues and the quarter with the lowest revenues is significantly smaller in book streaming services (where the ratio between Q4 and Q2 is 1:0.91) than in all other book sales channels: physical bookstores (Q4:Q2 = 1:0.46); internet retailers and book clubs (Q4:Q2 = 1:0.66); and shopping centres and grocery stores (Q1:Q2 = 1:0.57) (Wikberg, *Bokförsäljningsstatistiken: Helåret 2021*, 37–40).

[25] This means that all started streams in the Storytel platform on, for example, 1 January in the four years 2017, 2018, 2019 and 2020, have been added together and then divided by the total number of started streams for the entire four years. The date 29 February has been excluded in these calculations to not let the leap year 2020 affect the results.

are when many publishers release new books by big names, which is reflected in the data. Commercially important authors such as David Lagercrantz and Jan Guillou have their books released in the August/September period, Lars Kepler and Dan Brown in October/November and Sofie Sarenbrant and Mari Jungstedt in May/June. Since all formats including audiobooks are regularly released simultaneously, and since frontlist consumption is very important for commercially strong fiction – see the discussion in Chapter 3 – users start to read these titles on book streaming platforms immediately upon release. This explains the peaks and highlights a difference between audiobook streaming and book selling: *streaming patterns are more sensitive to publication dates than other forms of book sales, and they are less sensitive to other aspects of the book trade cycle.* Sales in relation to Christmas or the February book sale, for instance – important for the regular book trade, as noted by Forslid and colleagues above – do not seem to affect audiobook streaming. February and December show among the lowest rates of audiobook streaming during the entire year, significantly lower than in the summertime. In contrast, book sales of copies peak in December and in the first quarter, and are lowest during the summer.

Since streamed books are immediately available for the subscribing customer, their peaks of attention – and their peaks in consumption – will also be immediate in relation to the publication date. Although the consumption of backlist titles is a crucial part of book streaming, this does not contradict the importance of new releases, since these regularly increase the streaming rates for both the frontlist book and the related backlist books (see further the discussion in Chapter 3). Again, this should be contrasted to book sales of physical items, where the qualities of the book as a gift (Christmas sales) and pricing levels (the book sale) largely affect consumer behaviour. Audiobook streaming, on the other hand, is much more single-handedly driven by attention and presence in the media, which is naturally most intense close to the publication date.

While the daily peaks in audiobook streaming are explained by new releases by the most famous authors, the consumption drops on certain days are related to holidays. The most obvious drops in streaming that can be noted in Figure 5.12 are Christmas Eve (the most important day of Christmas celebrations in Sweden) and New Year's Eve. Upon closer inspection, there are also other dates where audiobook reading falls. New Year's Day has the lowest rate of audiobook consumption in January, and the days around Midsummer have the lowest in June.[26] The low reading rates on 30 April and 1 May are likely an effect of the Swedish tradition of celebrating Walpurgis Night and Labour Day, when most people are off from work. The same might apply for the low streaming rates towards the end of February, which is a period when schoolchildren in Sweden have a 'sports holiday', a winter vacation where people spend a lot of time together outdoors in the snow.

These patterns point in the same direction as the daily and weekly ones: audiobooks are read all the time but to the lowest extent when most people tend to spend time with their family and friends. On the level of the day, it means primarily around dinner time. On the level of the week, it means primarily during the weekend. On the level of the year, it means during major holidays, when it is common to be off work and hanging out with relatives. To sum up, the main competitor to audiobook reading seems to be people's need to socialize. Naturally, this is hard to do with an audiobook plugged in.

---

[26] The Swedish Midsummer is a holiday without a fixed yearly date. Instead, it is related to the summer solstice. In the period studied, Midsummer's Eve occurred on 19 June (2020), 21 June (2019), 22 June (2018) and 23 June (2017). If this day would have been the same for all the years studied, there would likely have been a drop in audiobook consumption in parity with Christmas and New Years for that day. The same goes for other holidays without fixed dates such as Easter.

6

Repeaters, swappers and constant readers: Expanded reading

When highlighting the complexities of popular genre fiction reading, Janice Radway once famously detested the metaphor of consumption when equated with reading. Reading is not a passive thing, she claimed.[1] I agree, and a multitude of readership scholars have convincingly proved this to be true.[2] However, this reasoning might be in need of an update since some of the audiobook practices surfacing in this study indeed seem to be exactly this: *passive*. Again, people are reading audiobooks while doing something else. What is also true in the age of streamed audiobooks is that a firm line between reading and book consumption is harder to draw than ever before. Since every streamed minute on Storytel and similar platforms renders money back to publishers and authors, consumption in book streaming services is inevitably tied to the reading practices involved. When people are streaming books on these platforms, they are simultaneously consuming them (in the sense of 'buying' them), minute by minute.

As I discussed in the introduction, it can be debated whether logged sessions of book streaming should be equated with reading or not. Book streaming is certainly book consumption, and it is certainly an example of some kind of literature use. But Storytel and other platforms can obviously not track users' engagement or level of cognitive processing of the content of books.[3] However, If one accepts that all possible activities a Storytel user can engage in while streaming audiobooks could be called 'reading' – that is, including sleeping, listening distractedly while talking to or texting someone, or leaving an audiobook playing aloud to calm down an anxious pet – then one ends up with what could be labelled as an *expanded concept of reading*. It is possibly quite far away from what is generally meant when reading is discussed, and likely

---

[1] Radway, 'Reading Is Not Eating'.
[2] For an overview of some important studies in this vein, see Murray, *The Digital Literary Sphere*, 148.
[3] Cf. Rowberry, 'The Limits of Big Data', 242.

closer to 'literature use', but it might prove effective for understanding the ways in which people are actually making use of audiobooks in their everyday lives. Or, if you will, passively reading them.

In the final chapter of this book, I follow this suggested trail and delve deeper into such expanded reading practices by examining readers who stream audiobooks to large extents. The empirical point of departure is 'the second dataset', described in detail in the introduction, covering reading consumption data per individual user and hour for one year (May 2020–April 2021). Two parameters essential in the reader consumption data are the focus of the analyses: the number of unique titles each reader has started to read and the number of minutes each reader has spent streaming books on the platform. In general, these parameters are positively correlated. It almost goes without saying that the more books you read on the Storytel platform, the more minutes you spend on it. But as the analyses will show, the reading patterns are highly varied and far more complex than this.

Based on these metrics and by going through the habits of thirty individual user cases, I will focus on three types of audiobook readers. I call them *repeaters*, *swappers* and *constant readers*. *Repeaters* are audiobook readers that over and over again listen to the same books. *Swappers* are readers who try out lots of books, only to abandon most of them early on and move on to others. *Constant readers*, finally, are binge-readers who listen to books all the time. In the following, I will analyse how these categories of readers make use of audiobooks, how common they are, how their behaviour can be explained and how they partly might alter the concept of reading as such.

I will also relate them to the longer history of reading and reading practices. In his seminal *Der Bürger als Leser* (1976), Rolf Engelsing observes a shift in reading patterns in the eighteenth century. Many readers went from an 'intensive reading' and rereading of very few texts – most often the Bible and a couple of other supra-canonical works – to an 'extensive reading' of many texts, which were not uncommonly read only once. Engelsing dubs this transformative shift 'the reading revolution' and understands it as the point in history when modern reading – in the way reading as a practice is commonly recognized today – emerged. The new form of extensive reading made us into modern readers, Engelsing claims.[4] This division between intensive and extensive

---

[4] Engelsing, *Der Bürger als Leser*; see also further Reinhard Wittmann, 'Was there a Reading Revolution at the End of the Eighteenth Century?', in *A History of Reading in the West*, edited by Guglielmo Cavallo and Roger Chartier (Oxford: Polity, 1999), 284–312.

reading practices is brought to the fore by the emerging streamed audiobook reading practices investigated here. Repeaters partly resemble the premodern intensive readers in Engelsing's terminology, while the swappers can be understood as extensive readers on steroids.

Three important groups of outliers

In Figure 6.1, all individual users who during the year studied streamed audiobooks for at least ten hours are visualized in a scatter plot.[5] Every single dot represents one of the roughly 356,000 readers in the analysis. The vertical y-axis measures the number of books read, and the horizontal x-axis the number of hours spent. The dashed line shows the result of a linear regression, which by statistical means calculates the correlation between the two variables. The positive curve makes perfect intuitive sense: in general, the more books you read, the longer you read. In statistical terms, the R-value of the regression analysis is

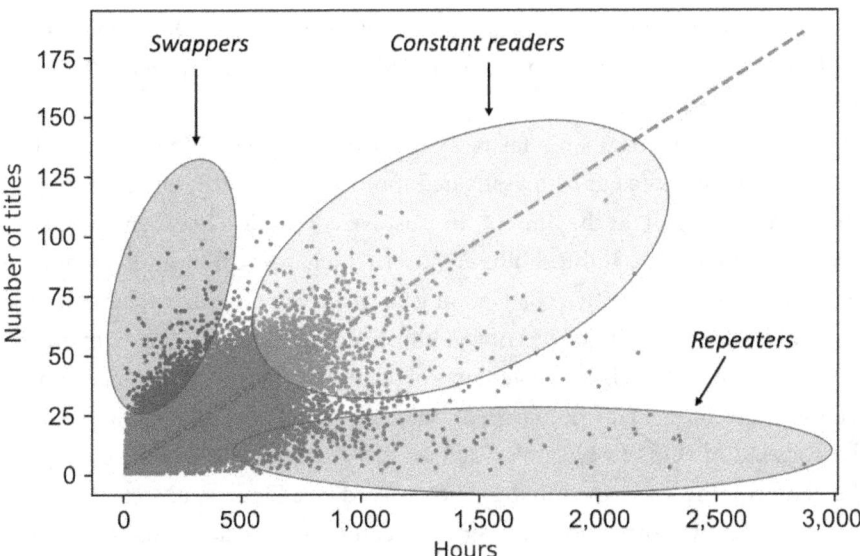

Figure 6.1 Individual audiobook users: number of titles per number of streamed hours (n=356,383).

---

[5] The ten hours threshold is used to get rid of users with little interaction with the books in the selection. Since there is so little data on these readers, they are not very helpful for analysing reading patterns.

0.86 and the p-value below 0.01, which suggests a statistically significant and strong correlation.

But what the scatter plot also shows is that the readers are indeed scattered – there are lots of readers with patterns far away from the regression line. The readers who are starting to read lots of books but without large amounts of hours spent on the platform are the ones that I call *swappers*. They are found in the upper left corner of the reader distribution. The opposite reading pattern, found in the lower right corner of the distribution, is what I call *repeaters* – the readers who read audiobooks a lot in terms of hours, but who are reading a few titles over and over again. These two reading patterns are outliers departing from the average reading practice (that is, the regression line). Nevertheless, they are interesting to discuss in more detail since they are to a large extent fostered by the audiobook medium and the subscription-based model of book streaming that Storytel uses. The same applies to the *constant readers* in the upper right corner of the reader distribution. They are not departing from the regression line in the same way, but their amount of reading makes them relevant to study. They are outliers due to scale. Importantly, a clear majority of the readers in Figure 6.1 is found in the lower left corner of the scatter plot, which has turned entirely blue due to the cluster of dots – 69 per cent of the readers have read at most twenty-five audiobooks for a maximum of 500 hours during the year studied.

What 'lots of readers' and 'far away from the regression line' mean in this context however needs to be investigated more thoroughly. Before returning to this, I want to highlight the limit of the positive correlation between number of titles and hours spent. If thresholds are inserted regarding minimum reading in terms of hours, the positive correlation gets weaker and weaker the higher the threshold. At the very high level of 684 hours of reading on the platform during the year studied, there is no longer any correlation between the number of titles read and the number of hours spent reading. And for thresholds above this, the correlation shifts to negative. That is, the more minutes spent reading on the platform, the lower the number of titles read (see Figures 6.2 to 6.4).

These negative correlations are very weak and not statistically significant, but what can be said for sure is that the positive correlation between number of books read and hours spent reading ceases to exist for the readers who spend many hundreds of hours with the books in the selection yearly. It needs to be emphasized that these 'super readers' are very few – only around 1 per cent of the readers spend over 500 hours on the platform with these books during the studied year. Still, these outliers point towards new and extended reading practices that

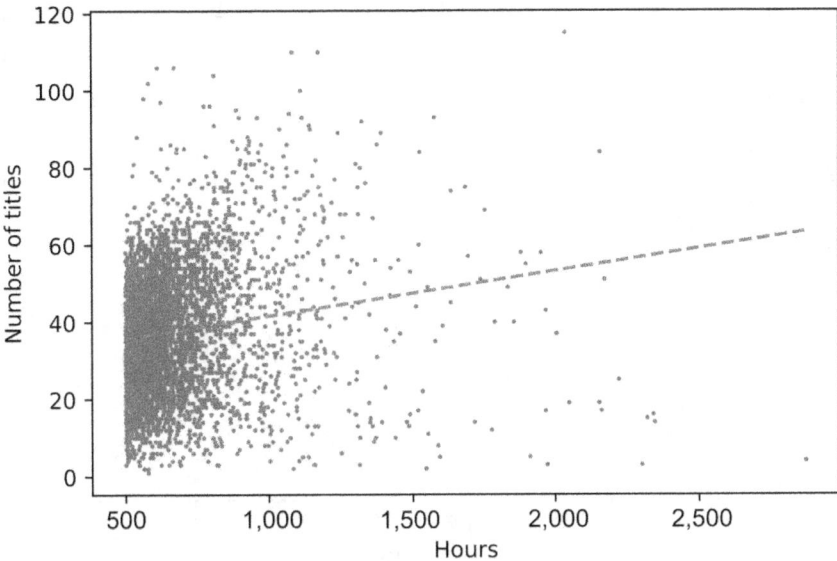

Figure 6.2 One of three high-consuming segments of individual audiobook readers (>500 hours of reading): number of titles per number of streamed hours.

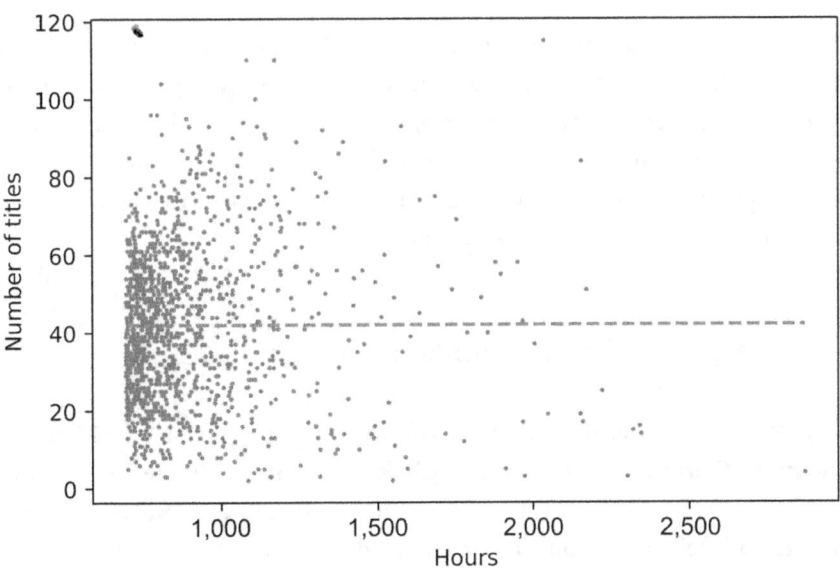

Figure 6.3 One of three high-consuming segments of individual audiobook readers (>694 hours of reading): number of titles per number of streamed hours.

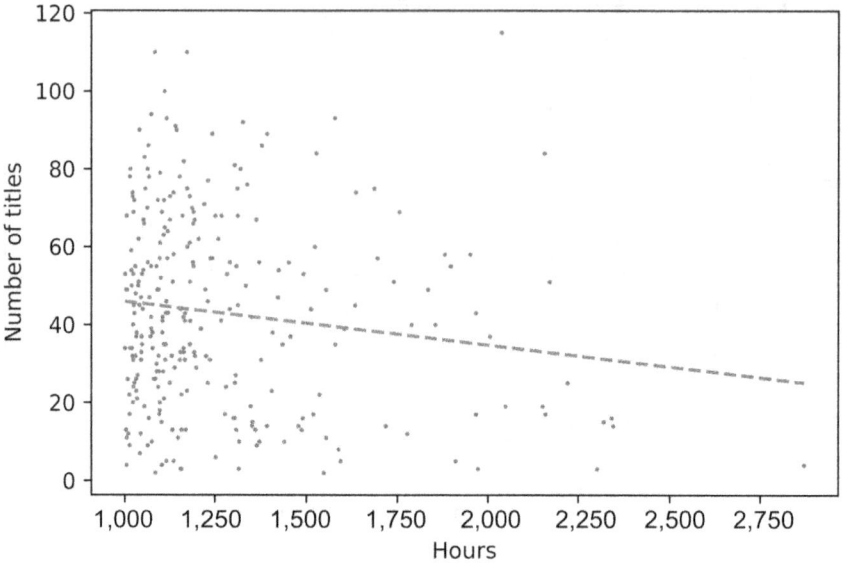

Figure 6.4 One of three high-consuming segments of individual audiobook readers (>1,000 hours of reading): number of titles per number of streamed hours.

differ from what is often taken for granted when the verb 'reading' is used. Similar to how Matthew Rubery argues that outliers on 'the reading spectrum' in terms of neurodivergence can shed light also on more normative reading practices and reading as such,[6] I investigate the outliers of audiobook reading to discuss both the average practices they depart from and the extremes themselves as effects of what reading can be in the age of streamed audio.

Typical audiobook reading?

How does the 'typical reader' of the commercial top segment of audiobooks read in the Storytel platform? As I concluded in Chapter 5, there are risks with trying to identify any kind of statistical normal reader. It can be calculated on an aggregated level when people in general read audiobooks the most during the day – it is between 2 pm and 4 pm (see Figure 5.1). But although this is highly relevant to know when tracking the generic trends in reading practices, it says

---

[6] Rubery, *Reader's Block*, especially 4–9.

less about individual reading practices, because they vary distinctly between readers. An aggregate or a mean is not saying that most readers behave in a way similar to the mean. It only says that all individual reading practices taken together forms it, statistically.

This is important to bear in mind when studying readers of any kind. It also resonates with previous historical reading studies, where this fact is constantly emphasized. In the introduction to the influential *A History of Reading in the West* (1999), for instance, Guglielmo Cavallo and Roger Chartier come back to this over and over again: '[t]he task of the historians who have contributed to this volume has thus been to reconstruct, in their differences and their singularities, the various ways of reading'; '[t]his approach requires that we recognize the existence of several sorts of contrasts'; '[a]ll those who can read texts do not read them in the same manner, and in every age there is an enormous difference'; 'there is a great disparity in the very different sets of expectations and interests that different groups of readers invest in the practice of reading'; and so forth.[7] Their emphasis on reading diversity makes sense given the impressive historical period covered in the anthology – it spans from reading in classical Greece to the nineteenth century. In more contextually limited studies of reading practices, such as this book, the lesson learned from book history is that one should be very careful of even speaking of lay reading or reading in the singular form.

With that said, by turning to the statistical measures *mean*, *median* and *standard deviation*, some hints about how most people spend time with these books can be given. On average, readers spent 104.6 hours with the audiobooks in the selection on the Storytel platform during the year studied. Such a mean value does not say that much, however, since the extreme users skew the mean. A better metric is the median, which equals 64.3 hours. It represents the 'middle' value in a dataset – that is, the value just in the middle of the lower and higher half of a dataset.[8] In statistics, the median is generally seen as a stable representation of a 'typical' value. The large difference between the mean and the median reflects the extreme audiobook readers in the upper end of the strata. The standard deviation, finally, measures the variations in a dataset. A small number indicates many values close to the mean, while a large standard deviation indicates the opposite. The standard deviation for the number of hours read in the population is 116.2, which indicates a widespread distribution of the

---

[7] Cavallo and Chartier, 'Introduction', 2–3.
[8] If there is an even number of values in a dataset, the median equals the mean of those two middle values.

Table 6.1 Number of Hours and Number of Books: Mean, Median and Standard Deviation

Variable	Mean	Median	Standard deviation
Number of hours	104.6	64.3	116.2
Number of books	9.4	7.0	8.7

variable. The corresponding values for the number of books read are 9.4 (mean), 7.0 (median) and 8.7 (standard deviation) (see Table 6.1).

An interpretation of this outcome goes something like this: the typical audiobook reader in the dataset spent around sixty-four hours during the studied year reading seven different audiobooks in the selection, but there is a large dispersion from this middle ground. The final subordinate clause sums up the problems with trying to identify typical reading practices. Yes, such practices can be found, but in so doing one risks concealing that most people actually depart more or less strongly from the typical pattern.

So, let's investigate the audiobook reading spectrum in full. The three categories of readers highlighted below will be discussed both from a bird's eye perspective and by zooming in on the reading patterns of ten randomly selected readers in each category.

Repeaters: Reading as entering the comfort zone

The repeaters are the readers who spend a lot of time reading audiobooks on the Storytel platform, but with their reading distributed over rather few literary works – they are repeating and rereading the same books over and over again, to various degrees. The repeaters are found in the lower right corner of the reader distribution in Figure 6.1. Exactly how the group of repeaters should be defined, however, is trickier. (And the same goes for the swappers and the constant readers.) Any demarcation line between repeaters and non-repeaters is in one sense an artificial and arbitrary construct. Still, there is a need to draw a line somewhere – or to draw multiple lines – to be able to discuss these readers, both as a group and as individuals.

One way to quantify repeaters is to depart from the slope in the linear regression, determined by the m value in the formula $y = mx + b$. With a cut-off point of ten hours – that is, if only the roughly 356,000 users with at least ten hours of audiobook reading during the year studied are taken into account – the

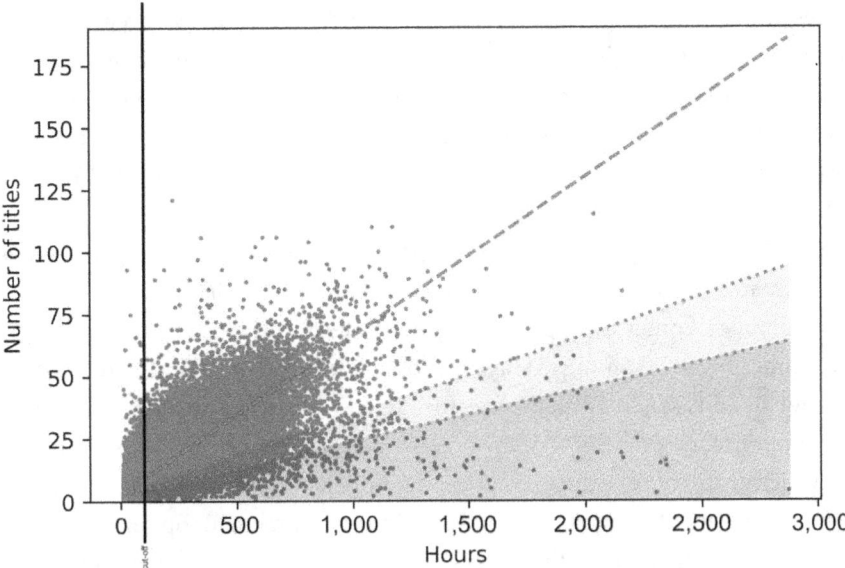

Figure 6.5 Audiobook users with at least 100 hours of reading and with two strata of repeaters highlighted: number of titles per number of streamed hours (n=128,038).

m-value in the regression analysis is 0.064. Simplified, it means that for each hour spent on the platform the average reader reads 6.4 per cent of a book. Or even more simplified: the average among these users is to spend around 15.6 hours per started audiobook. Since the average audiobook is shorter than this – the mean length for the 481 titles in the dataset is 12.9 hours and the median 12.3 hours – it indicates that audiobook rereading practices are affecting the mean.[9]

To single out only the subset of readers who repeat audiobooks more frequently, one can divide m by a certain value, depending on how narrowly defined the segment of repeaters should be. In Figure 6.5, I have divided it by two and three, respectively (the two dotted lines below the dashed general regression line), to define two strata of repeaters. I have also inserted a higher cut-off point of 100 hours to only measure the users who frequently use the Storytel platform for audiobook reading (in total, 128,038 readers). Returning to what these values mean in practice, a threshold of 0.5 m (0.032) groups all readers who spend roughly thirty-one hours or more per started audiobook, with a total minimum of 100 hours of reading. A threshold of 0.33 m (0.021),

---

[9] In fact, since users have the possibility to read at speeds above 1.0 times the recorded speed in the app (the Storytel app spans 0.75–2.0 times the recorded speed), this gap is in practice likely even bigger. Unfortunately, I have no data related to the chosen audiobook reading paces, so this factor is unknown.

correspondingly, groups all readers who spend around forty-seven hours or more per started audiobook, with a total minimum of 100 hours of reading. The wider definition of repeaters holds 7,411 readers, or a share of 5.8 per cent of all readers who read audiobooks for at least 100 hours during the year studied. The corresponding number for the narrower definition of repeaters is 3,111 readers, a share of 2.4 per cent (see Figure 6.5).

Which of these segments is the most precise in tracking repetitive audiobook reading can be debated, of course. To me, spending over thirty hours on average per audiobook comes through as repetitive indeed. It is close to a reading time three times higher than the average audiobook length.[10] It should also be added that not all books are read all the way through, which makes the thirty-one-hour average even more indicative of the practice of rereading certain books. But even the wider group of repeaters is a group of outliers – they make up only 5.8 per cent of all frequent readers of audiobooks in the commercial top segment.

As a group, apart from their repetitive reading practices they are united by their reading hours. Much related to the discussion of night readers in Chapter 5, the repeaters are distinct evening and night readers. In general, the reading starts off between 9 pm and 10 pm and peaks an hour later, but it remains at a high level during the entire night. From around 6 am it falls off to apparently lower levels during the daytime. This is anticipated and ties into the arguments raised in Chapter 5 – much of the repetition seems to connect to people reading the same book over and over again while going to sleep in the evening and/or while trying to sleep during the night. It appears that many of these readers have their own literary comfort zones to which they return for sleeping aid, or for comfort and company during long nights.

To get a better picture of how repeaters make use of fiction, I zoom in on a sample of ten of the 3,111 readers in this group of outliers, chosen in a randomized fashion. As they are few, they should not be seen as representatives for the group. But by examining their reading behaviour in detail, a complementary and concrete understanding of the repeating audiobook practices can be gained.

---

[10] 'Reading time' here refers to the tracked amount of hours read at the speed in which an audiobook is recorded. However, since the Storytel app enables their users to either speed up or slow down their reading on a scale between 0.75–2.0 times the recorded pace, users who frequently use a sped-up tempo in the audiobook player are reading more tracked hours than 'real hours' of the day. In 2.0 times the recorded speed, an hour of a recorded audiobook can be read in thirty minutes. Since an hour of reading logged by Storytel always refers to an hour of the original recording, the difference between 'tracked hours' and 'real hours' does not affect the categorizations in this chapter. However, it might explain further some of the audiobook practices of the most frequent users as it enables more books to be read in a shorter period of time. Unfortunately, I have no information about the sound tempo settings made by the users in the data I have access to.

All the ten readers in the selection fit into the characterization of repeaters as evening and night readers. Everyone's peaks of consumption are found between 10 pm and 6 am, albeit with variation both regarding evening versus night, and how much they read during the daytime. Some of the readers more or less only read audiobooks late in the evening and during the night, while others pair such practices with daytime reading.

Moreover, the ten repeaters can roughly be divided into two equally large groups based on their reading practices. The first are *distinct repeaters* in the sense that they show more or less only repetitive audiobook reading practices in the dataset. They also usually read a lot, and almost exclusively late in the evening and at night. 'Repeater A', for instance, reads audiobooks almost every evening and night, starting around 10 pm, and with the peak in consumption between 10 pm and 1 am. Between 6 am and 9 pm, they read almost nothing. The reading pattern is to repeat the same book for some weeks for up to a couple of months. Only nine books by five authors in the selection were read by this user during the year studied, and they were all Swedish crime fiction. The single most repeated book was Camilla Läckberg's *Häxan* (The Girl in the Woods). In total, 'Repeater A' read for 1,395 hours, which gives an average of 155 hours of reading time per book.

'Repeater B' has similar behaviour, but less extreme – a total reading time of 833 hours during the year is distributed over nine books written by five authors. On average, this gives ninety-two hours of reading time per audiobook started on the Storytel platform. The typical reading pattern is more of a list of favourite books, which are reread one at a time for a couple of days or weeks at most. Then the reader shifts to another title for some days, just to later return to the same books again in a cyclical pattern. 'Repeater B' prefers books in the 'other fiction' category, mostly books that in Sweden are labelled as 'feelgood', primarily by the two Swedish bestselling authors Fredrik Backman (the author of *A Man Called Ove*) and Jonas Jonasson (the author of *The Hundred-Year-Old Man Who Climbed Out the Window and Disappeared*).

The remaining repeaters pair rereading practices with reading in a more typical or expected way of completing one book at the time and then moving on to the next. 'Repeater C', for example, reads only Swedish crime fiction by authors such as Susan Casserfelt, Anna Jansson, Hans Rosenfeldt and Dag Öhrlund. The reader stays with a book between a couple of days and a couple of weeks, and then moves to the next. They never return to a previously read title, but what makes the reading pattern repetitive is that most books are given a reading time in the Storytel player that by far exceeds its running time: for example, 'Repeater

C' dedicated ninety-seven hours during two weeks to Anna Janssons *Dödslistan* ('The Death List', author's translation) (2020), followed by eighty-two hours during an additional two weeks to Susan Casserfelt's *Prästens lilla flicka* ('The Priest's Little Daughter', author's translation) (2013). Given the two audiobook's running time – roughly 12 and 11.5 hours, respectively – 'Repeater C' indeed seems to repeat these and other books several times before moving on.

A closer inspection of the streaming logs, however, indicates that they might rather be *rewinding books*.[11] Most of the time spent reading on the platform emanates from sessions that are exactly 180 minutes long. Since this coincides with the automatic stop of the Storytel player – if no interaction has been made during this period of time – and since most of these 180-minute sessions take place during the night time, it is highly likely that 'Reader C' has fallen asleep during this session, just to wake up and rewind the audiobook to the place where the cognitive aware reading stopped (but not the player), and pick up the reading again from that point in the next tracked session. If all 180-minute sessions are excluded from the Jansson and Casserfelt reading sessions described above, the reading time per book clocks in to amounts much closer to the two audiobooks running time. A similar reading practice appears to occur for 'Repeater D', whose reading takes place during most hours of the day, shifting between single stream-throughs and reading times of around two to three times the book length. Also, this user never returns to books after spending time with them but moves on to the next crime novel – the preferred genre for 'Repeater D' as well – and has frequently recurring 180-minute sessions.

The repetitive audiobook reading practices thus seems to occur for almost opposite reasons: one deliberate, where the audiobook is used for falling asleep or for company during insomnia; and one by mistake, where readers fall asleep or get distracted for other reasons while the player keeps playing but rewinds the audiobook in the next session to make sure not to miss parts of the narrative. The strong connection to reading and sleeping, discussed further in Chapter 5, however, seems to apply for both. Audiobooks function as sleeping pills, intentionally swallowed or not. A key difference is the importance these categories of readers give to following along in the narrative. While the distinct repeaters stick with their favourite story worlds to fall asleep, the rewinders instead read in a way that resembles reading of print books while going to bed,

---

[11] All remarks on rewinding audiobook reading practices are based on interpretations of the streaming logs. In the reader consumption data that I have access to, there are no parameters that track where in a narrative each session takes place; the granularity stops at ISBN, namely, on the level of the book.

where one reads a couple of pages before it is hard to keep one's eyes open. The rewinders represent old reading practices transformed for the age of streamed audiobooks. The reading practices of the distinct repeaters, on the other hand, are something new – a kind of literary use dependent on the medium specificity of the audiobook. People appear to be returning to well-known and familiar stories for comfort and company.

Drawing from previous studies of audiobooks, one could assume that the performing narrators play a key role for this group of readers, but I have seen no such patterns in my sample. Rather, it seems to be personal taste and well-known and safe story worlds that decides the choices of the repeated books preferred. And this, it perhaps goes without saying, differs from reader to reader. One repeater in the sample spent nearly 500 hours listening to Camilla Läckberg's crime novel *Häxan* (The Girl in the Woods) (2017), narrated by Katarina Ewerlöf. Another one favoured the Irish historical fiction and romance writer Lucinda Riley's Seven Sisters series (2014–21), especially the first title *The Seven Sisters* in Swedish narration by Gunilla Leining. Yet another repeated the well-renowned Swedish literary author Klas Östergren's novel *Renegater* ('Renegades', author's translation) (2020), a partly autobiographical account about the events leading Östergren to leave the Swedish Academy during its #MeToo-crisis in 2017–18, and narrated by the author himself. Literary tastes are personal things. Which audiobooks people constantly return to pronouncedly reflects this.

Swappers: Impatient customers in the digital economy

In the opposite corner of the ring from the repeaters one finds the *swappers*. (Or, to better relate it to the statistical findings, in the upper left corner of the reader distribution, as opposed to the lower right corner where the repeaters are found.) They are audiobook readers who start to stream a lot of books but without spending that much time on each of them. They are swapping between narratives, trying out lots of titles and only read some of them all the way through.

To quantify swappers, I proceed similarly as with the repeaters, but instead of decreasing the slope of the regression line by division, I increase it to the corresponding extent. In Figure 6.6, accordingly, I have multiplied the m-value by two and three, respectively (the two dotted lines above the dashed general regression line), to define two strata of swappers. I have also inserted a higher cut-off point on the y-axis to fifteen books read to only measure the users who

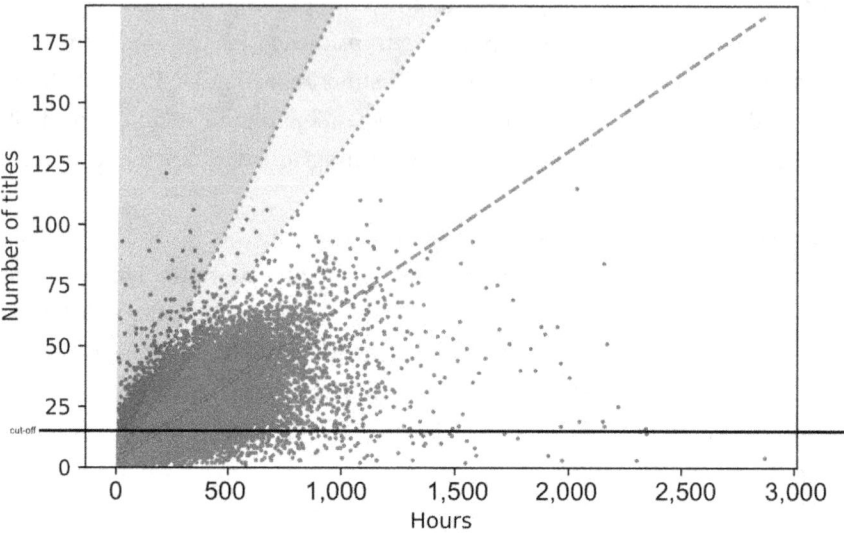

Figure 6.6 Audiobook users with at least fifteen books started, and with two strata of swappers highlighted: number of titles per number of streamed hours (n=74,695).

to a higher extent have started to read the books in the selection (in total, 74,695 readers).[12] A threshold of 2 m (0.13) groups all readers who spend roughly 7.8 hours or less per audiobook, and with at least fifteen books started. A threshold of 3 m (0.19) correspondingly, groups all readers who spend around 5.2 hours or less per audiobook, and with at least fifteen books started. The wider definition of swappers holds 5,923 readers, or a share of 7.9 per cent of all readers who started at least fifteen audiobooks during the year studied. The corresponding number for the narrower definition of swappers is 1,460 readers, a share of 2.0 per cent (see Figure 6.6).

Contrary to the repeaters, the swappers have no specific temporal pattern as a group. They correspond quite close to the average for all audiobook readers. In terms of genre preferences, it is the same thing – no significant genre biases can be found. What does stand out on the group level, however, regards the subsets in the selection. The swappers to a clearly larger extent than both audiobook readers on average and repeaters read audiobooks who are popular only on the Storytel platform (the 'beststreamers'), and Storytel Originals, that is, books written directly for the audiobook format and published by Storytel.

---

[12] Remember from Table 6.1 that the mean number of books started by a user in the dataset was 9.4, whereas the median was 7.0.

The reading of the latter is twice as high in the most distinct group of swappers compared to all users with at least ten hours of audiobook reading during the year studied.

One possible explanation is that the swappers to a greater extent than other audiobook readers are keen on trying out new and unfamiliar books. The born-audio narratives Storytel Originals were introduced in 2016 by Storytel, as a counterpart to Audible Original Audiobooks. It is newly written popular genre fiction, mostly crime fiction and romance, and by both well- and less-known authors. At least during the first years, the Storytel Originals were released as series consisting of episodes, much resembling the TV series format. The standard length for one series was ten one-hour episodes, which equals a total running time per season roughly corresponding to the running time of a standard novel in the audio format. Initially, each episode was also published as a standalone title on the platform. In the regression analysis used in Figures 6.1 to 6.6 and in all calculations regarding the groups of readers, one *season* of a Storytel Original title has been counted as one book. But the publications of episodes on the Storytel platform makes it possible to study in detail (on the level of the episode) how swappers read and progress within a series.

A look at ten randomly selected users in the group of most distinct swappers (1,460) gives further insights into such reading practices. 'Swapper A', for instance, started to read around twenty books in the selection during the year studied, without finishing any of them. The only possible exception is the three seasons of the Storytel Original series *Jordbunden* ('Earthbound', author's translation) (2016–19), a thriller marketed as 'hillbilly noir' written by the rather unknown author Erik Thulin and narrated by the Swedish actress Eva Röse. Each episode in the series has a running time of around one hour. The entire series is completed by 'Swapper A' in the sense that each of the thirty episodes in total in the series is started by this reader. A closer inspection of how long they spent reading each episode, however, paints a more complex picture. In Figure 6.7, the time spent per episode is visualized for this particular user. As can be noted, five episodes are read all the way through, another five episodes are read only a short way through, while the remaining twenty episodes lie somewhere in-between – they are read in part or in larger parts but not in their entirety.

The reading logs show an *impatient* reading behaviour, but an impatience still dedicated to the narrative in question. It seems that 'Swapper A' basically wants to find out what happens in the plot and how the story ends, but in doing this they are jumping in the narrative to more rapidly get to the finale. I find the

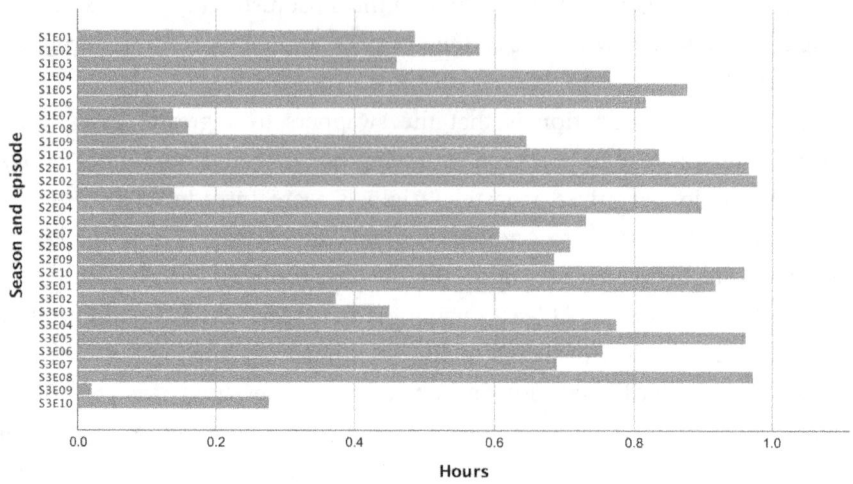

Figure 6.7 Streaming pattern of reader 'Swapper A' for the thriller series Jordbunden (seasons 1–3) by Erik Thulin: hours read per episode.

completion of episode eight in season three followed by the almost immediate jump to episode ten especially telling. After a rather high level of engagement, it seems that the reader as quickly as possible wants to finish the series by skipping episode nine entirely and reading only parts of the final episode to satisfy their urge to see how it all ends.

This kind of jumping *within* narratives is at the same time connected and dissimilar to swapping *between* narratives. Connected in the sense that many users in the swapper subset show these reading practices simultaneously, and that they are both examples of impatient reading. Such readers want to engage in as many narratives as possible but only spend time with what is most interesting. Dissimilar, because the *jumpers-within-narratives* show impatience with narratives they still want to finish, whereas the *swappers-between-narratives* instead want to find and only read books that they really want to read in full. The jumpers are thus optimizing their reading time by taking part in as many plots as possible, without caring too much about missing out on details here and there in the narratives. The readers swapping between books, on the contrary, are optimizing their time by trying to find their favourite books as quickly as possible, books which they then read in a more 'normal' way from the first word to the last.

Jumping in narratives is only possible to track for the Storytel Originals, which are divided per episode in the dataset. But similar practices of forwarding within narratives are likely to occur also for all the other books – just that it is not possible to see given the less-specific granularity of regular novels. One reader pointing towards possible jumping practices is 'Swapper B', who started to read fifty-one books in the selection during the year studied for a total amount of 223 hours. This gives an average of 4.4 hours per book, which indicates that most books are either left unfinished or forwarded through. On closer inspection of the logs of 'Swapper B', this user leaves most of the started titles unfinished but reads some of them all the way through – roughly nine of the fifty-one books started have a tracked reading time that corresponds to the audiobook's running time.

This user has a varied reading diet – crime fiction, romance, middlebrow literary fiction. They have also read one Storytel Original: Karin Janson's *Byvalla*, a romantic comedy set in the rural village Byvalla, 'a small community in the heart of Dalarna, far away from the pulse of the big cities', as parts of the translated text from the back cover reads. 'Swapper B' spent around three hours reading the first seven episodes before abandoning it for another book. Since the Byvalla series (2016–18) consists of three seasons with ten episodes each – plus a Christmas special episode, *Jul i Byvalla* ('Christmas in Byvalla', author's translation) (2016), thirty-one episodes in total – the decision to leave the series only after seven episodes must be understood as a swap to another book. Presumably, the reader found the narrative not to be exciting enough to carry on reading. But what can also be drawn out from the streaming logs is that 'Swapper B', before quitting reading the series, impatiently jumped forward in the narrative. They read the first episode in its entirety, skipped the second and read the third. Episodes four to six were read half-way through, while the story in the seventh episode of the first season was abandoned after eleven minutes of reading.

'Swapper B', then, seems to have given *Byvalla* a fair chance, but a rather impatient one. Again, reading practices of this granularity can only be investigated for the Storytel Originals in the selection, but it is likely that 'Swapper B' is engaged in similar reading behaviour also for other books. Their average time spent with an audiobook is 4.4 hours, which equals roughly a third of the running time of the average audiobook in the selection. The three hours spent with the Byvalla series is correspondingly around a third of the total running time of its first season. Thus, 'Swapper B' is simultaneously a swapper between narratives and a jumper within narratives. And, at times, also a more invested reader reading books in their entirety. Some of the audiobooks started are given up quickly (rapid trials), some are read to similar extents as *Byvalla* (serious trials) and some are read in their entirety (preferred books). A similar blend of swapping and jumping in relation to Storytel Original series is found in five of the ten readers in the sample.

These reading practices obviously have their counterparts in non-streaming book reading. Also, readers of print books are jumping into narratives to quickly reach the end, and also they are leaving books unfinished for other reads. The subscription-based streaming model, however, makes more intensive swapping practices possible, especially when it comes to swapping between books. Since the whole catalogue of books is available for the Storytel user, the mere accessibility of 'all books' might encourage readers to try out new books by unknown authors but also to leave them quickly if they are not instantly catching their interest. Much like how digital platforms work for other areas, book streaming services may foster impatient practices – readers always ready to move on to the next book.

For example, one swapper invested in Swedish crime fiction gives Dag Öhrlund's *Där inga ögon ser* ('Where No Eyes See', author's translation) (2016) five and a half minutes before they decide to move on to Mari Jungstedt's crime novel *Det andra ansiktet* ('The Other Face', author's translation) (2016). This book is in turn given almost an hour, before it is abandoned for Helene Tursten's *Snödrev* (Snowdrift) (2018), which is read all the way through. Another swapper, with a more eclectic reading taste spanning suspense to prize-winning fiction, spends less than five minutes each on Tara Westover's *Educated* (2018), Alex Schulman's *Bränn alla mina brev* ('Burn All My Letters', author's translation) (2018) and *Glöm mig* ('Forget Me', author's translation) (2016), and Jonas Gardell's *Till minne av en villkorslös kärlek* ('In Memory of an Unconditional Love', author's translation) (2018), before moving to B. A. Paris's psychological thriller *Behind Closed Doors* (2016). This book is in turn given one hour and eighteen minutes of the reader's time before they decide to swap to another book again. To nail down more precisely how long the attention span is for this group of impatient streaming audiobook readers on a more general level is hard. But as these examples show, it can at times in any case be short. It seems to be a matter of minutes.

Constant readers: The always plugged-in

The constant readers are the users who stream audiobooks a lot during the year studied, both in terms of number of books and number of hours spent on the Storytel platform. Accordingly, they are found in the upper right corner of the reader distribution in Figure 6.1. To quantify them, I group all users found between the outer delimitations of the repeaters and swappers, respectively. That is, readers closer to the regression line, within the span of 2–0.5 m. Moreover, lower thresholds regarding both number of books and number of hours of audiobook streaming need to be inserted to identify the group and separate them from any reader with streaming patterns following the regression line. I use two levels to gain some flexibility: a broader segment of constant readers who have started to stream at least thirty-five unique audiobooks in the selection during the year studied, for at least 500 hours; and a more niche segment of constant readers who have started to stream at least fifty audiobooks for at least 750 hours (see Figure 6.8). (Remember that these thresholds account only for the 481 books in the selection; they might have read far more books outside of this.) The wider group holds 2,645 readers, a share of 3.9 per cent of all readers who have streamed at least ten books for at least 100 hours during the year studied (see the two cut-off demarcation

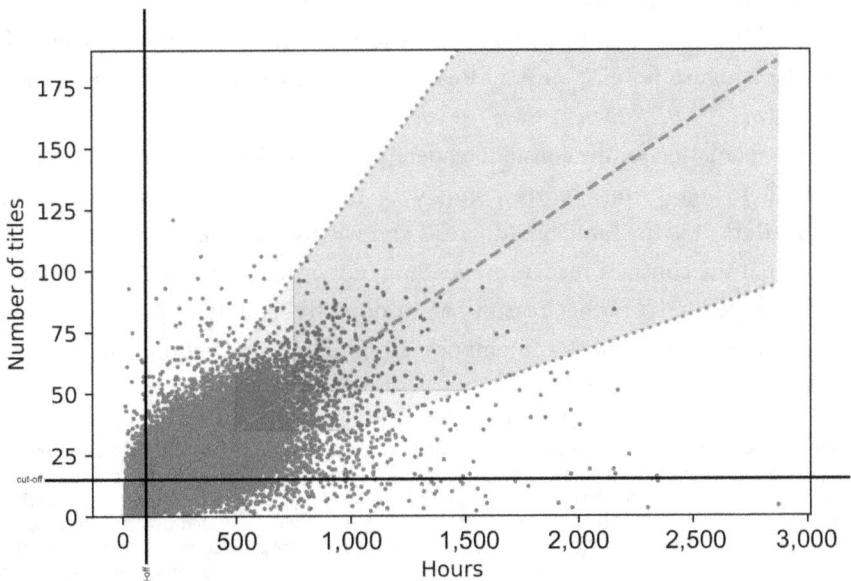

Figure 6.8 Audiobook users with at least 100 hours of reading and fifteen books started, and with two strata of constant readers highlighted: number of titles per number of streamed hours (n=67,924).

lines in Figure 6.8). The narrower group holds only 349 readers, a share of 0.5 per cent.[13]

On a generic level, the constant readers are not that different from audiobook readers in general, apart, then, from the sheer scale of their reading. They read during all times of the day, and their reading hours are very evenly distributed over both day and night. They can be characterized as anytime readers. In terms of the subset of books they read the most, they lie close to the average. In terms of genre, however, they are in relation to all other groups biased towards crime fiction reading. A total of 85 per cent of these users' reading time is devoted to crime fiction.

This preference for crime fiction is present in the sample of ten randomly selected constant readers. Of these ten readers, nine read crime fiction to a very large extent and six more or less only read crime fiction. One example of the latter is 'Constant Reader A', who read books only by Swedish crime writers, with one exception: Nobel Prize laureate Kazuo Ishiguro's dystopian science fiction novel *Never Let Me Go* (2005). But this novel was given up around half-way through, which departs from the reader's usual pattern of streaming through a novel in its entirety over a couple of days, then moving on to the next. 'Constant Reader A', thus, seems to once during the year studied have tried out a new and different kind of read of the titles in the selection, which was not appreciated. After the Ishiguro novel, 'Constant Reader A' continued reading Swedish crime fiction.

One explanation for the constant readers' preference for Swedish crime fiction is that their literary taste corresponds with the preferences of most Swedish book readers. It is the same broadly read and widely recognized Swedish crime writers that the constant readers are reading, not obscure or more niche names within the genre.[14] Another reason has to do with seriality. It is of course an important feature in most contemporary popular genre fiction, increasingly

---

[13] The constant readers, and especially so the narrower group, are thus rare, also in relation to the repeaters and swappers. The reason to still study them is partly because their status as outliers is interesting. Another reason has to do with how the dataset is set up. Since it only covers a selection of 481 titles in the commercial top segment, the constant readers identified here are the readers who rather precisely read a lot of books within this selection. If the dataset instead had covered the reading patterns of Storytel users in their entirety, many more constant readers would likely have been found. In one sense this is true also for the swappers and the repeaters, but the narrowing-down effects are stronger on the constant readers since they need to encompass two thresholds (number of books and hours) instead of one. Therefore I have chosen to study a smaller group of constant readers rather than lowering the thresholds to include more readers in the subset.

[14] For perspectives on the role of crime fiction on the Swedish book trade in general, see Berglund, 'Detectives in the Literary Market'; see further Berglund, 'Crime Fiction and the International Publishing Industry', for comparisons between different national book trades.

also for literary fiction.[15] But the series has a long and perhaps the strongest tradition in the crime fiction genre.[16] Today, crime fiction is almost by default published in the series form. Standalone crime novels are in fact uncommon in contemporary publishing.[17] The typical crime fiction series format enables two simultaneous narrative arcs: one on the level of the murder mystery – the case – which gets solved at the end of each novel; and one, much longer, arc on the level of the main protagonist – the hero/detective – whose life in terms of relationships, family, career, crises and other life-changing events the reader is invited to follow over three, five, ten or more books.[18]

This narrative set up seems to suit the constant readers perfectly, since most of them are engaged in binge-reading, where a whole series of books are read through at a rapid pace. And when one series is completed, the reader regularly, more or less seamlessly, moves on to another one. 'Constant Reader B' binge-read Stieg Larsson's Millennium trilogy and the succeeding three novels in the Millennium series written by David Lagercrantz in just over two weeks. 'Constant Reader C' similarly completed all ten by then published novels in Camilla Läckberg's Fjällbacka series in order – starting with *Isprinsessan* (The Ice Princess) from 2003 and finishing with *Häxan* (The Girl in the Woods) from 2017 – in roughly three and a half weeks.[19] Straight after finishing the last book in this series, they moved on to stream through the first six books in Mari Jungstedt's Anders Knutas series in just one week – from *Den du inte ser* (Unseen) (2003) to *Den dubbla tystnaden* (The Double Silence) (2009). Several others of the constant readers in the sample have similar reading habits.

Again, remember that these users might have read a whole lot more outside of the selection studied here. Judging by their streaming patterns, it seems to be a kind of reading that perhaps more closely resembles radio listening than traditional book reading. Thus, it is an extended reading practice, indeed, enabled both by the subscription-based and digital availability of 'all books', and by the oral nature of audiobooks, which enables readers to read while doing

---

[15] On serialization and contemporary bestsellers, see Steiner, 'Serendipity, Promotion, and Literature', 48–9.
[16] Some even understand the seriality to be foundational for the crime fiction genre as such, see Priscilla L. Walton and Manina Jones, *Detective Agency: Women Rewriting the Hard-Boiled Tradition* (Berkeley: University of California Press, 1999), 56–7.
[17] This does however not mean that standalone crime novels are non-existent. Two famous bestseller examples in the genre are Gillian Flynn's *Gone Girl* and Paula Hawkins's *The Girl on the Train* (2015).
[18] On this kind of storytelling in Swedish crime fiction, see further Karl Berglund, *Död och dagishämtningar: En kvantitativ innehållsanalys av det tidiga 2000-talets svenska kriminallitteratur* (Uppsala: Uppsala University, 2017), 118–20.
[19] In 2022, an eleventh title in the Fjällbacka series was published, *Gökungen*, not yet translated into English.

something else. To connect back to Janice Radway from the beginning of this chapter, the constant readers appear to rather *passively* stream through all these crime novels. What they get out of all these books is impossible to say by means of data analysis alone. It might be the comfort and relaxation of entering a fictional world and/or shutting out the outside world in creating their own sound bubble. It might be working as a company for people on sick leave. It might enhance focus for others. It might be something completely different. But it must be something – otherwise they would not continue this rather particular use of literature.

Conclusion: New reading practices and material effects

The reading practices discussed in this chapter emphasize that reading in the age of streamed audio can be something quite far from what is generally meant when talking about reading. Imagine all the examples above transferred from streamed audiobooks to print books. A person that reads the same book day after day, week after week. A person that spends five minutes per book before turning it down and moving to the next. A person that most days has a crime novel at hand and reads on all possible occasions. It is not impossible to visualize, but it does appear rather odd. But these and similar reading practices are what make up the contemporary audiobook reading culture.

Furthermore, most people would probably not count using books as sleeping pills or muzak as reading since the user is not actively engaged with the text. Yet, since Storytel and similar companies pay publishers per number of streamed minutes on their platforms, all audiobook consumption is in economic terms equally important for publishers and authors. The level of cognitive engagement in the text by the reader does not matter. It means that the repeater above who spent around 500 hours with Camilla Läckberg's *Häxan* (The Girl in the Woods) actually 'bought' the same crime novel roughly twenty-two times during the year studied. Or rather, that the reader generated revenues to the publisher and author just over twenty-two times the revenue of a single stream of the book. No one would buy twenty copies of the same print book. With book streaming, this is happening all the time.

As I highlighted in Chapter 2, payment per streamed minute will make publishers more interested in titles that are completed since they generate more revenues. It is reasonable to believe that a similar logic will apply for titles that are often repeated. How economically important such repeating practices will be for the publishing of the future is hard to say, but it will matter. The most extreme repeater in the dataset studied here streamed the same audiobook through over 100 times its running time. To get such readers for your books can prove to be very profitable. One hundred repeaters of this type generate revenues back to publishers and authors equal to 10,000 'normal' readers, who each stream through the book once.

I have not detected any strong signals regarding what *kinds* of books people tend to return to. It appears to be personal preferences that matter the most. Since people will repeat narratives that have stuck with them for some reason, one guess is that this in many cases will mean widely recognized and appreciated books: Harry Potter, the Hunger Games, Fifty Shades of Grey, the Millennium Trilogy and similar kinds of megasellers. The repeating reading pattern thus risks further widening the gap between already commercially successful books and more niche titles.

Many repeaters likely seek to enter a familiar fictional universe, where they feel at home. In one sense, it can be understood as a logical amplification of the intense reading of the two most popular genres of fiction: crime and romance. When reading crime fiction, you know from the start that the killer will get caught and the mystery solved in the end. When reading romance, you can be sure that the main protagonists will find love in the end and live happily ever after.[20] When repeating the same novel over and over again, this familiarity of the expected narrative events is taken to its extreme. You know everything that will happen, all steps in the plot and the dramatic curve.

Although far from Tzvetan Todorov's classical narratological scheme of what gets readers interested in crime fiction – basically either 'suspense' or 'curiosity'[21] – such reading practices lie quite close to Janice Radway's findings. The romance readers she investigates value 'simple relaxation' as the most important factor to why they are reading these novels.[22] And a clear majority of her informants are engaged in rereading practices, especially during times of stress or depression. The romance readers reread, Radway notes, 'when they feel sad or unhappy because they know exactly how the chosen book will affect their state of mind'.[23]

---

[20] As the informants in Radway's study emphasize, a happy ending is understood as the most important ingredient in a romance novel, while a sad ending is seen as one of the things that should never be included in the genre (Radway, *Reading the Romance*, 66–74).
[21] See Todorov, *The Poetics of Prose*, 42–52.
[22] Radway, *Reading the Romance*, 60–1.
[23] Radway, *Reading the Romance*, 62.

Curiously, it also reminds of the 'intensive' rereading of religious texts that Rolf Engelsing deemed as a premodern reading practice that got replaced by the modern and 'extensive reading' of our times.[24] How thorough the shift in reading practices that Engelsing identified actually has been can be debated. Likely, people have been rereading books all along from the eighteenth century and up until today. With streamed audiobooks, such reading practices surface, and – importantly – acquire economic significance for authors and publishers.

Books have been sold as entities for hundreds of years. This binary business model – either you sell a complete book or you do not – is now being challenged by a new one, where readers can choose to quit anywhere within a narrative and, albeit indirectly, only pay for the parts read. Or, as the repeaters, pay for the same book over and over again. When people are speaking of 'the audiobook revolution' in publishing, I would suggest that what is happening with streaming audiobooks can be characterized as a triple revolution – it takes place simultaneously on the levels of the medium, the distribution and the business model.

But perhaps the unlimited hours for reading that are currently possible on the Nordic book streaming services is a book historical parenthesis, a business model that in the longer run will not prove to be economically sound? The various levels of subscription offered, with different pricing levels and of which some have limitations in streaming time, launched by both Storytel and BookBeat with increasing marketing emphasis, point in this direction. Niclas Sandin, CEO of BookBeat, explicitly mentions heavy users as the reason behind the shift in strategy:

> It is no longer possible to wear blinders and ignore the fact that all the data we have collected over the past six years shows that what is driving down compensation and in some cases forcing questionable alternatives such as revenue share is the large consumption of a few percent by the users.[25] (My translation.)

The US book streaming service Scribd made a similar analysis some years ago. They realized that their heaviest users – especially readers of romance and audiobooks – cost them a lot of money each month, which made them insert limitations in streaming time in their subscription offers.[26] John B. Thompson calls this the *heavy-user paradox*: 'your best and most loyal users are also your

---

[24] See Engelsing, *Der Bürger als Leser*.
[25] Niclas Sandin, quoted in Sölve Dahlgren, 'BookBeat gör tidsbegränsade abonnemang till huvudprodukter', *Boktugg*, 23 August 2023, https://www.boktugg.se/2022/08/23/bookbeat-gor-tidsbegransade-abonnemang-till-huvudprodukter/ (accessed 7 January 2023).
[26] Thompson, *Book Wars*, 323–30.

most unprofitable users. The more they consume, the more they cost you, so the heaviest users become your biggest liabilities.'[27] Although unlimited subscriptions are still available in the Nordic countries, BookBeat, for instance, has in other national markets launched only various time-limited subscription alternatives. And as Thompson's account of book streaming services in the US market in the 2010s shows, it is currently only Amazon's Kindle Unlimited that offers a truly unlimited book streaming service. But KU holds mostly the vast body of self-published books from Kindle Direct Publishing. Apart from some special cases, the books from the major publishing houses are not present on the platform. Thompson's conclusion is that book streaming services will likely also henceforth play a marginal role in the Anglo-American book business.[28]

What will happen in the future is yet to be seen, but it is a fact that Storytel and their competitors in the Nordic region are offering to their readers exactly what Thompson believed to be impossible to achieve for the US market: an unlimited subscription for a monthly fee to audiobooks and ebooks by all major publishers. And they have been doing so for what is approaching a decade. In the meantime, audiobook readers in Scandinavia have become used to being able to stream as much as they like. Although it is a small minority that use this option in excessive amounts, taking away the unlimited subscription alternatives completely from the Nordic market is not without problems, not least since all the new reading hours enabled by the streamed audiobook has made the book market grow in total. The new audiobook reading practices that I have investigated in this chapter are closely connected to the success story of the streamed audiobook.

[27] Thompson, *Book Wars*, 327.
[28] See Thompson, *Book Wars*, 343–48.

Conclusion: Listen up to the reading data

In this book, I have analysed the current wave of streamed audiobooks in global publishing and reading culture through a dataset covering over 430,000 Swedish audiobook readers on the Storytel platform. These concluding remarks will not cover a comprehensive summary of the book's results and discussions. Instead, I will focus and expand upon three aspects that surfaced on this journey that I find especially significant, and novel, in the sense that they might alter the understanding of familiar concepts such as 'reading' and 'bookselling'.

The first is in one respect the most obvious: the boom in streamed audiobooks is *altering reading practices*. While such alterations have been reported by others prior to me, the reader consumption data backing up this book has made it possible to empirically and more concretely lay bare what is going on among audiobook readers. A result that reappears in many forms is that there are various and even contradictory audiobook reading practices at play simultaneously. Some read a lot during the night, others only during the evening and yet others during all hours of the day. Some are deeply invested in certain genres or authorships, while others have eclectic literary tastes and read a little bit of everything. Some finish every single story they embark on, while others jump between narratives in an impatient fashion. Some use the subscription-model in full resulting in rather excessive amounts of reading hours, while others read more sparsely.

The reading practices that come through in the data make an entire spectrum of kinds and modes of reading visible. While averages and aggregates on reading habits are key metrics for identifying patterns and for seeing the larger picture, it is crucial not to forget that these mean scores hide diverse and heterogeneous individual reading practices. There is no such thing as the 'typical' digital audiobook reader. The practices span from careful close listening to books used as muzak. When investigating reading of any kind, both these layers should ideally be considered. Only a discussion that includes the aggregate *and* the many practices forming the aggregate will be able to provide a more holistic account of what reading is and looks like in a certain format and historical/regional context. The kind of reader consumption data investigated in this book brings this dual mode of analysis to the fore.

It is vital to remember that the data considered here can never track if and how people cognitively perceive what the audiobook player is playing. What is measured is literary use and book consumption in terms of logged interactions with the Storytel platform. In most cases, this probably equals reading in the sense of a user cognitively processing the text to some extent. But it could also involve book streaming where no such mental engagement with the text occurs. The large number of users exhibiting patterns that indicate streaming while sleeping is the most obvious example in this direction, but theoretically any logged streaming session could be a tracking of an audiobook playing through headphones taken off from the user's head, earbuds not plugged in or speakers in an empty room.

Audiobooks trigger the grey area of practices in between the often-idealized focused reading and the non-reading. The format's unique selling point has to a large extent been that it is time-saving in the sense that it enables reading books while doing something else. This means that a lot of audiobook reading probably is somewhat distracted. With the rise of audiobooks, people are increasingly pairing their reading with other daily activities. This leads to an expansion of reading time, indicated by book sales figures: audiobook streams are increasing rapidly, while other forms of book sales are more or less steady.[1] Instead of a competition between formats, the audiobook boom so far appears to have expanded people's possibilities to read books. It also affects the understanding of what reading means and can be. To 'read books' today includes a broad array of practices ranging from distracted background listening while doing something else to focused reading of either print books or audiobooks.

These alterations in reading are visible in the reader consumption data on aggregate levels as well as among individual and niche subsets of readers. The most clear-cut bird's-eye-view 'proofs' of how audiobook reading diverges from print and ebook reading practices are offered in Chapter 5, where ebook but not audiobook reading shows significant peaks in consumption in the evening and at the weekend, and in Chapter 2, where prestige fiction is found to be mostly absent in the audiobook format. People listen almost exclusively to popular

---

[1] Wikberg, *Bokförsäljningsstatistiken: Helåret 2021*, 9.

genre fiction. In terms of individuals and smaller subsets, the new altered reading practices surfacing include constant audiobook streaming, readers who appear to be sleeping and readers returning to practices resembling premodern habits of repeatedly reading the same books.

It should furthermore be considered that most of the audiobook readers are probably also readers of print books and/or ebooks. A more precise description of how readers interrelate, combine and jump between book formats is however hard to achieve without resorting to guesswork. Solid statistics on book formats and reading behaviour is unfortunately scant. For Sweden, a couple of clues are given by 'The Media Barometer', a yearly survey study on people's daily media use. Regarding the relationship between audiobooks and print books, three findings are of special interest in this context. First, although increasing year by year, the group of respondents who read audiobooks on a daily basis (13 per cent) is far smaller than the group who read print books on a daily basis (34 per cent).[2] Second, of the daily readers, the audiobook readers spend significantly longer time on reading during an average day (eighty-two minutes) than print book readers (fifty-four minutes).[3] Third, both reading audiobooks and print books are clearly female-biased activities, but when it comes to age, there are large differences between the formats. Audiobook reading is most popular in the younger middle-age segment (35–54 years). Print book reading, on the contrary, is most popular among children (9–14 years) and in the oldest age segment in the survey (65–85 years).[4]

The study points out that audiobook readers still constitute a minority of the readers and an age-biased one. Extrapolating the results, females in the younger middle-age segment are the most clearly overrepresented group when it comes to audiobook reading, and they read a lot. This is a good illustration of the often-reported advantages of the audiobook medium – ideal for people in the middle of their working life and with kids at home, who have trouble finding traditional reading time in their daily lives. These overrepresented audiobook readers quite interestingly resemble the romance readers interviewed in Radway's study. They were also women in their younger middle-age with kids at home. They also strived to map reading time into their daily chores. They were also heavy readers.[5]

---

[2] Ohlsson, *Mediebarometern 2021*, 15. Audiobook reading is more common than ebook reading though (7 per cent), which is a notable difference to the Anglo-American context.
[3] Ohlsson, *Mediebarometern 2021*, 83.
[4] Ohlsson, *Mediebarometern 2021*, 80–1.
[5] Radway, *Reading the Romance*, 50–60.

Audiobook reading offers a practical way of combining reading with all the must-dos of everyday life. But one can wonder what this efficient doing-two-things-at-once approach misses out. It can lead to a more distracted kind of reading, as noted above. Another potential drawback connects to the explanations for romance reading in Radway's study: many respondents claim to read for relaxation and for the possibility to escape from their daily problems.[6] Also audiobook reading can offer relaxation and escape from daily problems. Still, it is relaxation of a different kind, and it is arguably not offering a *pause* from everyday life in the same respect as print book reading – at least not if one is to simultaneously do the laundry or work out. In a recent survey study of dedicated Swedish audiobook readers conducted by Sara Tanderup Linkis and Julia Pennlert, this double and partly contradictory nature of audiobook reading surfaces. Most respondents emphasize the format's efficiency and time-saving qualities, but many also mention 'relaxation' as an important asset.[7] In this respect, audiobooks and the new reading practices emerging with them can be considered a good example of contemporary hectic life. People have so much to do that the best way to relax is the possibility to do two things at once.

The second aspect that I want to highlight is that book streaming affects the core of bookselling in what can be labelled as *data-driven publishing on the narrative level*. Throughout publishing history, the principal idea of most publishers has been to sell books to make a profit. Whether the book buyer reads the book once, ten times or not at all has not attracted too much interest among publishers since they have already been paid. The act of selling and buying books is in an economical respect disconnected from the act of reading. 'We know that the purchase of a book is not to be confused with its reading', as Robert Escarpit succinctly points out.[8]

With the pay-per-minute business model introduced by several book streaming services – including all the major Nordic platforms as well as Anglo-American counterparts such as Kindle Unlimited – this changes. Suddenly, publishers and authors are no longer getting paid in a binary way (per sold work) but in a continuous one (per streamed minute). This concretely connects book reading to sales figures. It makes books that are completed and reread by large groups of readers more attractive to publish, since they will generate more profit. On the other hand, books that readers tend to leave partly unfinished will

---

[6] Radway, *Reading the Romance*, 60–2.
[7] Tanderup Linkis and Pennlert, 'En helt annan upplevelse', 45–7.
[8] Escarpit, *Sociology of Literature*, 89.

be less attractive. And because publishers will know these reading patterns in detail (through the reader consumption data fed back to them from the book streaming service), it is likely to affect which books are chosen for publication. In the longer run, it might change how literature is written in the first place.

As I have shown in this study, there are numerous data points on book streaming practices that contemporary and future publishers may consider when they evaluate a book's commercial impact. Some readers repeat the same book twenty, fifty or even a hundred times during a year. Such readers are gold for publishers as they are literally getting twenty, fifty or a hundred times the revenues of a single stream-through out of one single book reader. If a writer gets a hit that is frequently repeated among larger groups of readers, publishers will notice this and ask the question if and how similar books could be written. Certain authorships and genres, moreover, are streamed all the way through by readers to larger extents than others. Most notably, crime novels are finished significantly often, while prestige fiction works are rarely completed. Publishers will notice this as well and may adjust their decisions.

If the market share of book streaming continues to grow, metrics of rereading, completion and number of streamed minutes will be increasingly valued in the trade. Exactly how this will affect the literary culture of the future is a matter of speculation, but I believe that it is beyond doubt that it will have effects. Currently, bookselling is turning into a data-driven enterprise, where reader consumption data is collected and analysed by book trade actors. While sales data for long has been key in the publishing business, the streaming data increase the granularity immensely. It represents a move from the level of the book to the level of literary scenes – a ten-hour audiobook is 600 minutes long, which gives 600 analysable narrative positions along the plotline, from the first word to the last. In the near-future (if not already), publishers will start to make use of this information to make data-driven publishing decisions concerning narrative structure and dramatic curves. The next step is a data-driven writing process, where authors are getting exposed to this kind of data to improve their books in line with what most of their readers seem to appreciate.

This could be considered as dystopian science fiction, but think about it: if a writer gets to know from data that 10 per cent of their readers quit reading at a certain point in their last novel, wouldn't they be curious to understand why this happened and if similar 'weak spots' in the plotline could be avoided in the next book? Of course, such crass commercial thinking does not apply to all kinds of books and writing processes. But at least for popular genre fiction, I believe the willingness amongst authors to please the crowd to be crucial enough to let reader's behaviour at least to some extent affect what they write.

As the pay-per-minute business model blurs the line between bookselling and reading, it simultaneously blurs the line between publishing studies and reading studies. Reader consumption data shows both sales patterns and reading patterns. Consequently, I have advocated for a mixed approach, with three chapters mostly focused on publishing matters and three mostly on reading matters, but where the perspectives are constantly intertwined.

The final aspect that I want to draw attention to is *the reader consumption data and the computational methods* used in this book, and what such approaches can bring to publishing and reading studies from a long-term perspective. As I argued in the introduction, the scale and level of detail of this data opens vast possibilities for reading studies, and for sociology of literature in general. I have examined some of them, including when people are reading, which books and genres they tend to finish, and practices of rereading and swapping. Still, I am only scratching the surface. There are plenty of other possible angles available for studies based on similar data. One thing that this book does not cover at all is similarity patterns and network analyses of books and readers. That readers of Camilla Läckberg (a contemporary popular Swedish crime writer), for instance, also to a large extent prefer Mari Jungstedt (another contemporary popular Swedish crime writer) will not alter the understanding of reading preferences, but imagine all the more nuanced and fine-grained possibilities at hand. Which are the most distant books to Läckberg's, in the statistical sense, that still show a reader overlap? How do readers within this overlap read? Is there such a thing as a common literary ground for Läckberg readers? If yes, what does it look like? Such computational approaches can furthermore be combined with other methods for reading studies that create knowledge about why readers behave a certain way. Envision mixed-methods setups with reader consumption data paired with surveys, qualitative interviews or focus groups that examine the relationship between what people do with books (reader consumption data), what they say that they do with books (surveys) and their explanations for what they say that they do (interviews). Endless possibilities indeed.

The problem is that this kind of reading data is far from accessible to scholars. On the contrary, most companies, including Amazon, do not share any parts of their data with researchers, which risks becoming an increasing problem for publishing studies. As larger parts of the book trade transfer to digital streaming platforms, academia will know less and less of the contemporary book trade if these cannot be studied. 'How are scholars to document, much less critique, algorithmic culture's self-reinforcing effects on cultural selection if denied access?' Simone Murray rightly asks, proceeding to paint a rather depressing picture of the future of publishing studies: 'Proprietary data are thus unlikely ever to be regarded as sufficiently historical to be discarded or gifted to public institutions.'[9]

With this book, I have shown that proprietary reader consumption data from commercial actors in the trade indeed *can* be accessed and used for scholarly purposes. In doing this, *Reading Audio Readers* is the first book of its kind. But will it also be the last? Will Storytel's data sharing be a Swedish exception with no followers? I believe not. Although Amazon might perhaps not share data, there are other possibilities and agents that could be more willing. For instance, a group of researchers from the University of Chicago, Duke University and McGill University recently started a collaboration with Parrot Analytics to analyse cross-regional successes in video streaming services through their audience demand data.[10] There is also library data, which is not the same thing but can provide insights.[11] And then there is digital social reading data, and the possibility to build your own 'counterdata' through various kinds of manual collection and markup, scraping and reverse-engineering.[12] As Melanie Walsh points out, '[w]hile all of this data is powerful in its own right, it becomes even more powerful if we can combine it all together.'[13]

I end this book on a similar note to the beginning. Since the future of reading and publishing most probably will continue to be increasingly data-driven, the future of reading and publishing studies needs to be too. It is a development not without obstacles, but the possibilities by far outshine the difficulties. My hope is that this book has managed to convince a few others of this.

Thank you for listening.

---

[9] Murray, 'Secret Agents', 976.
[10] Parrot Analytics, 'How are OTT platforms and streaming services shaping audience tastes around the world?', press release, 20 December 2022, https://www.parrotanalytics.com/press/how-are-ott-platforms-and-streaming-services-shaping-audience-tastes-around-the-world/ (accessed 11 January 2023).
[11] See, for instance, Melanie Walsh's use of library lending data from Seattle Public Library (Melanie Walsh, 'Where Is All the Book Data?', *Public Books*, 4 October 2022, https://www.publicbooks.org/where-is-all-the-book-data/ (accessed 11 January 2023)). In the article, she also discusses the problem that BookScan – an important actor in US publishing, and also elsewhere – are reluctant to share data with researchers.
[12] For an example of some reverse engineering practices concerning Amazon's Kindle platform, see Rowberry, *Four Shades of Gray*, especially 167–75.
[13] Walsh, 'Where Is All the Book Data?'.

References

Albert Bonniers förlag. 'Lars Keplers Spegelmannen – en bok, två röster.' Available online: https://www.albertbonniersforlag.se/nyheter/lars-keplers-spegelmannen-en-bok-tva-roster/ (accessed 17 August 2022).

Allington, Daniel, Sarah Brouillette, and David Golumbia. 'Neoliberal Tools (and Archives): A Political History of Digital Humanities.' *LA Review of Books* (1 May 2016).

Altick, Richard D. *The English Common Reader: A Social History of the Mass Reading Public 1800–1900*. Chicago: University of Chicago Press, 1957.

Anderson, Chris. *The Long Tail: How Endless Choice Is Creating Unlimited Demand*. London: Random House, 2006.

Anderson, Porter. 'AAP StatShot: The United States' Publishing Industry Gained 12.2 Percent in 2021.' *Publishing Perspectives* (26 January 2022).

Anderson, Porter. 'France's "Digital Barometer": 27 Percent Trying Audiobooks.' *Publishing Perspectives* (4 May 2022).

Apple Books. 'Every Book Deserves To Be Heard.' Available online: https://authors.apple.com/support/4519-digital-narration-audiobooks (accessed 25 April 2023).

Audible. Available online: https://www.audible.com (accessed 25 January 2022).

Audible. 'Ray Porter: Narrators' Greatest Hits. Volume 4.' Available online: https://www.audible.com/ep/NarratorsGreatestHitsVol4_Porter (accessed 30 November 2022).

Audio Publishers Association. '2022 Audie Awards.' Available online: https://www.audiopub.org/2022audieawards (accessed 30 November 2022).

Audio Publishers Association. '2023 Audie Awards Categories.' Available online: https://audieawards.secure-platform.com/a/page/Submit/categories (accessed 27 June 2022).

Baron, Naomi. *How We Read Now: Strategic Choices for Print, Screen, and Audio*. New York: Oxford University Press, 2021.

Berglund, Karl. 'Crime Fiction and the International Publishing Industry.' In *Cambridge Companion to World Crime Fiction*, edited by Jesper Gulddal, Stewart King and Alistair Rolls, 25–45. Cambridge: Cambridge University Press, 2022.

Berglund, Karl. 'Detectives in the Literary Market: Statistical Perspectives on the Boom in Swedish Crime Fiction.' *Scandinavica: An International Journal of Scandinavian Studies* 51, no. 2 (2012): 38–57.

Berglund, Karl. *Död och dagishämtningar: En kvantitativ innehållsanalys av det tidiga 2000-talets svenska kriminallitteratur*. Uppsala: Uppsala University, 2017.

Berglund, Karl. 'Genres at Work: A Holistic Approach to Genres in Publishing.' *European Journal of Cultural Studies* 24, no. 3 (2021): 757–76.

Berglund, Karl. 'Killer Plotting: Typologisk intriganalys utifrån fjärrläsningar av 113 samtida svenska kriminalromaner.' *Tidskrift för litteraturvetenskap* 48, no. 3–4 (2017): 41–68.

Berglund, Karl. *Mordförpackningar: Omslag, titlar och kringmaterial till svenska pocketdeckare 1998–2011*. Uppsala: Uppsala University, 2016.

Berglund, Karl and Mats Dahllöf. 'Audiobook Stylistics: Comparing Print and Audio in the Bestselling Segment.' *Journal of Cultural Analytics* 11 (2021): 1–30.

Berglund, Karl, Mats Dahllöf, and Jerry Määttä. 'Apples and Oranges? Large-Scale Thematic Comparisons of Contemporary Swedish Popular and Literary Fiction.' *Samlaren* 140 (2019): 228–60.

Birkerts, Sven. *The Gutenberg Elegies: The Fate of Reading in an Electronic Age*. Boston, MA, and London: Faber and Faber, 1994.

Björkén-Nyberg, Cecilia. 'Hearing, Seeing, Experiencing: Perspective Taking and Emotional Engagement Through the Vocalisation of Jane Eyre, Heart of Darkness and Things Fall Apart.' *International Journal of Language Studies* 14, no. 1 (2020): 63–88.

Björkén-Nyberg, Cecilia. 'Tolkning, tydlighet och tolkande tydlighet.' In *Från Strindberg till Storytel: Korskopplingar mellan ljud och litteratur*, edited by Julia Pennlert and Lars Ilshammar, 137–61. Gothenburg: Daidalos, 2021.

Björkén-Nyberg, Cecilia. 'Vocalising Motherhood: The Metaphorical Conceptualisation of Voice in Listener Responses to The Girl on the Train by Paula Hawkins.' *International Journal of Language Studies* 12, no. 4 (2018): 1–28.

Bloom, Clive. *Bestsellers: Popular Fiction Since 1900*. Basingstoke: Palgrave, 2002.

Bloomsbury. 'Harry Potter The Complete Audio Collection.' Available online: https://www.bloomsbury.com/uk/harry-potter-the-complete-audio-collection-9781408882290/ (accessed 30 November 2022).

Bondi, Gabrielle. 'How Trans and Nonbinary Actors Are Revolutionizing Audiobooks.' *BuzzFeed News*, 6 May 2021. Available online: https://www.buzzfeednews.com/article/gabriellebondi/ya-trans-nonbinary-fiction-ownvoice-writers-actors (accessed 2 December 2022).

BookBeat. 'BookBeat.' Available online: https://www.bookbeat.se/ (accessed 17 November 2022).

BookNet Canada. 'Listening In: Audiobook Use in Canada 2021.' Available online: https://issuu.com/booknetcanada/docs/listening_in_2021 (accessed 25 November 2022).

Bottomley, Andrew. *Sound Streams: A Cultural History of Radio-Internet Convergence*. Ann Arbor: University of Michigan Press, 2020.

Bull, Michael. *Sound Moves: iPod Culture and Urban Experience*. New York: Routledge, 2007.

Cavallo, Guglielmo, and Roger Chartier, editors. *A History of Reading in the West*. Oxford: Polity, 1999.

Cecco, Leyland. 'Death of the Narrator? Apple Unveils Suite of AI-Voiced Audiobooks.' *The Guardian* (4 January 2023).

Clark, Giles, and Angus Phillips. *Inside Book Publishing*, 6th edn. London and New York: Routledge, 2020.

Colbjørnsen, Terje. 'The Streaming Network: Conceptualizing Distribution Economy, Technology, and Power in Streaming Media Services.' *Convergence* 27, no. 5 (2021): 1264–287.

Colclough, Stephen. 'Readers: Books and Biography.' In *A Companion to the History of the Book*, edited by Simon Eliot and Jonathan Rose, 50–62. Malden, MA, and Oxford: Wiley-Blackwell, 2007.

Da, Nan Z. 'The Computational Case Against Computational Literary Studies.' *Critical Inquiry* 45, no. 3 (2019): 601–39.

Dahlgren, Sölve. 'BookBeat gör tidsbegränsade abonnemang till huvudprodukter.' *Boktugg*, 23 August 2023. Available online: https://www.boktugg.se/2022/08/23/bookbeat-gor-tidsbegransade-abonnemang-till-huvudprodukter/ (accessed 7 January 2023).

Dahlgren, Sölve. 'JK Rowling mest lyssnad på Storytel men Laila Brendan visar värdet av långa bokserier.' *Boktugg*, 2 December 2019. Available online: https://www.boktugg.se/2019/12/02/jk-rowling-mest-lyssnad-pa-storytel-men-laila-brenden-visar-vardet-av-langa-bokserier-2019/ (accessed 25 November 2022).

Darnton, Robert. 'The First Steps Toward a History of Reading.' *Australian Journal of French Studies* 51, no. 2–3 (1986): 152–77.

Darnton, Robert. *The Great Cat Massacre*. London: Allen Lane, 1984.

Darnton, Robert. 'What Is the History of Books?' *Daedalus* 111, no. 3 (1982): 65–83.

Desrochers, Nadine, and Daniel Apollon. 'Introduction.' In *Examining Paratextual Theory and Its Applications in Digital Cultures*, edited by Nadine Desrochers and Daniel Apollon, xxix–xxxix. Hershey, PA: IGI Global, 2014.

'Do you count listening to audio books as reading?' Reddit.com. Available online: https://www.reddit.com/r/books/comments/24pykt/do_you_count_listening_to_audio_books_as_reading/ (accessed 26 January 2022).

Editeur. 'Thema Current Version 1.5.' Available online: https://www.editeur.org/151/thema/ (accessed 30 November 2022).

Engelsing, Rolf. *Der Bürger als Leser: Lesergeschichte in Deutschland 1500–1800*. Stuttgart: Metzlersche Verlagsbuchhandlung, 1976.

English, James F., and Ted Underwood. 'Shifting Scales: Between Literature and Social Science.' *Modern Language Quarterly* 77, no. 3 (2016): 277–95.

Escarpit, Robert, *The Book Revolution*. 1965; London: Harrap, 1966.

Escarpit, Robert. *La révolution du livre*. Paris: United Nations Educational, Scientific and Cultural Organization, 1965.

Escarpit, Robert. *Sociology of Literature*. 2nd edn. 1958; London: Cass, 1971.

Felski, Rita. *Uses of Literature*. Malden, MA, and Oxford: Blackwell, 2008.

Finn, Ed. 'New Literary Cultures: Mapping the Digital Networks of Toni Morrison.' In *From Codex to Hypertext: Reading at the Turn of the Twenty-First Century*, edited by Anouk Lang, 177–202. Amherst: University of Massachusetts Press, 2012.

Forslid, Torbjörn, Jon Helgason, Lisbeth Larsson, Christian Lenemark, Anders Ohlsson and Ann Steiner. *Höstens böcker: Litterära värdeförhandlingar 2013*. Gothenburg and Stockholm: Makadam, 2015.

Fuller, Danielle, and DeNel Rehberg Sedo. *Reading Beyond the Book: The Social Practices of Contemporary Literary Culture*. New York: Routledge, 2013.

Furuland, Lars. 'Litteratur och samhälle: Om litteratursociologin och dess forskningsfält.' In *Litteratursociologi: Texter om litteratur och samhälle*, edited by Lars Furuland and Johan Svedjedal, 16–50. Lund: Studentlitteratur, 1997.

Genette, Gérard. *Paratexts: Thresholds of Interpretation*. 1987; Cambridge: Cambridge University Press, 1997.

Gruzd, Anatoliy, and DeNel Rehberg Sedo. '#1b1t: Investigating Reading Practices at the Turn of the Twenty-first Century.' *Mémoires du livre/Studies in Book Culture* 3, no. 2 (2012). https://doi.org/10.7202/1009347ar.

Gunder, Anna. *Hyperworks: On Digital Literature and Computer Games*. Uppsala: Uppsala University, 2004.

Hanner, Hedda, Alice O'Connor and Erik Wikberg. *Ljudboken: Hur den digitala logiken påverkar marknaden, konsumtionen och framtiden*. Stockholm: Svenska Förläggareföreningen, 2019.

Hansson, Gunnar. *Dikten och läsaren: Studier över diktupplevelsen*. Stockholm: Bonniers, 1959.

Hansson, Gunnar. *Inte en dag utan en bok: Om läsning av populärfiktion*. Linköping: Linköping University, 1988.

Have, Iben, and Mille Raaby Jensen. 'Audio bingeing.' *Passage* 83 (Summer 2020): 101–18.

Have, Iben, and Birgitte Stougaard Pedersen. 'The Audiobook Circuit in Digital Publishing: Voicing the Silent Revolution.' *New Media & Society* 22, no. 3 (2020): 409–28.

Have, Iben, and Birgitte Stougaard Pedersen. *Digital Audiobooks: New Media, Users, and Experiences*. New York: Routledge, 2016.

Hayles, N. Katherine. *Writing Machines*. Cambridge, MA: MIT Press, 2002.

Helgason, Jon, Sara Kärrholm and Ann Steiner (editors). *Hype: Bestsellers and Literary Culture*. Lund: Nordic Academic Press, 2014.

Hertel, Hans. *500.000 £ er prisen: Bogen i mediesymbiosens tid*. Stockholm: Svenska Bokförläggareföreningen, 1996.

Joyce, Michael. *Of Two Minds: Hypertext, Pedagogy, and Poetics*. Ann Arbor: University of Michigan Press, 1995.

Kirschenbaum, Matthew, and Sarah Werner. 'Digital Scholarship and Digital Studies: The State of the Discipline.' *Book History* 17 (2014): 406–58.

Knip-Häggqvist, Elizabet. *Den talande bokens poetik: En studie med fokus på olika unga vuxnas reception av tre fiktiva texter inlästa på band*. Åbo: Åbo Akademi University Press, 2010.

Koepnick, Lutz. 'Figures of Resonance: Reading at the Edges of Attention.' *Sound-Effects* 8, no. 1 (2019): 4–19.

Koepnick, Lutz. 'Reading on the Move.' *PMLA* 128, no. 1 (2013): 232–7.

Koolen, Corina, Karina van Dalen-Oskam, Andreas van Cranenburgh and Erica Nagelhout. 'Literary Quality in the Eye of the Dutch Reader: The National Reader Survey.' *Poetics* 79 (April 2020). https://doi.org/10.1016/j.poetic.2020.101439.

Kovač, Miha, Angus Phillips, Adriaan van der Weel and Rüdiger Wischenbart. 'What Is a Book?' *Publishing Research Quarterly* 35 (2019): 313–26.

Lenas, Sverker, and Georg Cederskog. 'Konflikt om ljudböcker på Bonniers: "Nobelpristagare underpresterar digitalt".' *Dagens Nyheter* (22 March 2018).

Llinares, Dario, Neil Fox, and Richard Berry. 'Introduction: Podcasting and Podcasts – Parameters of a New Aural Culture.' In *Podcasting: New Aural Cultures and Digital Media*, edited by Dario Llinares, Neil Fox and Richard Berry, 1–13. Cham: Palgrave Macmillan, 2018.

Long, Elizabeth. *Book Clubs: Women and the Uses of Reading in Everyday Life*. Chicago and London: University of Chicago Press.

Long, Hoyt. *The Value in Numbers: Reading Japanese Literature in a Global Information Age*. New York: Columbia University Press, 2021.

'Love It or Leave It: What To Do When You Can't Stand the Narrator.' Goodreads.com. Available online: https://www.goodreads.com/topic/show/1954770-love-it-or-leave-it-what-to-do-when-you-can-t-stand-the-narrator (accessed 26 August 2022).

Lundh, Anna. '"I Can Read, I Just Can't See": A Disability Rights-Based Perspective on Reading by Listening.' *Journal of Documentation* 78, no. 7 (2022): 176–91.

Malm, Mats. 'Ljudlig läsning – ett historiskt perspektiv.' In *Från Strindberg till Storytel: Korskopplingar mellan ljud och litteratur*, edited by Julia Pennlert and Lars Ilshammar, 31–50. Gothenburg: Daidalos, 2021.

Mangen, Anne, and Adriaan van der Weel. 'The Evolution of Reading in the Age of Digitisation: An Integrative Framework for Reading Research.' *Literacy* 50, no. 3 (2016): 116–24.

Manovich, Lev. *Cultural Analytics*. Cambridge, MA: MIT Press, 2020.

Marche, Stephen. 'Literature Is Not Data: Against Digital Humanities.' *LA Review of Books* (28 October 2012).

McGann, Jerome. *The Textual Condition*. Princeton, NJ: Princeton University Press, 1991.

McGurl, Mark. *Everything and Less: The Novel in the Age of Amazon*. London and New York: Verso, 2021.

McKinney, Wes. 'Data Structures for Statistical Computing in Python.' In *Proceedings of the 9th Python in Science Conference*, edited by Stefan van der Walt and Jarrod Millman, 55–61. Austin, TX, 2010.

Mildorf, Jarmila, and Till Kinzel (editors). *Audionarratology: Interfaces of Sound and Narrative*. Berlin: De Gruyter, 2016.

Miller, Laura J. 'The Best-Seller List as Marketing Tool and Historical Fiction.' *Book History* 3 (2000): 286–304.

Murray, Simone. *The Adaptation Industry: The Cultural Economy of Contemporary Literary Adaptation*. New York and London: Routledge, 2012.

Murray, Simone. *The Digital Literary Sphere: Reading, Writing, and Selling Books in the Internet Era*. Baltimore, MD: Johns Hopkins University Press, 2018.

Murray, Simone. 'Secret Agents. Algorithmic Culture, Goodreads and Datafication of the Contemporary Book World.' *European Journal of Cultural Studies* 24, no. 4 (2021): 970–89.

Murray, Simone. 'Varieties of Digital Literary Studies: Micro, Macro, Meso.' *Digital Humanities Quarterly* 16, no. 2 (2022). Available online: http://www.digitalhumanities.org/dhq/vol/16/2/000616/000616.html (accessed 29 June 2023).

Määttä, Jerry. 'Kvalitetslitteraturen i luren: Utbudet av Nobelpristagare och Augustnominerad skönlitteratur som strömmande svenska ljudböcker.' In *Från Strindberg till Storytel – korskopplingar mellan ljud och litteratur*, edited by Julia Pennlert and Lars Ilshammar, 295– 326. Gothenburg: Daidalos, 2021.

Määttä, Jerry, Ann Steiner and Karl Berglund. *Skilda världar: Kvalitetslitteraturens villkor i Sverige idag*. Stockholm: Swedish Publishers' Association, 2022.

Noorda, Rachel, and Stevie Marsden. 'Twenty-First Century Book Studies: The State of the Discipline.' *Book History* 22 (2019): 370–97.

Ohlsson, Jonas (editor). *Mediebarometern 2021*. Gothenburg: Nordicom, 2022.

Ong, Walter J. *Orality and Literacy: The Technologizing of the Word*. London: Methuen, 1982.

Pandas Development Team, The. *pandas-dev/pandas: Pandas*. Zenodo, 2020.

Parnell, Claire. 'Mapping the Entertainment Ecosystem of Wattpad: Platforms, Publishing and Adaptation.' *Convergence* 27, no. 2 (2021): 524–38.

Parrot Analytics. 'How are OTT platforms and streaming services shaping audience tastes around the world?' Press release, 20 December 2022. Available online: https://www.parrotanalytics.com/press/how-are-ott-platforms-and-streaming-services-shaping-audience-tastes-around-the-world/ (accessed 11 January 2023).

Penguin Random House Audio Publishing. 'Daisy Jones & The Six (TV Tie-in Edition).' Available online: https://www.penguinrandomhouseaudio.com/book/577211/daisy-jones-and-the-six/ (accessed 30 November 2022).

Phillips, Angus. 'How Books Are Positioned in the Market: Reading the Cover.' In *Judging a Book by Its Cover: Fans, Publishers, Designers and the Marketing of Fiction*, edited by Nicole Matthews and Nickianne Moody, 83–92. Aldershot: Ashgate, 2007.

Pianzola, Federico. *Digital Social Reading: Sharing Fiction in the 21st Century*. Cambridge, MA: MIT Press, 2021.

Pianzola, Federico, Simone Rebora and Gerhard Lauer. 'Wattpad as a Resource for Literary Studies: Quantitative and Qualitative Examples of the Importance of Digital Social Reading and Readers' Comments in the Margins.' *PLoS ONE* 15, no. 1 (2020): 1–46.

Piper, Andrew. *Book Was There: Reading in Electronic Times*. Chicago: Chicago University Press, 2012.

Piper, Andrew. *Enumerations: Data and Literary History*. Chicago: University of Chicago Press, 2018.

Price, Leah. *How to Do Things with Books in Victorian Britain*. Princeton, NJ: Princeton University Press, 2012.

Price, Leah. 'Reading: The State of the Discipline.' *Book History* 7 (2004): 303–20.

Price, Leah. *What We Talk About When We Talk About Books: The History and Future of Reading*. New York: Basic Books, 2019.

Pritchard, Alan. 'Statistical Bibliography or Bibliometrics?' *Journal of Documentation* 25, no. 4 (1969): 348–49.

Radway, Janice. 'Reading Is Not Eating: Mass-Produced Literature and the Theoretical, Methodological, and Political Consequences of a Metaphor.' *Book Research Quarterly* 2 (1986): 7–29.

Radway, Janice. *Reading the Romance: Women, Patriarchy, and Popular Literature*. 1984; London: Verso, 1987.

Rebora, Simone, Peter Boot, Federico Pianzola, Brigitte Gasser, J. Berenike Herrmann, Maria Kraxenberger, Moniek M. Kuijpers, Gerhard Lauer, Piroska Lendvai, Thomas C. Messerli and Pasqualina Sorrentino. 'Digital Humanities and Digital Social Reading.' *Digital Scholarship in the Humanities* 36, no. 2 (2021): 230–50.

Riddell, Allen, and Karina van Dalen-oskam. 'Readers and Their Roles: Evidence From Readers of Contemporary Fiction in the Netherlands.' *PLoS ONE* 13, no. 7 (2018). https://doi.org/10.1371/journal.pone.0201157.

Rimm, Anna-Maria. 'Conditions and Survival: Views on the Concentration of Ownership and Vertical Integration in German and Swedish Publishing.' *Publishing Research Quarterly* 30 (2014): 77–92.

Rose, Jonathan. *The Intellectual Life of the British Working Classes*. New Haven, CT: Yale University Press, 2001.

Rowberry, Simon. *Four Shades of Gray: The Amazon Kindle Platform*. Cambridge, MA: MIT Press, 2022.

Rowberry, Simon. 'The Limits of Big Data for Analyzing Reading.' *Participations* 16, no. 1 (2019): 237–57.

Rubery, Matthew. 'Introduction: Talking Books.' In *Audiobooks, Literature, and Sound Studies*, edited by Matthew Rubery, 1–21. New York: Routledge, 2011.

Rubery, Matthew. *Reader's Block: A History of Reading Differences*. Stanford, CA: Stanford University Press, 2022.

Rubery, Matthew. *The Untold Story of the Talking Book*. Cambridge, MA: Harvard University Press, 2016.

Scribd. 'How many books does Scribd have? Are you adding more.' Available online: https://support.scribd.com/hc/en-us/articles/210135406-How-many-books-does-Scribd-have-Are-you-adding-more- (accessed 28 November 2022).

Spjeldnæs, Kari. 'Platformization and Publishing: Changes in Literary Publishing.' *Publishing Research Quarterly*, September (2022). https://doi.org/10.1007/s12109-022-09912-2.

Spotify. 'A new chapter for listening: Audiobooks on Spotify.' Available online: https://www.spotify.com/us/audiobooks/ (accessed 28 November 2022).

Squires, Claire. 'The Global Market 1970–2000: Consumers.' In *A Companion to the History of the Book*, edited by Simon Eliot and Jonathan Rose, 406–18. Malden, MA and Oxford: Wiley-Blackwell, 2007.

Squires, Claire. *Marketing Literature: The Making of Contemporary Writing in Britain.* Basingstoke: Palgrave Macmillan, 2007.

Squires, Claire, and Padmini Ray Murray. 'The Digital Publishing Communications Circuit.' *Book 2.0* 3, no. 1 (2013): 3–24.

Statista. 'US Book Market – Format Market Shares 2011–2019.' Available online: https://www.statista.com/topics/1474/e-books/ (accessed 13 October 2020).

Steiner, Ann. 'The Global Book: Micropublishing, Conglomerate Production, and Digital Market Structures.' *Publishing Research Quarterly* 34 (2018): 118–32.

Steiner, Ann. 'Serendipity, Promotion, and Literature: The Contemporary Book Trade and International Megasellers.' In *Hype: Bestsellers and Literary Culture*, edited by Jon Helgason, Sara Kärrholm and Ann Steiner, 48–50. Lund: Nordic Academic Press, 2015.

Steiner, Ann, and Karl Berglund. *Barnlitterära strömningar: Om ljudböcker för barn.* Stockholm: Swedish Publishers' Association, 2022.

Storytel. 'Bokslutskommuniké 2015.' Press release, 26 February 2016. Available online: https://investors.storytel.com/sv/bokslutskommunike-2015/ (accessed 5 January 2023).

Storytel. 'Om Storytel.' Available online: https://www.storytel.com/se/sv/om-storytel (accessed 17 November 2022).

Storytel. 'Om Storytel Awards.' Available online: https://awards.storytel.com/se/sv/storytel-awards-4/ (accessed 21 June 2022).

Storytel. 'Passerar 300 000 betalande abonnenter.' Press release, 27 June 2016. Available online: https://investors.storytel.com/sv/passerar-300-000-betalande-abonnenter/ (accessed 5 January 2023)

Storytel. 'Storytel.' Available online: https://www.storytel.com/se/sv/ (accessed 4 January 2023).

Storytel. 'Storytel Enters Strategic Partnership with ElevenLabs and Announces Upcoming Launch of New VoiceSwitcher Feature.' Press release, June 13, 2023. Available online: https://investors.storytel.com/en/storytel-enters-strategic-partnership-with-elevenlabs-and-announces-upcoming-launch-of-new-voiceswitcher-feature/ (accessed 29 June 2029).

Storytel. 'Storytel Original.' Available online: https://publishing.storytel.com/storytel-original/ (accessed 27 June 2022).

Storytel. 'Storytel passerar 500 000 betalande abonnenter.' Press release, 17 August 2017. Available online: https://investors.storytel.com/sv/storytel-passerar-500-000-betalande-abonnenter/ (accessed 5 January 2023).

'Storytel Enters the U.S. with Acquisition of Audiobooks.com.' *Reuters* (12 November 2021). Available online: https://www.reuters.com/business/media-telecom/

storytel-enters-us-with-acquisition-audiobookscom-2021-11-12/ (accessed 28 November 2022).
Stougaard Pedersen, Birgitte, Maria Engberg, Iben Have, Ayoe Quist Henkel, Sarah Mygind and Helle Bundgaard Svendsen. 'To Move, to Touch, to Listen: Multisensory Aspects of the Digital Reading Condition.' *Poetics Today* 42, no. 2 (2021): 281–300.
Striphas, Ted. 'Algorithmic Culture.' *European Journal of Cultural Studies* 18, no. 4–5 (2018): 395–412.
Striphas, Ted. *The Late Age of Print: Everyday Book Culture from Consumerism to Control*. New York: Columbia University Press, 2009.
Sundet, Vilde, and Terje Colbjørnsen. 'Streaming Across Industries: Streaming Logics and Streaming Lore Across the Music, Film, Television, and Book Industries.' *MedieKultur: Journal of Media and Communication Research* 37, no. 70 (2021): 12–31.
Sutherland, John. *Bestsellers: Popular Fiction of the 1970s*. London: Routledge & Kegan Paul, 1981.
Sutherland, John. *Bestsellers: A Very Short Introduction*. Oxford: Oxford University Press, 2007.
Svedjedal, Johan. 'Författare och förläggare.' In *Författare och förläggare och andra litteratursociologiska studier*, 9–34. Hedemora: Gidlunds, 1994.
Svedjedal, Johan. *The Literary Web: Literature and Publishing in the Age of Digital Production*. Stockholm: Kungl. biblioteket, 2000.
Svedjedal, Johan. 'Det litteratursociologiska perspektivet: Om en forskningstradition och dess grundantaganden.' In *Litteratursociologi: Texter om litteratur och samhälle*, edited by Johan Svedjedal, 73–102. 2nd edn. 1996; Lund: Studentlitteratur, 2012.
Svedjedal, Johan. 'Läsning och lyssning i en mångmedial tid.' In Anna Nordlund and Johan Svedjedal, *Läsandets årsringar: Rapport och reflektioner om läsningens aktuella tillstånd i Sverige*, 9–42. Stockholm: Svenska Förläggareföreningen, 2020.
Svenbro, Jesper. 'Archaic and Classical Greece: The Invention of Silent Reading.' In *A History of Reading in the West*, edited by Guglielmo Cavallo and Roger Chartier, 37–63. Oxford: Polity, 1999.
Svensk Bokhandel. 'Årets viktigaste händelser enligt bokbranschen.' 27 December 2019. Available online: https://www.svb.se/nyheter/arets-viktigaste-handelser-enligt-bokbranschen (accessed 24 November 2022).
Tanderup Linkis, Sara. 'Reading Spaces: Original Audiobooks and Mobile Listening.' *SoundEffects – An Interdisciplinary Journal of Sound and Sound Experience* 10, no. 1 (2021): 42–55.
Tanderup Linkis, Sara, and Julia Pennlert. 'Episodic Listening: Analyzing the Content and Usage of Born Audio Serial Narratives.' *Journal of Electronic Publishing* 23, no. 1 (2020). https://doi.org/10.3998/3336451.0023.102.
Tanderup Linkis, Sara, and Julia Pennlert. 'En helt annan upplevelse: Ljudbokens band till sina läsare.' *Tidskrift för Litteraturvetenskap* 52, no. 1 (2022). https://doi.org/10.54797/tfl.v52i1.2227.

Tattersall Wallin, Elisa. 'Audiobook Routines: Identifying Everyday Reading by Listening Practices Amongst Young Adults.' *Journal of Documentation* 78, no. 7 (2022): 266–81.

Tattersall Wallin, Elisa. 'Reading by Listening: Conceptualising Audiobook Practices in the Age of Streaming Subscription Services.' *Journal of Documentation* 77, no. 2 (2021): 432–48.

Tattersall Wallin, Elisa, and Jan Nolin. 'Time to Read: Exploring the Timespaces in Subscription-based Audiobooks.' *New Media and Society* 22, no. 3 (2020): 470–88.

Thomas, Bronwen. *Literature and Social Media*. London and New York: Routledge, 2020.

Thompson, John B. *Book Wars: The Digital Revolution in Publishing*. Cambridge, UK: Polity Press, 2021.

Thompson, John B. *Merchants of Culture: The Publishing Business in the Twenty-First Century*. Cambridge, UK: Polity Press, 2010.

Todorov, Tzvetan. *The Poetics of Prose*. 1971; Ithaca, NY: Cornell University Press, 1977.

Trettien, Whitney. 'Tracked.' In *Further Reading*, edited by Matthew Rubery and Leah Price, 311–24. Oxford: Oxford University Press, 2020.

Underwood, Ted. 'A Genealogy of Distant Reading.' *Digital Humanities Quarterly* 11, no. 2 (2017). Available online: http://www.digitalhumanities.org/dhq/vol/11/2/000317/000317.html (accessed 29 June 2023).

Walsh, Melanie. 'Where Is All the Book Data?' *Public Books*, 4 October 2022. Available online: https://www.publicbooks.org/where-is-all-the-book-data/ (accessed 11 January 2023).

Walsh, Melanie, and Maria Antoniak. 'The Goodreads "Classics": A Computational Study of Readers, Amazon, and Crowdsourced Amateur Criticism.' *Journal of Cultural Analytics* 6, no. 2 (2021): 243–87. https://doi.org/10.22148/001c.22221.

Walton, Priscilla L., and Manina Jones. *Detective Agency: Women Rewriting the Hard-Boiled Tradition*. Berkeley: University of California Press, 1999.

Weel, Adriaan van der. *Changing Our Textual Minds: Towards a Digital Order of Knowledge*. Manchester: Manchester University Press, 2011.

Whelan, Julia. *Thank You For Listening: A Novel*. New York: HarperCollins, 2022.

Wikberg, Erik. *Bokförsäljningsstatistiken: Helåret 2021*. Stockholm: Swedish Publishers' Association and Swedish Booksellers' Association, 2022.

Wilkins, Kim, Beth Driscoll, and Lisa Fletcher. *Genre Worlds: Popular Fiction and Twenty-First-Century Book Culture*. Amherst and Boston: University of Massachusetts Press, 2022.

Williams, Mark. 'Spotify's Move Into Audiobooks Is a Seismic Shift in the Publishing Landscape, but the Ripples Will Take Time To Be Felt.' *The New Publishing Standard*, 18 August 2020. Available online: https://thenewpublishingstandard.com/2020/08/18/spotifys-move-into-audiobooks-is-a-seismic-shift-in-the-publishing-landscape-but-the-ripples-will-take-time-to-be-felt/ (accessed 25 November 2022).

Wischenbart, Rüdiger. 'Deposing the King of Content: Understanding the Shift Triggered by Audiobooks and Subscription.' *LOGOS: Journal of the World Publishing Community* 32, no. 2 (2021): 29–33.

Wischenbart, Rüdiger, and Michaela Anna Fleischhacker. *The Digital Consumer Book Barometer 2021: A Report on Ebook and Audiobook Sales in Canada, Germany, Italy, Spain, Brazil, Mexico*. Vienna: RWCC, 2021.

Wittmann, Reinhard. 'Was there a Reading Revolution at the End of the Eighteenth Century?' In *A History of Reading in the West*, edited by Guglielmo Cavallo and Roger Chartier, 284–312. Oxford: Polity, 1999.

Zuboff, Shoshana. *The Age of Surveillance Capitalism: The Fight for a Human Future at the New Frontier of Power*. London: Profile Books, 2019.

Index

Adler-Olsen, Jussi 98
Ahndoril, Alexander, *see* Kepler, Lars
Alakoski, Susanna 125–6
Altick, Richard D. 8, 16
Alvtegen, Karin 105
Amazon 3, 7, 15, 17–18, 36–7, 46–7, 61, 66, 71, 169, 176–7
Anderson, Chris 69
Antoniak, Maria 11, 17–19
Anyuru, Johannes 56, 99
Apple Books 117
Audible 3, 46–8, 71–2, 95–6, 159
Audie Awards 95
Audio Publishers' Association 95
Audiobooks.com 46
Augustpriset (August Prize) 25, 56

Backman, Fredrik 98–9, 101, 155
Baron, Naomi 11–13
Bengtsson, Kjell 101
Berglund, Karl 15, 35–6, 60, 134
Bible 146
'Big Five' publishers 48
Björkén-Nyberg, Cecilia 102, 104–5, 116
Bjurwald, Lisa 88
Bloomsbury 93
Bokinfo 35
Bolme, Tomas 98, 108
Bondi, Gabrielle 102
Bonnier Books 20–1, 56–7, 108
BookBeat 20–1, 30, 35, 46, 67, 72, 122, 139, 168–9
Booker Prize 25, 56
BookScan 25, 177
Bookstagram, *see* Instagram
BookTok, *see* TikTok
Bookwire 35
Bottomley, Andrew 15
Brown, Dan 98, 124, 140, 143
Bågstam, Anna 135
Börjlind, Cilla & Rolf 135, 138

Casserfelt, Susan 88, 139, 155–6
Cavallo, Guglielmo 16, 151
Chartier, Roger 16, 151
Clark, Giles 70
Coelho Ahndoril, Alexandra, *see* Kepler, Lars
Colbjørnsen, Terje 32–3, 42, 48
Colgan, Jenny 74, 76, 81
Collins, Suzanne 100
Correa, Armando Lucas 56
Cumberbatch, Benedict 118

Dahllöf, Mats 25, 57, 60
Dalengren, Sara 104
Darnton, Robert 14, 16, 32–3
Disney, *see* Walt Disney
Divergent series 100
Doerr, Anthony 56
Doughty, Louise 56
Driscoll, Beth 23

Engelsing, Rolf 16, 146–7, 168
Escarpit, Robert 60–1, 72–4, 119, 174
Ewerlöf, Katarina 94, 97–9, 103, 105–7, 157

Felski, Rita 10, 104–5, 119
Ferrante, Elena (pseud.) 22, 64–5
Fifty Shades of Grey series 118, 167
Fletcher, Lisa 23
Flynn, Gillian 98, 165
Forman, Gayle 95
Forslid, Torbjörn 141–3
Forssén Ehrlin, Carl-Johan 134
Fry, Stephen 93, 118
Fuller, Danielle 17
Furuland, Lars 32

Gardell, Jonas 99, 162
Genette, Gérard 24–5, 31, 44–5
Gerhardsen, Carin 64
Goodreads 11, 13, 17–18, 38, 116

Google 36
Gothenburg Book Fair 141
Grimwalker, Caroline 104
Grimwalker, Leffe 104
Guillou, Jan 64, 74–5, 81, 98–9, 108, 135, 143
Gummerus 21
Gunder, Anna 33–4, 43

Hansson, Gunnar 17
Have, Iben 32–3, 57, 87, 94, 96, 98–9, 115, 120, 122
Harry Potter series 47, 93, 167
Hawkins, Paula 165
HBO 48
Hemse, Rebecka 100
Hertel, Hans 32
Holmquist, Mikael 53
Holt, Anne 101
Hoover, Colleen 132
Hosseini, Khaled 79–80
Hunger Games series 47, 100, 167

Iggulden, Conn 98
Ingelman-Sundberg, Catharina 101
Ingemarsson, Kajsa 99, 108
Instagram 13, 38–9
Ishiguro, Kazuo 164

Jackson, Stina 135
Janson, Karin 161
Jansson, Anna 98, 135, 139, 155–6
Jenkins Reid, Taylor 93
Jonasson, Jonas 124, 155
Jones, Manina 165
Jungstedt, Mari 99, 107, 135, 143, 162, 165, 176

Kallentoft, Mons 77, 98, 108
Kepler, Lars (pseud.) 28, 55, 64, 97–8, 108–12, 135, 143
Kindle 6, 18–19, 37, 177
Kindle Direct Publishing (KDP)61, 66, 71, 117, 169
Kindle Unlimited (KU)35, 46–8, 67, 71–2, 169, 174
Kirkus Prize 56
Knip-Häggkvist, Elizabet 104
Koepnick, Lutz 96, 120, 122

Kovač, Miha 14
Kovács, Angela 110
Kubicek Boye, Helena 132
Käll, Anna Maria 98, 101, 105–7
Körberg, Anton 104

Lagercrantz, David 55, 64, 74–5, 98, 143, 165
Larsson, Christina 101
Larsson, Stieg 51, 124–5, 165
Leining, Gunilla 98, 105–6, 108–12, 157
LibraryThing 17
Lind & Co 21
Lindemalm, Albert 104
Lindgren, Torgny 99
Long, Elizabeth 17
Long, Hoyt 140
Lundell, Ulf 99
Lundström, Klas 104
Läckberg, Camilla 55, 64, 78, 80–1, 85–6, 88, 98–9, 139, 155, 157, 165–6, 176

Malmsjö, Jonas 94, 98, 108–12
Mangen, Anne 13
Manovich, Lev 6
Marche, Stephen 8
Marklund, Liza 98
Marsden, Stevie 7, 10–11
McGann, Jerome 31, 43, 45, 49
McGurl, Mark 18–19, 23, 61
Meyer, Stephenie 100
Millennium series 74–5, 124, 165, 167
Mohlin, Peter 135
Moyes, Jojo 64, 79, 81–2, 98
Müller, Herta 57
Murray, Simone 5, 7, 10–11, 13, 18, 52, 89, 176–7
Määttä, Jerry 35–6

Nesbø, Jo 81–2, 98, 108
Nesser, Håkan 81–3, 99
Netflix 35, 41, 45–6, 48, 133
Nielsen BookScan, *see* BookScan
Nobel Prize in literature 25, 56–7, 106, 124, 164
Nolin, Jan 122
Noorda, Rachel 7, 10–11
Nordic Noir 51, 139

Nordiska rådets litteraturpris 25
Norstedts 20-1
Nyström, Peter 135

Owens, Delia 98, 135

Pandas 22
Paris, B. A. 162
Parnell, Claire 30
Parrot Analytics 177
Pennlert, Julia 115, 174
People's Press 21
Persbrandt, Mikael 134
Phillips, Angus 70
Pianzola, Federico 18-19
Piper, Andrew 140
Porter, Ray 95
Price, Leah 10, 13
Pritchard, Alan 22
Publit 35
Publizon 35
Pulitzer Prize 25
Python 22, 59

Raaby Jensen, Mille 87
Radway, Janice 2, 9-10, 17, 26, 104, 119, 145, 166-7, 173-4
Ray Murray, Padmini 32-33
Rebora, Simone 18
Reddit 13
Rehberg Sedo, DeNel 17
Richardson, Marie 98
Riley, Lucinda 98, 135, 157
Rimm, Anna-Maria 40
Robinson, Peter 98
Rose, Jonathan 16
Rosenfeldt, Hans 135, 155
Roth, Veronica 100
Rowberry, Simon 7-9, 11
Rubery, Matthew 8, 13, 15, 30, 94, 96, 103, 112-13, 115-17, 122, 150
Rudberg, Denise 106
Röse, Eva 159

Sandin, Niclas 168
Sarenbrant, Sofie 107, 135, 138-9, 143
Sauk, Stefan 98, 103, 108
Schepp, Emelie 135
Schulman, Alex 99, 162

Scribd 46-7, 168
Skeppstedt, Lotten 70
Skoog, Helge 101
So, Richard Jean 22
Soulis, Anastasios 104
Soundcloud 41-2
Spjeldnæs, Kari 29
Spotify 35, 41-2, 46-7, 133
Squires, Claire 19-20, 32-3
Steiner, Ann 15, 35-6, 134
Sten, Viveca 105-7
Storyside 21
Storytel Originals 23, 40-1, 87, 158-61
Storytel Awards 95
Stougaard Pedersen, Birgitte 32-3, 57, 94, 96, 98-9, 115, 120, 122
Streep, Meryl 118
Striphas, Ted 89
Sundet, Vilde 42, 48
Svedjedal, Johan 6, 32, 35
Svenbro, Jesper 14
Svensk Bokhandel 23
Swedish Academy 157
Swedish Crime Fiction Academy 24
Swedish Publishers' Association 20, 23, 53, 142

Tanderup Linkis, Sara 115, 174
Tattersall Wallin, Elisa 41, 120, 122, 126, 133
Thema (subject category scheme) 24
Thulin, Erik 159-60
Thompson, John B. 26, 38-9, 45-47, 70-1, 83, 99, 168-9
TikTok 38-9
Todorov, Tzvetan 64
Tokarczuk, Olga 55-7, 106
Turestedt, Mirja 108
Tursten, Helene 162
Twilight series 100

Wahlund, Torsten 98, 101
Walsh, Melanie 11, 17-18, 177
Walt Disney 48
Walton, Priscilla L. 165
Wattpad 17, 30
Weel, Adriaan van der 13
Weir, Andy 95
Westover, Tara 162

Whelan, Julia 1–2
Wilkins, Kim 23
Wischenbart, Rüdiger 4
Witherspoon, Reese 118
Wähä, Nina 99

Yanagihara, Hanya 56

Zuboff, Shoshana 5

Åkerblom, Viktor 104

Öhrlund, Dag 64, 155, 162
Öqvist Ragnar, Anna 40–2
Östergren, Klas 99, 157

www.ingramcontent.com/pod-product-compliance
Lightning Source LLC
Chambersburg PA
CBHW052119300426
44116CB00010B/1714